KILRENN
AND CELLARDYKE

KILRENNY AND CELLARDYKE

800 Years of History

HARRY D WATSON

JOHN DONALD PUBLISHERS LTD
EDINBURGH

To all my family, past and present,
and to Dykers everywhere

This edition published in 2003 by
John Donald Publishers
an imprint of Birlinn Limited
West Newington House
10 Newington Road
Edinburgh
EH9 1QS

www.birlinn.co.uk

First published in 1986 by John Donald Publishers Ltd, Edinburgh

ISBN 1 904607 08 X

British Library Cataloguing-in-Publication Data
A catalogue record of this book is available from the British Library

Printed and bound by Antony Rowe Ltd, Eastbourne

Acknowledgements

Many individuals and institutions have helped in the making of this book. At Register House, West Register House and the Scottish Record Office the expertise of the staff makes research a positive pleasure. At St. Andrews Univerity Library the Keeper of Muniments, Mr. Robert Smart, gave me access to the Kilrenny Burgh Records and to a century-long run of old Anstruther newspapers. The library of the Dictionary of the Older Scottish Tongue and Edinburgh University Library were other sources of useful material, and it was from books in the latter institution that I obtained the illustrations on pages 14, 24 and 74. The map on page 99 appears by courtesy of the Central Public Library (Scottish Room) at George IV Bridge, Edinburgh, the Royal Commission on the Ancient and Historical Monuments of Scotland supplied the photograph of Melville's Manse on page 30, and the Wemyss Environmental Education Centre in Buckhaven generously sent me free copies of their photographs of Caiplie Coves. The photograph on page 3 was reproduced from an original lent me by Mary Gourlay, widow of my second cousin Salter Watson jun.

Thanks to Richard Wemyss and Garth Sterne of the Scottish Fisheries Museum in Anstruther, I have spent some happy hours in that museum's fine photographic archive, and I am grateful to John Doig, the museum's photographer, for so promptly responding to all my requests for prints. Illustrations from the museum's collection can be found on pages 5, 7, 16, 18, 22, 96, 97, 104, 122, 128, 130, 138, 139, 143, 148, 157, 163, 170, 173, 175, 177, 179, 198, 203, 207 and 215. Mr. Andrew Wallace of the Customs & Excise Office at 270 High Street, Kirkcaldy, allowed me to consult the early Boats Registers of the Anstruther Fishery Office, and kindly made an office available for me to work in on each of my visits. Miss Alison E. Denholm, B.A., F.S.A. Scot., took my roughly-drawn family-trees and converted them into the elegant charts in Appendix 1. I must also thank my good friend Norma Brown of Nepean, Ontario, for an often amusing and always informative correspondence on the subject of Cellardyke genealogies. John Tuckwell of the publishers, John Donald, was unfailingly encouraging, and oversaw the transition from typescript to print with tact and good humour.

Among local people who have helped with information or advice, I must single out Peter Smith, author of *The Lammas Drave and the Winter Herrin'*, for special mention. Peter, being of my parents' generation, has a longer memory than mine, and he has shared his knowledge with me in conversation, in numerous letters and on tape. There can be few former fishermen who are also trained mathematicians, and this book has benefited both from his deep knowledge of and love for the sea, and from his rigorous insistence on accuracy. I am also indebted to Peter for allowing me to quote from his father's poems. Other fellow-Dykers who helped, directly or indirectly, include Jimmy Barclay (Glenburn Road), Jimmy Brunton (James Street), my aunt Margaret Watson (Mrs. Alex. Cunningham), Gardner Doig (Rodger Street), Alex. Gardner (East Forth Street), Robert Gardner (Burnside Place), Mary Gourlay (Mrs. Salter Watson jun.), Mary Murray (Murray Square), Peter Murray sen. (Rodger Street), Alex. Rodger (Rodger St.), David Smith sen. (East Forth Street), John Watson (Tarvit) (Gardner Avenue), Prof. Alex. Gardner Watson (son of John Salter Watson and Lilias Gardner), my second cousin John Watson (son of Salter Watson sen. and Jean Anderson) and my second cousin William Carstairs Watson, skipper of the *Gleanaway II* (son of Jocky Watson jun. and Jen Hughes). Their advice and information were invaluable, and any errors that remain are mine and mine alone.

My late father Henry Watson was often in my thoughts as I worked on this book, for he was my first playmate and mentor at the seaside. My mother Jessie Peebles can claim some credit too, for she is a born storyteller, and it was her inexhaustible store of anecdotes about old Crail and Cellardyke that first awakened my interest in our local history. Finally, I must pay tribute to my wife Sue, whose interest, encouragement, patience and good humour never flagged, and to my sons Andrew and Michael, who take me down the seaside at regular intervals for a clamber over the skellies. This book is for all of them.

                                                      Harry D. Watson

Contents

Introduction

Born in Crail, at my maternal grandmother's house in the Nethergate, I was barely a fortnight old when my parents took me back to the family home at 12 East Forth Street, Cellardyke; and it was in that house, where my paternal great-grandparents had lived almost a century before, that I grew into childhood. James and Margaret Watson must have been among the first fisherfolk to desert the fever-ridden straggle of cottages by the shore for the airy new terrace on the Braehead, and they were joined at No. 12 by Margaret's sister Mary Watson and her husband George Moncrieff. At No. 8 lived another sister, Isabella, with her husband Charles Marr ('Auld Chairlie the Laud'), and at No. 16 their brother Adam Watson with his wife Mary Brown and their large brood.

My great-grandfather James Murray Watson, being a second son, was named after his mother's father. But there were many James Watsons in Cellardyke, and only by their fisherman's nickname or 'by-name' could they be distinguished. My great-grandfather was neither 'Patchie', 'Fiddler' nor 'Star Jeems' – but 'Ruser'. A placid man, he was never seen to lose his temper and become angry, or in Cellardyke parlance 'rused' – hence the by-name. After returning from a trip to the Australian gold-diggings he never went back to sea; or so I was told.

As in most of the fisher-families it was the woman who met life head-on and became the raw material of anecdote, and my father's 'Granny Mags' was, by all accounts, a terror: a ferocious bantam with a withering tongue, always happier mending nets or baiting lines than performing the more menial chores of housework. A Watson married to a Watson – no unusual occurrence in that tightly inbred community – she was the daughter of William Watson and Margaret Reid and a granddaughter of that William Watson who had earned himself the by-name 'Water Willie' one February morning in the year 1800, when he had seemed to walk across the waves which had buried his boat and his seven comrades to the safety of the Craw Skelly, hard by Cellardyke harbour. A Greek chorus of eyewitnesses saw his young wife Mary Galloway wade in and pluck him out of the water, and years later they relived the experience for the local chronicler George Gourlay, the author of *Fisher Life, or the Memorials of Cellardyke and the Fife Coast*. Ironically, when Mary Galloway died in 1848, her death was recorded in the parish register with

1

the laconic comment, 'died of water'.

My grandfather William Watson was another second son, but as William Watsons were no rarer than James Watsons he was better known as 'Puckie'. Though dead these four decades, 'Puckie' lives on in the memories of the older generation of Dykers, who remember with affection his pawky ways and dry sense of humour. In the 1890s, before the rise of the steam-drifter, he was skipper of the sailing Fifies *W. E. Gladstone* and *Herbert Gladstone*. Before and during the First World War he had the bauldies *Andrews* and *Boatie Rows* and sailed on Alex. Rodger's drifter *Morning Star* and the motorboat *Fisher Lassie*, with skipper Rob Stewart. Later still came his famous partnership with 'Puggy Patch' or 'Patchie' (James Watson), and their fellow-'worthies' of the *Goldfinch*: a crew immortalised by a local wag in the rhyme, 'There wis King Jeems and Crukkie, Puggy Patch and Puckie'.

Among the oldest retired fishermen of Cellardyke there are still some who can quote verses about 'Patchie' and 'Puckie', verses like:

> The sail was blowing to and fro,
> And Patch went forward and let it go.
> And Puckie says, 'That's awfae wark!
> We'll no get in afore it's dark!'

Or another, hinting at a favourite pastime of the two cronies:

> The Goldfinch sailed from Buckhynd toon,
> And a' Patch hid wis ae half-croon.
> He says tae Puckie, 'We cannae drink!
> We'll shin be runnin short o clink!'

My grandfather was a kindly man, not averse to a nip and a pint, and a flutter on a horse at Hughie Gourlay's boot-repairing and (unofficial) betting establishment in the East Green. He died the year before I was born, to my everlasting regret. My granny, on the other hand, I remember all too well. I will return to her in a moment.

My earliest memory is of a seemingly endless succession of summer days – the cold logic of adulthood labels it the summer of 1949 – playing out in the paved area or 'brick' at the front of the house. I remember minor tyrannies: knocking over a row of tiny cars which a playmate had lined up along the wall; threatening the same longsuffering playmate with a handful of dessicated dog-dirt (it had been a remarkably dry summer), my mother intervening frustratingly (as mothers will do) at the crucial moment; and, of course – the seaside.

(L. to R.) Mary Brown (Mrs. Adam Watson) and her sisters-in-law Isabella Watson (Mrs. Charles Marr) and Margaret 'Granny Mags' Watson (Mrs. James Murray Watson), the author's great-grandmother. Taken around the turn of the century in the garden at 'Craigholm', home of their niece Betsy Waterston and her husband Alex. Watson of Watson's factory.

Exactly when the seaside claimed me, I cannot tell, for it goes back beyond consciousness, but the stretch of shoreline from Cellardyke harbour along George Street and John Street to James Street, where my Granny Watson lived, was my nursery and playground. When I was four my mother tried to enrol me at the nursery-school up the road, but when the teacher came to the door and their backs were turned I ran back down the hill, and that was that. Later I would be offered various inducements: a bike – but I desired no means of escape from that small world; a train-set – after the first day it lay abandoned until finally it was given away; the Cubs – but I had no fancy for a uniform, and I was in no need of healthy distractions, for there were 'dergies' to catch with the simplest of rods, crabs under every rock, rusty tins to heap into a pile and demolish with a well-aimed pebble, smooth slivers of slate to 'skiff' in the water. My father taught me that 'pelns' were the best crabs for bait, and together we fished off the rocks near the shore where he had fished as a boy: preparing himself, like the children of so-called 'primitive' societies, for the tasks of manhood.

Other boys fished there too, of course. One day I watched with horrified fascination as Billy Taylor pulled a sea-monster out of the incoming tide. Even after he cut its head off it managed to bite his finger, or so he claimed, so we hacked it up, laboriously, into little pieces which went on wriggling with nauseating autonomy. It was the first, and biggest, conger-eel I ever saw.

At high tide on stormy days the spray would crash over the seawall into my granny's garden. I took the same route, clambering over the door in the wall into the catmint-smelling garden, skirting the disused well, with its flimsy covering of a herring-barrel lid, and through the cold stone passage to the daylight of James Street. Round the corner of the house the outside steps led to the winding staircase which led in turn to the interior, the inner sanctum where the two elderly widowed sisters lived out their days in uneasy partnership. 'Auntie Kate' Cunningham, my great-aunt, had been married to the St. Andrews-born golfer Harry Duff, whom I was named after. Perhaps that accounted for the bond between us. Kate would give me a pandrop, paper and pencil, and sucking and scribbling I would lie on my belly on the floor of her room until a whispered 'Ye'd better gan through and see yer granny' would send me reluctantly to the darkened bedroom where my arrival, however quietly managed, had been registered, and my non-appearance at the bedside grimly noted. The ritual seldom varied. Was I going 'ist or wast?' (i.e. back home to Cellardyke or down to Anstruther). What was my father 'saying to it' today? More insidiously, how long had I been through beside Kate? I was too young to realise that jealousy will flourish and feed off itself when all the other wellsprings of feeling have dried up. Daunted by her massive presence, and by the Victorian clutter of the room – the interrogatory stare of stuffed birds in their glass cases – I would answer as best I could, uncomfortably aware of the patina of legend that clung to my granny like barnacles. Only years later did I learn how to piece together her story.

Her Cunningham forbears, Cellardyke fishermen like the Watsons with whom they had been intermarrying for centuries, had shrugged off cholera, shipwreck and storm-tossed seas to survive to prodigious old age. Robert Cunningham, my great-great-great-grandfather, had reached 88; his son Alexander, 86. Alexander's father-in-law, the whaler Lock Horsburgh, had escaped time and again from the infamous channel of the Davis Strait to die in his home by the peaceful haven of Pittenweem. Alexander Cunningham and Janet Horsburgh's son,

East Forth Street *c*. 1908, looking west towards Tolbooth Wynd and West Forth Street. The woman on the right, at No. 16, is Kate Smith, wife of skipper William Watson of the *Midlothian*. The boy nearest the camera is their son William. The babes-in-arms are Philip Anderson and Jimmy Smith (cousins of the author's father).

another Robert, attained the venerable age of 92. Now my granny, Jessie Horsburgh Cunningham, lay stranded in the shallows of her bed: Moby Dick in lacing cap and round, peering spectacles. In her young days, according to hearsay, she had been 'wan o' the twa cheekiest women in the toon' (the other was her best friend), and her pride had brought the tut to many a tongue. As a wife and mother her frugality had been striking, even by the canny standards of the day. Finding once that my grandfather had overpaid a crewman for his 'deal', she immediately sent him out to retrieve the money: a twelve-mile walk, there and back, to Craighead, by Fife Ness. Old age had only slightly mellowed her. My father, the youngest of her ten children, stood in awe of her to the end, so how could I do less? She spoke, unselfconsciously, the tongue of her ancestors, and when she died in her 89th year it was like the death of a culture.

The formalities once over, I would make my escape upstairs to the garret, with its neat piles of elderly 'Sunday Posts' and its box of carefully-preserved postcards with exotic stamps. A Meldrum uncle had struck gold in New Zealand's South Island, and my granny's wedding

5

ring was carved out of a nugget from Matakanui. A younger sister had emigrated to Australia. A son, my American uncle John, played professional golf in South Bend, Indiana. The postcards spoke of a network of relations which had spanned the globe. Even better, though, was the abandoned pair of binoculars which nobody but myself ever claimed, and with which I could perch at the eyrie of the garret window and look out at fishing-boats passing down the firth and, beyond, the white-flecked cliffs of the May Island, as the gulls wheeled past and shrieked on the roof.

Next to the garret was the gear-strewn loft where Toby, a neighbour's tomcat, stalked mice on a freelance basis for little reward other than the thrill of the chase and an occasional swig of days-old milk which would glug yellowly from the bottle. Once I brought him a crab, a big 'saftie', and offered it to him in the sunlit, seasprayed garden. One of my chums, in an experimental mood, had dropped a rock on its back, and I watched as the poor smashed creature slowly revolved, the cat licking gingerly at its yellow pulp. Even the pathetic 'dergies' which had dried out in the bottom of my bucket were received with appreciation, in those pre-'Kitekat' days. I took Toby to be representative of the whole cat tribe, and later, when we had cats of our own at home, I would be offended when they backed away fastidiously from my well-intentioned offerings.

When I was four and a half we moved the few hundred yards to Toll Road, where in a few years' time an R.A.F. camp would be built, to be converted later still into Anstruther Holiday Camp: the N.C.O.s' married quarters becoming the present March Place and Crescent. Then, we looked out over a field of cows to the Pictish humps of Kellie and Largo Laws. One Christmas time our attention was caught by a huddle of cows over by the drinking-trough. When they parted, a snow-white calf had been born. In blissful ignorance of its true nature we dubbed it 'Christmas', but after my first panic-stricken flight from its jovial charge I shunned it like the plague.

Behind the house a cornfield stretched down towards the sea. On nights when the haar crept in over the land the revolving light on the May would pierce the curtains of my room, and I would snuggle down under the bedclothes to escape the banshee howl of the foghorn, like a wild creature far out at sea.

Sometimes instead of haunting the seashore I would be drawn to the quiet backwater of Kilrenny, and the crowded churchyard where long-dead Watsons far outnumbered the Cunninghams, Reids, Salters, Tarvits, Fowlers, Meldrums and Murrays on the tilting rows of head-stones. Only years later would I realise the part these others too had

Kilrenny church and churchyard from the Crail road.

played in shaping me, and in a flash of revelation perceive the whole churchyard to be peopled with my kin.

Beyond the churchyard lay the common or 'commontry' of Kilrenny, dominated by the house and grounds of Innergellie, with its frog-infested 'Puddock Dub'. Local legend spoke of nocturnal suicides in that dark, still pool, now long since filled in. Memory can be deceptive when there is no reality left to curb the imagination, and perhaps the pool in the woods was less sinister than my fancy paints it. Yet I recall an acorn-gathering expedition which ended in a dense blanket of fog, when even my ever-reassuring elder sister seemed less confident of her bearings than I could have wished. In retrospect childhood was a succession of sunbursts and fogs, of panics and joys.

Further on, a wooden bridge flanked by dog-roses and a wild luxuri-ance of greenery hung over a railway-line where steam-trains still ran. From that vantage-point I could scan the horizon from the Forth past the distant spires of Anstruther and Pittenweem to Kellie Law, and east-wards almost to Crail – the bounds of my world. This spot and my chosen strip of shoreline were the two fixed points of my existence, the two places to which I could always return and be out of Time: in the brooding days of adolescence; in the tense weeks of late summer before

7

examination results arrived; and later, on the eve of a new life in a new country.

Nowadays, on all too infrequent visits, I walk these places with my own children and see them, as for the first time, through their fresh, unbiased eyes. Their roots, through force of circumstance, lie elsewhere, and they have arrived too late in time to know the ageless rhythms of the traditional fishing community which was still alive in my childhood. Nevertheless, I will do what I can to pass on to them some of that heritage which is theirs as well as mine, for there is much truth in the old cliché that we must know where we have come from before we can know where we are going. In a society which increasingly seeks to urbanise, standardise and homogenise, a sense of identity becomes ever harder to hang on to, especially for the young: hence the need to hand down to them the gift of their past. And to write books like this one.

1

From Dark-Age East Fife to Mediaeval Kilrenny

Cellardyke is a paradoxical sort of place. Despite its long history as a fishing-port, culminating in a brief period of prominence as 'the cod emporium of Scotland', [1] it has never enjoyed an independent existence. From earliest times until 1929 it hid behind the bland official title of 'Nether Kilrenny'; in that year of local government reorganisation it was swallowed up by neighbouring Anstruther. Now only an incorrectly-positioned signpost on the Crail road marks its continuing existence.

The ancient parish of Kilrenny itself extends for about three miles along the coastline of the East Neuk of Fife, bounded on the west by Anstruther and Carnbee, on the north by Carnbee and Crail, on the east by Crail and on the south by the Firth of Forth. For as far back as written records go this has been a fishing community, and a romantic legend out of the Dark Ages purports to explain the origins of the rich fishing-grounds around the May Island, some five miles offshore.

Loth, pagan British king of Lothian, had a daughter, Thaney or Thenaw, who was violated and made pregnant by a prince named Ewan. Enraged by her refusal to marry her violator, her father ordered her to be hurled in a chariot from the summit of Traprain Law. Miraculously, she survived the ordeal unharmed. Loth's Christian subjects tried to inter-cede on her behalf, but pagan counsels prevailed. If she was worthy to live, declared Thenaw's father, let her be handed over to Neptune, and let her God free her from the peril of death if he so wished (*si vita sit digna, Neptuno tradatur, et liberat eam a mortis periculo deus ejus si vult*).

The unfortunate Thenaw was accordingly placed in a leather coracle, which was then towed out beyond the May Island and cast adrift, followed only by shoals of fish from the teeming waters of Aberlady Bay, who had taken pity on the young princess. Luckily, a favourable wind sprang up and carried the coracle up the Forth to Culross, where Thenaw's son Kentigern, the future patron saint of Glasgow, was born. The fish, however, once they saw that their mistress was out of danger, remained in the vicinity of the May, where they have flourished ever since. [2]

This charming miracle is dated with precision to the year 518 A.D.,

A sandstone outcrop at Caiplie. The entrance to one of the 'Coves' can be seen on the right.

and commemorated on the island itself in such place-names as 'the Lady's Bed', 'the Lady's Well' and 'the Maiden Rocks'.[3]

If the story of St. Thenaw is wholly fanciful, however, the other surviving legend from Dark-Age East Fife seems to have at least some basis in fact. A Hungarian missionary named Adrian, together with six thousand, six hundred and six followers, was believed to have come on an evangelising mission to the Picts of the East Neuk sometime in the ninth century, setting up his headquarters at Caiplie Coves on the eastern fringe of Kilrenny parish. Excavations in these caves by the seashore have indeed revealed signs of human habitation, not least in the shape of crosses cut into the inner walls of the so-called 'Chapel Cave'.[4] From this base the saint's ascetic followers spread out along the length and breadth of this rugged coastline, some eventually taking refuge on the May. Here, we are told, the Blessed Adrian himself suffered martyrdom at the hands of marauding Vikings on March 4th, 875.

So powerful was the tradition of the martyred saint that the May eventually acquired a rich monastic foundation, and became the goal of pious pilgrims from all classes of mediaeval Scottish society: from barren women in search of a cure for their affliction, to the Stewart kings themselves. So potent is the legend even today that a street in Anstruther was named after the saint only a few years ago.

How much substance is there in the Adrian legend? Modern scholars,

The entrance to this cave looks man-made.

from the nineteenth-century historian W. F. Skene onwards, have accepted that a mission of some kind took place at that time, but have found no evidence of any such Hungarian incursion into ninth-century Fife. The real missionary is more likely to have been the Irish St. Ethernan, from Clonfert in County Galway, and it is surely no coincidence that he and his followers arrived in East Fife shortly after Clonfert, along with many other Irish monasteries and churches, is known to have been burnt and ravaged by the Danes (i.e. between 841 and 845). Moreover, the Gaelic-speaking Scots of Dalriada, descendants of fifth-century Irish invaders, had recently succeeded in conquering the warlike Picts – Kenneth MacAlpin became joint king of Dalriada and Pictland in 843 – and the land that henceforth would be known as 'Scotland' must have seemed a home from home to the fleeing Irish monks.

According to the Adrian legend, one of the saint's Hungarian followers was a certain Monanus, the reputed founder of St. Monans; but

Incised crosses in the 'Chapel Cave', with a double perforation or 'holdfast' above and to the right. This cave may have contained a rudimentary altar.

in fact St. Moinenn, who died in 571, was an early bishop of Clonfert, and it may well be that his ninth-century successors carried his relics with them to Fife and interred them at Inverie – the old name for St. Monans – thus creating the legend of the saint's ministry there. Another possibility is that the six-thousand-odd followers of 'Adrian' are simply a folk-memory of the Scottish invasion-force itself – of the war-bands with their attendant clergy; the mythical Hungarian missionaries being a later invention designed to please the half-Hungarian Queen Margaret, wife of Malcolm Canmore.[5]

From the ninth century onwards the whole of eastern Scotland north of Forth must have experienced an unprecedented mingling of races, cultures and traditions. The dominant Scots seem to have erased all traces of the Pictish language, although in the process they adopted some Pictish place-name elements. Foremost among these was the prefix *pit-*, a 'share' or 'piece' of land; a 'place', which in combination with various Gaelic words gives us such typically Fife Picto-Gaelic compounds as *Pittenweem* (place of the cave), *Pitbladdo* (place of flour), *Pitliver* (place of the book), *Pittencrieff* (place of the tree) and *Pitcorthie* (place of the standing-stone). The standing-stones of Easter and Wester Pitcorthie in the parishes of Carnbee and Kilrenny respectively are mute witnesses to an even earlier race than Pict or Scot – but from that dark period of prehistory not even a legend has come down to us.

Equally tantalising is the Skeith Stone, a rectangular boulder of sandstone in a field near Rennyhill farm. On one side of the stone is an incised double-ringed wheel design enclosing eight petal-shaped spokes, which are arranged in four pairs to form the arms of a cross. Such 'crosses of art' occur in the West Highlands, but are much rarer in our corner of Scotland. Similar crosses are thought to have been erected as early as the sixth century and as late as the twelfth. The stone formerly gave its name to the land round about, for in 1606 Archbishop Spottiswoode of St. Andrews granted John Strang of Balcaskie 'the quarter toune and lands of Killrynnie callit the Skeith's quarter'. It was the only part of Kilrenny to evade the grasp of the Beaton family.[6]

The next few centuries after the Scottish conquest saw the expansion of the Gaelic language throughout most of Scotland, and not until the twelfth-century influx of Angles, Normans and Flemings did it face a serious challenge. Its gradual decline as the sole tongue of the bulk of the population in East Fife must have begun in this century, as Norman barons acquired lands in the county and communities of merchants and fisherfolk developed into what would later become the first royal burghs. The anonymous author of the Latin *Vita Kentegerni* (Life of St. Kentigern), who gave us the story of St. Thenaw, goes on to say that, even in his day (about 1150) fishermen from all the coasts of Northern Europe were flocking to the rich fishing-grounds of the May Island, for '*ab illo quippe tempore in hunc diem tanta piscium fertilitas ibi abundat ut de omni littore maris, Anglici, Scottici, etiam a Belgie et Gallie littoribus, veniunt gratia piscandi piscatores plurimi quos omnes insula May in suis rite suscipit portibus*' (for, to be sure, from that time to this day there has been such an abundance of fish there that from every coastline – English, Scottish, even Belgian and French – very many fishermen come for the sake of the fishing, all of whom the May Island duly receives in its harbours).[7]

It is not impossible that some of these foreign fishermen may actually have settled on the nearby coast, and it seems more than likely that contacts between the different nationalities would have encouraged the use of a Northern English (i.e. early Scots) dialect by the East Fife men, if only as a lingua franca or neutral medium of communication.

By the 1170s much of the East Neuk was in the possession of the Norman Countess Ada, daughter-in-law of King David I and mother of Malcolm IV and William I; and it is in a charter drawn up on her behalf in or around the year 1170 that the name of Kilrenny first emerges

The 'Skeith Stone', from J. Stuart's *The Sculptured Stones of Scotland* (1856–67). The stone has since been moved slightly nearer the farm track and pushed further into the ground, and the face has suffered considerable weathering.

into recorded history. The charter records the grant of the church of 'Kylrethni', together with half a 'carucate' or ploughland of 'Petcorthi' and a 'toft' or house-site in 'Carele' (Crail), to the Premonstratensian canons of Dryburgh Abbey in Berwickshire. This house of 'White Canons', so styled because of their white cassocks, cloaks and felt bonnets, had been founded only twenty years before, the first canons being imported from the abbey of Alnwick in Northumberland; and the register of the abbey, or *Liber Sanctae Mariae de Dryburgh*, contains copies of the abbey's original charters, some of which are invaluable sources for the early history of Kilrenny.[8] No. 19, for example, dated 1266, contains the following grant by Bishop Gamelin of St. Andrews: 'Know us to have rented to our beloved sons in Christ the abbot and convent of Dryburgh that site on the south side of the church of Kilrenny which Bishop David of good memory granted to them when he dedicated the church [i.e. in 1243], and which they themselves then had enclosed and walled round: To be held by them from us and our successors in perpetuity with the houses which they had built there, freely, peacefully and undisturbed. Paying thence to us and our successors three shillings annually, one half at the Purification of the Blessed Virgin, and the other half at the Assumption of the Virgin'.

From this charter, then, we learn that the land to the south of Kilrenny church was walled-in and built on by 1266. A further charter of 1268 tells us that the vicar of Kilrenny was to be responsible for the annual payment of 3 shillings to St. Andrews, and that he would receive 10 marks sterling as his stipend from Dryburgh.

As for the fishermen of Kilrenny, a charter of 1222 reveals an agreement between the monks of Dryburgh and the Augustinian canons of St. Andrews to the effect that the fishermen of Kilrenny and those of St. Andrews may use each others' harbours without the necessity of paying tithes or 'teinds' there, these being payable only to the church in their native parish. Another dispute from this period was, however, less easily settled. This was the well-known wrangle between Dryburgh and the Benedictine monks of the May Island over anchorages in the Dreel Burn – the boundary between Kilrenny and (West) Anstruther parishes. The monks of Dryburgh complained to Pope Honorius himself about the Anstruther fishermen who moored their boats on the Kilrenny side of the burn, then refused to pay the appropriate teinds to Kilrenny church. In 1225 a compromise solution was reached whereby Dryburgh's right to the teinds of the Kilrenny men was confirmed, the monks of the May receiving the rest of the teinds on condition that they paid an annual tribute of a mark of silver within the parish church of Kilrenny. This thirteenth-century legal wrangle may have been the first dispute between the two parishes: it was certainly not the last.

An early reference to the modern 'Innergellie' occurs in charter no. 20, *Super terra de Invergelly*, dated 1281. This records the grant by Margareta of Ardross of part of the estate of Innergellie to Dryburgh Abbey; the donor being the wife of Hugo de Perisby, Sheriff of Roxburgh, and the

Innergellie House, Kilrenny, built in 1740 on the site of an older house. A century earlier the estate belonged to Sir James Lumsdaine, who commanded an army for the Swedish King Gustavus Adolphus in the Thirty Years War in Germany. Until recently the grounds were heavily wooded, and formerly they contained a number of cottages tenanted by estate-workers and tradesmen.

daughter of Merleswain, former lord of Innergellie. Merleswain may have been descended from a Saxon lord of that name who accompanied Prince Edgar Atheling to Scotland in 1068.[9]

What can we deduce from the Gaelic names *Kilrethny* or *-renny* and *Inver-* or *Innergelly*? The latter is quite simply 'mouth of the river Gelly' – the stream which runs through Kilrenny – but the name Kilrenny itself is more of a puzzle. *Kil-* is a common prefix, meaning a church or hermit's cell, and is most often found in conjunction with the name of a Celtic saint.[10] Could the second element then be connected with Ethernan, the original 'Adrian'? Or is it, as the Celtic scholar W. J. Watson has suggested, a corruption of *urnuigh* (Middle Gaelic *irnaide*) 'an oratory'?[11] A former minister of Kilrenny, the Rev. William Beat or Bett, writing in 1791, mentions that the fishermen of his day referred to the church as 'St. Irnie', and adds that in pre-Reformation days '. . . the devotees at Anstruther, who could not see the church of Kilrenny till they travelled up the rising ground to what they called the Hill, then pulled off their bonnets, fell on their knees, crossed themselves, and prayed to St. Irnie'.[12]

As this implies, the parish of Kilrenny formerly (until 1641) included Anstruther Easter, which had no church of its own until 1634. Mr. Beat almost certainly errs in deriving the name of 'St. Irnie' from St. Irenaeus, Bishop of Lyons, but his anecdote reveals that the legend of the site's former sanctity survived the disappearance from the parish of the Gaelic language, and the change of religion at the Reformation, to link the eighteenth-century fishermen of Cellardyke, however tenuously, with their remote ancestors.

Of the remainder of the mediaeval period there is little to relate. We can be sure that Kilrenny, like other parts of the Scottish Lowlands, would have suffered in the various outbreaks of civil strife which were characteristic of the age, and we know for example that the East Neuk was ravaged in 1445 by the Earl of Crawford, the sworn enemy of Bishop Kennedy of St. Andrews. According to the *Auchinleck Chronicle*, 'Ther was ane richt gret herschipe (i.e. armed raid) maid in Fyff ... on Sanctandrois land. ... And incontinent eftir bischope James Kennedy cursit solempnitlie with myter & staf buke and candill contynually a yer And interdytit all the placis quhar thir personis war'.[13] The raiders, it seems, harried 'nocht onlie the bischopis landis bot also the haill landis adjacent thairto, and brocht great pryssis of goodis out of Fyfe unto Angus'. It is unlikely that Kilrenny would have escaped this savage onslaught, although what 'pryssis of goodis' it could have yielded its attackers is hard to imagine.

Seven years after the Crawford raid King James II granted the Bishop of St. Andrews the so-called 'Golden Charter', which confirmed and ratified all previous grants of land to that rich see. Included in the long list are the names 'Kilrynny' and 'Invergelly', [14] and according to local tradition Bishop Kennedy went so far as to have a house erected for his use hard by the present Cellardyke harbour: 'This was in 1452, and the change is immediately signalised, if we believe the old fathers, by the erection of the 'Bishop's House', a stately tenement built, like the grange house of an old abbey, on a tier of massive arches, and shielded by the pier, which was originally designed, they also tell us, to save it from the storm'.[15]

When the 'stately tenement' was demolished in the late nineteenth century to make way for the present 9/10 Shore Street, workmen found frescoes on the walls.[16] Nor had Bishop Kennedy been the last prelate to live there, as an old man recalled for the readers of the *East Fife Observer* in 1927, drawing on the traditions of his childhood: 'There was a large house opposite the steps leading to the bulwark at the harbour. I think it had been the house of the Bishop of Orkney, or some distinguised

Shore Street, Cellardyke, in the 1920s, looking west towards George Street. Kirsty Murray and Jessie Murray Jack, with Tom Murray and W. Jack. The three-storey building in the background occupies the site of the former Bishop's Palace.

personage in the olden days. The park where Dove Street now stands was the grounds of it, and the Shore Wynd was the avenue or approach to the house'.[17] George Gourlay fleshes out the story for us on page 84 of *Anstruther: or Illustrations of Scottish Burgh Life*: 'Andrew Bruce, bishop of Orkney ... [was]one of the most remarkable men of his age. ... History tells the heroic sacrifice that led to his retirement to the castle built by Bishop Kennedy at the harbour of Cellardyke, where he died 18th March, 1699, in the 70th year of his age, and the 34th of his ministry. He was buried (in Anstruther Easter churchyard) by the side of his wife Elspeth Bethune of the house of Balfour. No stone was ever erected to his memory'.

Cellardyke must surely be unique among the fishing-villages of Scotland in having had an episcopal residence in the lee of its little harbour; and indeed even the name of the local bathing-pool – the 'Cardinal's Steps' – serves as a reminder that here the redoubtable David Beaton would board the ferry carrying pilgrims to his city of St. Andrews.

These prelates were of course keenly aware of the commercial advantages of the tiny East Neuk ports, and we should not underestimate the importance of the fisheries, even at this early date, to the lairds and churchmen of the district. In Anstruther the monks of Balmerino Abbey built a chapel for the fishermen who supplied them with the 'cream of

18

the sea'.[18] In Crail, the original settlement near the harbour grew into 'a sizeable and prosperous urban community'[19] which by the early sixteenth century could house well-to-do lairds and merchants in stone-built houses. In Pittenweem the 'virtuous labours' of the local fishermen provided vital revenues for the priory of the May Island.[20] In the sixteenth century enterprising individuals in each community would take steps to improve their local harbour facilities, thereby creating the thriving little fishing-towns which would become immortalised as the 'golden fringe on the beggar's mantle'. It was just such entrepreneurial activity which would transform a sheltered pocket of water behind tidal rocks at Nether Kilrenny into the fishing-village of Cellardyke, as we shall see in the next chapter.

2

From Skinfasthaven to Silverdyke

The period leading up to the Reformation was one of the most turbulent in Scottish history, and perhaps nowhere more so than in the East Neuk of Fife, with its metropolitan see of St. Andrews. Heresy-hunting reached its apogee here during the reign of Cardinal David Beaton, and the crofter-fishermen of the coastal parishes must have learned to hide any traces of dissent behind a cloak of filial obedience to Mother Church. In Kilrenny, where Master John Lauder was vicar perpetual, they would have been particularly well-advised to do so.

To the early Reformers like John Knox, for whom he was a 'sergeant of Satan', Lauder represented all that was worst in the pre-Reformation church. A pluralist, he held, in addition to his Kilrenny vicarate, a prebend of the collegiate church of Crichton, the parsonage of More-battle and the archdeaconry of Teviotdale. After serving as secretary to Archbishop Forman of St. Andrews from 1517 to 1521, Lauder spent many years in Glasgow, where he built up a formidable reputation as an ecclesiastical curser. The famous excommunication of the Border reivers, penned in 1525 and preserved in the *St. Andrews Formulare*, is thought to be a specimen of Lauder's work, and as one modern scholar has commented: 'If John Lauder himself drew up this document, some new light is thrown on his association with heresy trials and on the significance of the description of his behaviour when prosecuting George Wishart. Lauder may have been famed throughout the land as an expert in malediction'.[1]

When in 1539 David Beaton succeeded his uncle as Archbishop of St. Andrews, Lauder returned from Glasgow to be his secretary, and to enter the annals of Protestant demonology. As the above quotation implies, the trial in 1546 of George Wishart – the friend and mentor of John Knox – made a particularly strong impression on the public mind, and a contemporary account of the proceedings gives a lurid insight into John Lauder's prosecuting technique: 'Rycht against him (i.e. Wishart) stood up one of the fedd flok, a monstere, Johnne Lawder, ladin full of cursingis writtin in paper, of the which he took out a roll boyth long and also full of cursingis, threatnynges, maledictionis and wordis of devillesh spyte and malice, saying to the innocent Maister George so many cruell and abhominable wordis, and hit him so spytfullie with the Popis thunder, that the ignorant people dreded least the earth then wold have swallowed him up qwick. . . . When that this fedd sow had red throwghout all his lying minasingis, his face runnyng doune with sweat, and frothing at the mouth lyik ane bayre, he spate at Maister George his face, saying, "What ansuerist thow to these sayingis, thow runnigat, tratour, theef, which we have dewlye proved by sufficient witnes against thee?" '[2]

Wishart had much to answer, but to no avail. His accusers erected a stake for him beside the walls of St. Andrews Castle, and as Cardinal Beaton reclined on cushions to watch the spectacle, Wishart was strangled and burnt to death, bags of gunpowder strapped to his body to aid the combustion process. Atrocity breeds atrocity, however, and a mere eight weeks later the Cardinal's mutilated body hung gaping over the same castle walls, while, according to the Fife historian Robert Lindsay of Pitscottie: '. . . ane callit Guthrie pischit in his mouth that all the pepill might sie'.[3] John Lauder, whether by good luck or good management, survived to die a natural death five years later.

Monster or not – and we must allow for Protestant bias in contemporary descriptions of him – Lauder was probably an able cleric and administrator, and without doubt a subtle diplomat, for we know of his involvement in diplomatic missions to Flanders and Rome. Nor was he concerned solely with high affairs of state, for only three years before the horrors of St. Andrews, on behalf of his master the Cardinal, he had drawn up the charter which survives as no. 497 in the *St. Andrews Formulare*, and which in effect is the blueprint for the future port of Cellardyke.

The document is a curious mixture of the self-seeking and the philanthropic. Lauder's concern is to ensure the repair and upkeep of the new harbour of 'Skinfasthaven', previously little used by mariners (*novi portus marini olim lie Skynfasthavyne vulgariter nuncupati anteaque minime frequentati*), in order to provide a safe haven for ships and boats, especially for fishing-boats which will provide the vicar of Kilrenny with a regular income from catches of herring (*allecum*) and other fish. Furthermore, the building of the harbour will encourage more people to settle in that deserted place (*terra vasta et deserta*), which in turn will guarantee a steady flow of funeral dues and other emoluments to the parish church (. . . *cujus novi portus constructi et completi occasione plurimi inhabitandi gratia convenient qui michi et successoribus meis dicte ecclesie . . . oblationes jura funeralia finantias paschales jura ecclesiastica et alia emolumenta solvent* (*etc.*)). To implement John Lauder's intended improvements, no-one has

'Skinfasthaven', the interior of Cellardyke's tidal harbour, with Harbourhead and the east end of Shore Street. Undated, probably pre-1900. The outside stairs have long since been demolished.

been found more suitable (*nemo magis ydoneus aut convenius inveniri poterat*) than an honourable man, John Beaton of Kilrenny, who, with the consent of Thomas, Abbot of Dryburgh, and David, Archbishop of St. Andrews, is accordingly granted the tenth part of all fishes landed at Kilrenny's new harbour by the fishers of the parish; with the exception of the teinds of fish landed by citizens of the east part of the burn of the town of Anstruther, which Lauder reserves to himself and his successors. However, the teinds of fish landed at Anstruther by Kilrenny boats are to go to the Beatons. The laird of Anstruther at this time seems to have controlled the teinds of Anstruther Wester, and there was an agreement between the two lairds that neither would interfere with the other's fish teinds. It was a complicated business, and would be the source of much bitterness and feuding between the parishes in centuries to come.[4]

That Lauder's (or rather Beaton's) choice should have fallen on the laird of Kilrenny, former captain of St. Andrews Castle and nephew of the Cardinal, comes as no surprise. Nepotism, whatever its ethical shortcomings, is often an efficient way of doing business, and for confirmation that John Beaton took his responsibilities seriously we have only to leap forward a generation in time to 1579, and the act of the Scottish parliament which confirmed John Beaton's hereditary tenure of 'the port and heavyne callit the Skynfast Heyvne'.

'To his greit chairges and expensis', we are informed, John Beaton has 'buyldit and reparit the said heavyne to the confort and commoditie of all personis frequentand navigatioun alsweill within this realme as they quha salhappyne to repair to the samyne (same) Being chieflie movit thairto for the preservatioun of divers the liegis off this realme quhome he has sene with thair schippis and boittis in greit hazard with tempest of evill wathir quha hes had thair releif be the commoditie of the said heavyne'.

Beaton petitions his sovereign to ratify the erection of the little creek into a proper port, with himself as feuar being entitled to all the profits therefrom; and the petition is duly granted. There follows a Latin Charter by Patrick Adamson, Archbishop of St. Andrews at the time, conferring on John Beaton's lands of Kilrenny the status of a free burgh of regality, with the power to buy and sell wine, wax, linen, wool and other merchandise. The laird and his heirs are to receive all burghal rents, together with lesser customs, tolls, stall-keepers' fees and fines for bloodshed (*omnes et singulas firmas burgales dicti burgi cum parvis custumis thelonijs stallangijs bludewittis*). Permission is granted for the erection of a market cross, for a weekly market, and for annual fairs.[5] A distinctive coat-of-arms was adopted: 'On the sea a fishing-boat with four men rowing and one steering and letting down a line and hook. The sun above emerging from clouds. Legend: SEMPER TIBI PENDIAT HAMUS KILRENNY'.[6] This Latin sentence was freely translated by future generations of Cellardyke fishermen as 'May ye aye hae a hyuck in the watter'. It was an appropriate motto for the newly-fledged little burgh, whose fortunes would depend upon the chancy harvest of the sea.

John Beaton's concern for the fishers of Skinfasthaven was not an isolated phenomenon, for the late sixteenth century seems to have been a boom-time for harbour construction and repair. In 1541 both Anstruther and Pittenweem had been granted the right to build one or more harbours, and Anstruther's was completed in time for the hanging of two English pirates there in 1587.[7] In 1575 the harbour at Crail was in dire straits, and 'almaist altogidder unhable to ressave or keip in saulftie schip or boit resorting thairto'.[8] It was, deemed King James VI, 'maist necessar that the said port and havin be bet and repairit with all expeditioun, specialie in consideratioun that fyve boittis seikand thairto have laitlie perist in the mouth of the harberie'; and the treasurer of the burgh was therefore given powers to exact tolls and taxes from ships using the haven in order to raise funds for essential repairs. Similar works were under way or projected at St. Andrews, St. Monans, Kirkcaldy and other coastal towns up and down the Firth, for this was

The burgh seal of Kilrenny, from Lewis's *Topographical Dictionary*.

James's 'Golden Fringe', the resort of exotic 'strangearis' from France, Germany and the Baltic lands as much as of seamen and traders from nearer home.[9]

It would of course be wrong to imagine that these developments took place in a political vacuum. In 1547 many Fife lairds and doubtless many more of their tenants had fallen in battle against the English at Pinkiecleuch near Musselburgh. The following year an English invasion force landed in the East Neuk, and engaged the local inhabitants in pitched battle on St. Monans muir.[10] French and English ships did battle in the Forth, and every harbour and creek must have shared in the general frenzy of activity.[11] In 1565, Queen Mary deputed 'the keping of the havynnis and commoun passagis' to local magnates and councils, all of whom were charged with keeping known rebels out and potential ones in. 'Sanct monanis, Kilmynane and Pettinweme' were allotted to James Sandilands; 'Anstruder on bayth the sydis of the burn' to John Anstruther of that Ilk; 'Craill and Kilrynny' to the baillies of Crail, and 'Fyffis Ness and Balcomy' to Myrtoun of Cambo.[12] In June 1572 all men of property in Fife were ordered to join in the siege of Edinburgh, bringing with them a month's supplies, under pain of losing 'lyff, lands and guidis'.[13] No provision was made for conscientious objection.

Apart from the obvious toll in human lives and maimed bodies, this constant warfare and civil strife was attended with looting, burning and loss or destruction of crops and property. Plague and virulent fevers were also no strangers to these maritime communities, and there are many references to ships returning to the Forth with plague on board, only to be ordered to make for Inchcolm and lie there until 'cleansed'. In 1580 this was the fate of the *William*, skipper John Downy, whose crew were forbidden to set foot on the mainland until further notice.[14]

War, religious strife, invasion, famine and plague – these were the grim realities of life in the East Neuk in the sixteenth century. Yet then, as so often in succeeding centuries, there were occasions when the 'silver darlings' appeared in the Forth in such mysterious profusion that all other thoughts were driven from men's minds. In August 1574, for example, so Pitscottie relates, 'thair came in our firth ane scuill of heirinng (herring) that the lyk was nevir of befoir in thir wattiris in this tyme of the yeir'.[15] One only hopes the Kilrenny fishermen got their fair share of the bonanza.

It might be appropriate at this point to consider just *who* the inhabitants of Kilrenny and Anstruther were in the late sixteenth century. As far as the landed gentry are concerned, the question is easily answered. They were in fact the descendants of a small group of families who had been established in that corner of the kingdom for many centuries, and who were related to each other by sedulous intermarriage in a way which prefigures the convoluted patterns of inter-relationship within the later fishing-communities themselves. In Kilrenny the Beatons, Betouns or Bethunes – the name is variously spelt – were descended from a Sir Robert Beaton who by 1378 had inherited from his father-in-law the lands of Balfour in Markinch parish. The John Beaton mentioned above was married to Agnes Anstruther, sister of the Laird of Anstruther, whose Norman ancestors had arrived in the East Neuk shortly after the Conquest. Sir John Anstruther's second wife was a scion of the Learmonth family of Dairsie and Balcomie, and a daughter married into the family of Monipenny, one of whom had been the mother of Cardinal David Beaton. John Beaton's charter of Skinfasthaven was witnessed by Robert Strang, portioner of Kilrenny, who seems to have been related to the Strangs of Balcaskie. This family was resident at Balcaskie by, at the latest, 1362, when we first encounter John Strang of Balcaskie, husband of Cecilia Anstruther. Robert Strang married Agnes Beaton of Balfour, and their son John married Margaret Barclay of Innergelly, whose family also owned Pitcorthie. The daughter of an earlier Barclay had married Alexander Inglis or Tarvit, whose lands included Caiplie and Thirdpart. Add to this the names Forret, Sandilands, Sibbald, Durie, Melville –

and scarcely one illustrious Fife name is missing from the communal
pedigree.[16]

Less easily discernible in the records are the class of tenant farmers,
although the *Register of the Privy Seal* for 1575 does record a grant to
John Gledstanis of oats from lands in Kilrenny occupied by 'Johne Blak
and William Schevis'. Interestingly enough, a cottage to the west of
Kilrenny churchyard bears on its east gable a panel representing the
arms of Archbishop Schevis of St. Andrews (1478–96), and it may be
that some of his family lived nearby.

Even more interesting, because more real to us in his human frailty, is
the unfortunate 'Andro Weland in Kilrynne' who in the year 1565
emerges briefly from obscurity in the pages of the *St. Andrews Kirk-
Session Register*, where both he and Anne Anderson, 'inhabitant in
Sanctandrois', are 'delated, callit and accused as huyrmongaris'.[17] Andro
is only the first in a long line of his fellow-parishioners who were to fall
foul of kirk-session and presbytery, and it is ironic that, for so many of
our ancestors, only the written record of their various delinquencies
preserves their names and the fact of their existence for posterity. Andro
Weland's crime, that of having had premarital relations with a woman
who subsequently became pregnant, would hardly be regarded as a
'crime' today; but in 1565 it was sufficiently grave to merit several
mentions in the presbytery records. Andro and Anne's baby, we learn,
was born in St. Andrews, the mother confessing before witnesses that
Andro was the father. The couple were married, the baby was baptised,
and we hear no more of Andro Weland.

Yet another source of information about the early inhabitants of our
parish is provided by the Register of Testaments in the *Commissariot
Record of St. Andrews*.[18] This is a record of the last wills and testaments
of citizens of the East Neuk from 1549 onwards, and although few of
those listed can have had much to leave to their descendants, we read
here the names of Margaret Fuird (Ford) in Kilrenny; Janet Howieson in
'Caiplove-myll' (Caiplie-mill); David Paterson at 'Overgelle' and John
Kinninmonth at 'Enirgellie', all in 1551; David Lessels at 'Standand-
stane of Pitcorthy', in 1589; Alexander Geordie and his wife Bessie
Robertson in the 'Cottoune of Barns', in 1594; William Grub, 'sometime
in Kilrenny' and John Smart, 'sometime in Kepla' (Caiplie), both in
1595 – and several others.

More important than all these, however, are the earliest records of
births, marriages and deaths in Kilrenny parish, preserved for future
generations in the old parish registers of Anstruther Wester parish. Why
Anstruther Wester? The reason is quite simple. After the Reformation in

1560 it was some time before every parish in the country could be supplied with a qualified minister, and in the meantime many parishes made do with an inferior clergyman or 'reader' who was licensed to read aloud to the congregation from the Scriptures, catechise, sometimes even baptise children, but not to preach. Often the reader would simply be the priest who had been serving in that particular church before the Reformation, for many of the old clergy were happy to embrace the doctrines of the reformed faith. Such a one was Master John Forman, vicar of Kilrenny in 1560 and subsequently reader. Churches served by such incumbents were visited regularly by the nearest fully-qualified minister, who would preach and administer Communion. In the Anstruther area only Anstruther Wester church had a 'proper' minister – Mr. William Clark – who remained in office until his death in 1583, and his responsibilities included ministering to the congregations of Kilrenny, Pittenweem and Abercrombie as well as his own. Each place had its own kirk-session, but the minutes of all their meetings, together with the birth, marriage and death records of each parish, were alike entered in the Anstruther Wester register, which commences at the unusually early date of 1577.

For a modern native of old 'Kilrynny' it is a moving and exciting experience to search these ancient records, and to see, dimly outlined in fading ink and through the twentieth-century barrier of a microfilm-reader, names, including his own, which are still current in the parish. The following list represents a selection of entries for the years 1577 to 1580, and presents them in the form in which they were written down – with the addition of modern equivalents in brackets where the original may be hard to recognise. (If the present writer's surname seems to be over-represented here, this is not entirely deliberate! In fact, 'Watson' seems to have been one of the commonest names in the parish from a very early date.) Many birth entries give the names of 'witnesses' (god-parents); others, though not all, name the mother of the child – a practice which was still not common in inland parishes such as Kings-barns two centuries later. Where one or more words have through the passage of time become illegible, this is indicated below by means of three dashes:

1577   androw watsone of his wyf ––– ane sone bapt. callit androw
(July 23) James Kyngow of his wyf ane sone bapt. callit Thomas
(August)   John Wod (Wood) of his wyf maron anderson ane dochter
           bapt. callit agnes Witnesses john anderson allexander blak
           jhon thomsone of his wyf margret blak ––– Witnesses allex[r].
           blak willyem watsone thomas watsone

(Sept.)	Sir James of Balfour ane sone bapt. callit James Witnes erl of crawfurd

(Dec.)	robert cuik of his wyf jonat watsone ––– Witnesses thomas watsone charles Lessels thomas gray allane findlay

1578	(many entries indecipherable) thomas andersone ane sone bapt. callit allex^r. Witnesses androw andersone john andersone

william brown of his wyf elspet davidsone ane dochter bapt. callit janet Witnes jone king

1579

(April)	Androw Watsone of his wyf ane sone bapt. callit Wilyem Witnesses willeam th––– john allex^r. younger john kaird younger

(June 3)	John King of his wyf ––– Pacock ane sone bapt. Witnes george pacock in pittenweem

(June 11)	Thomas Watsone of his wyf Jonet thomsone ane sone bapt. Wilyem fairfull of his wife Isbell Jonson ––– Witnes Wilyem Watsone

androw smart with betrix greif mariet

(Aug. 23)	James Anstruther of that ilk of his wyf ––– ane son bapt. callit James Witnes John Beton of Balfour

(Aug. 26)	jhon wyd (Waid) of his wyf agnis gardnir ane dochter bapt. callit agnis Witnesses jhon wyd Jhon Leth wilyem myllir

(Sept. 6)	Allex^r. Anderson of pittenweem paroch (parish) with grissell mychel (Mitchell) mariet

(Nov. 25)	peter Watsone of his wyf jonet blak ane sone bapt. callit peter Witnesses William Watsone John Allex^r. John blak

(Dec.)	david barclay of his wyf jonet adamsone ane sone bapt. callit david Witnes Thomas Jak

william watsone of his wyf Nans garland ane sone bapt. callit Thomas

1580

(Feb. 19)	Thomas muir of his wyf geils michel a sone baptised. Witnesses andrew wyde William paterson

(May 17)	John gib(son?) of his wyf bessie watson a sone bapt. Witnes William Watson

(May 18)	Thomas Watsone of his wyf Jonet Thomsone a son bapt. Witnesses William Watsone Robert Watsone

(Aug. 3)	Jhon Watsone of his wyf ––– Anderson a dochter bapt. callit Rebecca Witnesses Thomas Watson William Watson.

There are many points of interest in these early parish registers. Already we can distinguish clearly a pattern of relationship between Watsons, Thomsons, Alexanders and Blacks. Marriage with 'outsiders' from Pittenweem is not unknown. One entry for 1578, not quoted above, mentions 'androw sater in innergellie', and is interesting by virtue of the fact that Saters or Salters continued to live on the Innergellie estate until well into the nineteenth century. The older spelling of the name reflects a pronunciation still heard today.

Sometimes a particular entry gives rather more information than is the norm. Under January 27th, 1580, for instance, we read:

> Symon philp of his wyf Euphane grub ane dochter bapt. callit —— Witnesses William grub her fader James philip his broder.

On one occasion the parish clerk took a charitable view of an irregular birth:

> voll (Will) yung of his future wyfe Isbell ——— a dochter bapt. Witnes Peter Watson.

On another occasion his suspicion shows through:

> (March 1580) William gowrlaye (Gourlay) stranger with his wyf as he allegit Issobell ane sone callit Williame.

But most significant of all for our purpose is this semi-legible entry for the last day of August 1579:

> penult. augusti 1579 in kylrynnie
> John Willsone in the siller dyk of his wyf ——— ane dochter callit ———.

This, as far as can be ascertained, is the first recorded mention of Cellardyke: the earliest surviving evidence of the fisher community which, in accordance with the wishes of priest and laird, had grown up around the old creek of Skinfasthaven in Nether Kilrenny. Later the same year there are references to Allex^r. Kynninmonth and William Spindie in 'Sellerdyke', and just over a decade later the *Commissariot Record of St. Andrews* is recording the wills of Andrew Spindie and his wife Agnes Henderson 'in Silverdyke' (1596); John Alexander, 'mariner in Silver Dykes' (1597), and James Mortoun, 'in Silverdykes' (1599).

Despite modern theories about cellars and dykes, the first element in the name is obviously 'silver' – in Scots, 'siller' – which in turn is modified by the Fife dialect into 'seller', the Fife pronunciation of -i- tending to be an open -e- sound. At some later stage, either through genuine ignorance of the older Scots tongue or out of a desire to anglicise

The Rev. James Melville's manse, built in 1590–91 in Anstruther Easter, then still part of Kilrenny parish.

what had begun to sound too rudely 'Scotch', the 'seller' was officially converted into the neater, if historically less accurate, 'cellar'.

As the sixteenth century drew to a close, Kilrenny acquired its first, and arguably its finest, full-time minister. James Melville's achievements were many and varied, but perhaps the deed for which he is best remembered is his succouring of a stray ship from the Spanish Armada in 1588, with its crew of 'for the maist part young berdles men, sillie, trauchled, and houngered'. After coming ashore at Anstruther the sailors were given 'keall, pattage and fische', and were hospitably entertained by the townsfolk until they were in a condition to return home. The kind deed bore fruit, for on his return the Spanish captain, Juan Gomez de Medina, found that an Anstruther boat had been interned in the port of his home town and the crew imprisoned. Mindful of his reception in Anstruther, de Medina lost no time in having the Anstruther men set free and returned to their home town with messages of goodwill to Mr. Melville and the laird of Anstruther.[19]

James Melville was a powerful and expressive writer, and his *Diary* is one of the ornaments of Older Scots prose. In an entry for the year 1596, for example, he give a typically vivid description of a phenomenon which will become all too familiar to us in the course of this story – a raging storm in the East Neuk:

> This yeir had twa prodigius things, quhilk I marked amangs us, on the coste syd. Ane in the Seinyie ouk efter Pace (in the week of the Synod, after Easter), the day being fear, about noone, ther fell a cloud of rean upon Kellie Law, and the mountains besyd, that for a space covered them with rinning water, the quhilk descending thairfra, rasit sa at ane instant the strypes and burns, that they war unpassable to the travellars, whowbeit weill horst ('horsed', mounted). The burn of Anstruther was never sein sa grait in man's memorie, as it rase within an hour. The read speat of fresche water (i.e. red with soil from the fields) market the sie mair nor a myll and a halff. That brought grait barrenness upon the land the yeirs following. The uther (prodigious thing) was a monstruus grait whaale, befor the hervest cam in, upon Kincrag Sandes (i.e. Kincraig, nr. Elie).[20]

The scene springs before our eyes: Caddies Burn and the Dreel Burn hurtling in spate to the shore, the spreading red stain in the Forth, and Leviathan – hurled out of his natural element – gasping on Kincraig Sands.

But whales and the weather were the least of James Melville's problems. From the outset he had realised that each parish church in the district needed its own resident minister, and he was single-minded in his efforts to secure outright possession of the various fish-teinds, in order to guarantee his successors a regular income. The laird of Anstruther was prevailed upon to sell his teind-rights to Melville for a fixed sum of money. His uncle, another John Anstruther, was by now vicar and reader at Kilrenny, and he proved less tractable. Persistent bargaining finally helped James Melville to achieve his goal, but his exasperation at the obduracy of the Anstruther family and his lack of faith in their goodwill found expression in the form of a curse: as if to illustrate that the art of malediction had not died with John Lauder:

> And namlie I man ernestlie admonische the hous of Anstruther never to mein to acclame againe the tytle or possessioun of thay teinds, whowbeit they might find a corrupt and sacrilegius perjured persone to put in the roume (i.e. in my place), be whome they might gett a new sett and possessioun of thay teind fishes; for I pronunce heir a curse and maledictioun from God upon whosoever sall introvert (i.e. intervene, meddle) and draw away the commodities thairof from the right use of susteining of the ministerie of God's worschipe and of the salvatioun of God's peiple's saulles within the town of Anstruther and congregation of Kilrynnie. And God forbid that ever that hous (i.e. the family of Anstruther) sould bring on it the feirfull effect of this curse, quhilk of dewtie I man love best of anie hous in the land.[21]

For his congregation in Kilrenny, to whom alone he chose to devote himself from October 1590 (much to the anger and dismay of his original Anstruther Wester congregation), James Melville had kinder words. He was badly off financially, and had considered accepting various better-paid offers elsewhere:

> Yit, finding my deir peiple's hartes, their obedience to my ministerie, and wounder-full blessing of God growing alwayes with me, I durst na wayes waver or mint away (i.e. try to leave), bot stand stedfast in that roum and station wher He haid placed me.[22]

This loyalty to his chosen congregation of Kilrenny would be recipro-cated years later when Melville found, in King James VI and I, a more formidable adversary than John Anstruther. Summoned to London in 1606, along with his uncle Andrew Melville, James found himself on the receiving end of that monarch's severe displeasure. Both Melvilles had been leaders of the resistance among Scottish churchmen to King James's policy of bringing the Scottish church into line with the Church of England, and Andrew Melville, in a famous gesture of exasperation, had even dared to pluck the king by the sleeve and remind him that he was but 'God's sillie vassall'. The upshot for James Melville was per-petual banishment to the North of England; and although his faithful parishioners in Kilrenny would make repeated appeals for the rescinding of his sentence, he would die at Berwick-upon-Tweed in the year 1614 without ever again setting foot in his native land.

3

Seventeenth-Century Kilrenny: War, Witchcraft and Want

The beginning of the seventeenth century found Kilrenny, with its port of Silverdyke, enrolled in the ranks of royal burghs and enjoying the dues and privileges which went with that coveted status. Each burgh was the trading centre for an extensive hinterland, and it was only from royal burghs that fish and such 'staple goods' as wool and hides could be exported. Into their harbours, by contrast, came '. . . vessels laden with the fine cloth and manufactures of Flanders and Lombardy, the wines of France, timber from the Baltic, oriental luxuries, and the spices that made a winter diet of salt beef palatable'.[1]

There were thirty-six royal burghs by this time, all of which regarded themselves as vastly superior to the ordinary 'burgh of regality or barony' which had been founded by a local laird or churchman, and which was therefore merely 'thrallit to serve ane raice of pepill'.[2] Nevertheless, Kilrenny itself had developed out of precisely this kind of 'inferior' burgh, and indeed the expense of sending a paid delegate or 'commissioner' at regular intervals to meetings of the Convention of Royal Burghs, together with the oppressive taxes exacted from royal burghs in return for their privileges, would eventually force the presumptuous little seaport to petition the Scottish parliament for restoration to its former status of a burgh of regality.

As for the fishermen themselves, their calling has perhaps never been more dangerous than it was at this period, when Dutch, German, French, Spanish, English and Scottish vessels disputed the seas around Britain. It is difficult for us nowadays to appreciate the importance of the fisheries at the end of the Middle Ages, when for a small country like Holland they could hold the key to unmatched wealth and political power amongst the nations of Northern Europe. The Scottish kings were not slow to realise the potential of the industry, and in 1493 Parliament in Edinburgh had passed an act enjoining the burghs to build fishing-boats of 20 tons, and to man them, if need be, with the idle able-bodied men of the parish.[3] The following century saw a spate of legislation concerned with the catching, selling and export of salmon, herring and 'keeling' (cod), and by 1600 fleets of small, half-decked 'crears' were sailing from Cellardyke, Anstruther, Crail and Pittenweem to the herring grounds of the Western Isles and the rich cod and ling banks of Orkney and Shetland.

Long before their appearance in these fishing-grounds, however, the Dutch and North Germans – confusingly described in contemporary records as 'Hollanders' and 'Dutch' (from *Deutsch*, i.e. German) respectively – had made those waters their own. As early as 1177 the Dutch had drawn up regulations prescribing the correct manner of salting herrings, and by 1295 they were fishing for herring off Yarmouth.[4] A century later it was a Dutchman who invented the curing process, an innovation which led directly to the great Dutch salted herring trade of the later mediaeval and early modern period. The type of boat favoured by these highly professional fishermen was the huge, squat 'buss' crewed by up to 24 men; and by 1614 the Dutch fishing-fleet had grown to over 1,000 of these vessels, all protected by an auxiliary convoy of heavily-armed warships from the attacks of Spanish galleons, French privateers, or any other jealous aggressor. Dutch law laid down that the Shetland fishery should start on June 24th, and from that date until September the Dutch fleet would work its way down past Fair Isle, Buchan Ness and the Dogger Bank, to finish up at Yarmouth.

On their passage south, despite the agreement of 1594 whereby they undertook not to come '. . . within the sight of the shoar, nor into any of the loughs nor in the seas betwixt islands', these arrogant rulers of the waves would frequently invade the harbours and creeks of the East Neuk, where they met with stubborn resistance from the natives. In George Gourlay's picturesque phrase, 'Mynheer, vaunting in his big bus, which floated like a tower amongst the boats, would sweep into the Auld Haikes or the Traith, from which he would only be beaten, if beaten at all, by cutlass and pike'.[5]

If the Dutch were no friends of the East Neuk fishers, no more were the men of the Western Isles. The *Register of the Privy Council* for the year 1605 records the 'barbarous and deteastable murthers, slauchters and uthers insolencies' perpetrated by the Lewismen on Lowland fishermen, and describes them as 'professit and avowit enemies to all his Majesties guid subjects, and to all strangers quha aither in thair lawfull trade of fishing or be contrarious winds are set upon thair coist, swa that be reason of thair barbaritie and tyrannie the trade of fisheing in these pairts is neglectit and oursein, to the grite hurt of the commonweill'. The same theme is taken up at a meeting of the Convention of Royal Burghs, where the commissioners complain that 'the maist profitabill and easie fisching at all tymeis is to be haid in the ileis, and lochis thairof', from which the fishermen of the royal burghs are 'debarrit be the wiolence and barbarous crueltie, abusis and extortiouns of the hielandis and cuntre men'.[6] They have no desire to risk their boats and their lives out on the open sea, for '. . . it war in wane to tak them to fische in the mayne sey quhen thai may gett mair easie and mair profitabill fischeing in the lochis and neir the schore att all seasounis in grit aboundance baith somer and wynter'.

Modern disputes over fishing-limits pale into insignificance compared to these near-warlike conditions, and, sad to say, the aggressive instincts of the East Neuk fishermen were not directed solely against the foreign 'Hollander' or the almost equally foreign Gaelic-speaking Highlander. In 1613 a missive from Sir Alexander Drummond, admiral-depute of the Forth, to the Convention of Royal Burghs, complained of the disorder among the seafaring men attending the herring fishing at Dunbar, and suggested a levy on all the burghs along the Forth to pay for an armed fly-boat which would be in constant attendance during the herring season to apprehend '. . . sik as steills thair nichtbours geir, schaks thair netts, maks quarrels and fechts, and dois uther iniuries'.[7] More than once the fishermen of Kilrenny parish are named in complaints of harassment by other burghs, and when they were not fighting aggressors or attacking rivals at sea, they were busy defending their burghal rights by land against the covetousness of their neighbours. In Gourlay's words: 'It is a curious characteristic of the times that the merchants of Cupar and St. Andrews, and even Dundee, would come marching across the hills armed to the teeth, though on no more hostile errand than to buy and cure herring like their neighbours of the coast. In doing so, however, they forgot, or rather defied, the jealous laws and still more jealous spirit of the burghs, and the intruders were at once resisted as pirates and robbers'.[8] For our Dyker ancestors of four hundred years ago, the pistol, pike and cutlass must have been tools as indispensable as hook, net and line in the struggle to win a living from the sea.

Yet all was not disaster and loss in those years. The first Cellardyke town hall was built in 1624, to be followed some years later by a belated market cross. The Kilrenny burgh records, which survive in fragmentary form from the year 1613, commence with lists of local men admitted to be 'freemen and burgesses' of the town, and the variety of crafts exemplified points to a thriving little community of merchants and craftsmen. In 1625 the Crail laird Sir James Learmonth of Balcomie undertook to set up a beacon for mariners on his estate, which overlooked the rich herring ground known as the 'Auld Haikes'; and in 1636 his fellow-laird John Cunningham of Barns, whose estate lay near the modern Barnsmuir, between Crail and Cellardyke, erected the first light-house on the May Island 'for the saiftie and directing of sailleres in thair incomeing and outgoeing of the said firth in the darke nightes'.[9] Among the skippers who signed the petition to have a light erected were Alexander Beaton and Alexander Alexander of Kilrenny. In 1641 Anstruther Easter was disjoined from Kilrenny and erected into a separate parish, with the new church of St. Adrian's as its centre of worship. Overnight Kilrenny, deprived of a large slice of its population, shrank to almost its modern proportions, and the churchgoers of Anstruther broke with an ancient tradition of hazarding their health and footwear in the weekly tramp through mud or worse to St. Irnie's distant chapel on the hill.

Just as these peaceful developments were in progress, however, things took a turn for the worse both nationally and locally. In 1642, according to the burgh records, 'There was a scarcity of white fish along the east coast ... to the hurt and hunger of the poor and beggaring of the fishermen. It was reported that when the fishers had laid their lines and taken fishes abundantly there came ane beast called the sea dog to the lines, and ate and destroyed the haill bodies and left nothing on the lines but the heads'. Over a century earlier, the historian Boece had written of monstrous fish called 'bassinatis' with 'blak skinnis hingand on thair bodyis', whose appearance in the Forth signified 'gret infortuniteis to mortall pepill'.[10] No doubt then as now the East Neuk fishermen were a superstitious breed, and the plague of dogfish may have been seen as a portent of evil days to come.

In retrospect they would have been justified in their pessimism, for the long and bloody civil war between Royalist and Roundhead was looming on the horizon. In 1645 the Fife levies marched off to the carnage which was the Battle of Kilsyth, and although we have no definite information regarding the losses sustained by Kilrenny parish, we *do* know that Pittenweem lost over a hundred adult males, with the result that seventeen boats rotted at their moorings and the families of the dead seamen were reduced to the direst pauperdom.[11] Crail's losses amounted to 'fourscore ten of oure choisest men', and in an appeal addressed to the Parliament in Edinburgh the townspeople described themselves as '... bot a verie poore people haveing no meines to live upoun bot quhat the sea and oure Commers does affoord, yea the most pairt of us (have) not a bitt of meat to put in oure bellies quhil (i.e. until) the samyn be first gottin furth of the sea, frae quhich the pestilence and troubles did debar us'.[12] More significantly still, the Reverend John Brand's *A Brief Description of Orkney, Zetland, Pightland-Firth & Caithness*, written half a century after the battle, contained the following passage: 'Herrings do sweem here (Orkney) in abundance, which formerly occasioned several ships frequenting these Isles, but since the Battle of Kilsyth they say that Trade hath failed, many of the Enster men, who were ordinary fishers upon these Coasts, being killed there. When I was in Papa Westra, they pointed out to me a Holm upon the East side of the Isle, where I saw the ruines of some Huts or little Houses, whereunto these Enster Men sometimes resorted during the Herring-fishing'.[13]

Then, as later, the Kilrenny men were often lumped together with the men of Anstruther by those who were strangers to both burghs, and there can be little doubt that Kilrenny and Cellardyke men would have accompanied their Anstruther cousins to the Orkneys and, disastrously, to Kilsyth.

When in 1650 a levy of 80,000 marks was raised from the burghs to pay for the army, Kilrenny's contribution was a mere £80; a paltry sum when set beside Crail's £586/13/4d., or Anstruther Easter's £426/13/4d., but an eloquent statement of the depths to which the town had sunk. Units of Cromwell's army, who occupied and plundered Anstruther during the 1650s, are unlikely to have spared the little fisher town across the burn, and, to fully assure the people of God's wrath, a spell of exceptionally severe weather caused great damage to life and property, not least to the little harbours of the East Neuk. In December 1655, we learn from the Largo chronicler John Lamont, gales and heavy seas put paid to the piers of 'St. Androus, Enster, Craill, Weymes and Leith', and sank 'small barkes and other vessells . . . laying in harbrees (harbours), as in Enster, Dysart 20, Craill 30'.[14] Two years later Lamont was recording that 'This yeare, after Lammis, ther was few or none hearing (herring) gotten ether in Fyfe or att Dunbar in Lowthian; so that the like of this drave was not for many yeares past, viz. for badnese'. Similar gloomy comments followed in 1658, 1662 and 1663.

But there was an even blacker, more sinister aspect to those decades. In 1643 the Solemn League and Covenant had been drawn up, and adherence to its rigidly Presbyterian principles enforced throughout the land. Moral and spiritual lapses came to be seen in a graver light, as treason against God himself, and the most heinous of all moral lapses was the sin of witchcraft.

The tightly-knit, inbred communities of the East Neuk had long been strongholds of witchcraft, as the term was then understood – one of the most notorious practitioners being Agnes Melville, the witch of Anstruther.[15] But when in 1643 religious fanaticism entered the arena, the trickle of accusations became a terrible flood, with no fewer than thirty victims burnt in Fife within a few months. Prominent among the clerical inquisitors was the Reverend Robert Bennett, son of the minister of Monimail, who had been admitted to the ministry of Kilrenny and Cellardyke only the previous year; and associated with him in this work were such colleagues in the ministry as Colin Adam (Anstruther Easter), George Dewar (Anstruther Wester), James Wood and Robert Blair (St. Andrews), John Melville (Pittenweem), Robert Wilkie (Abercrombie), James Bruce (Kingsbarns), Arthur Myrton (Crail), Robert Traill (Elie), and various others. The Presbytery of St. Andrews minute-book for 1643-4 gives some idea of the scope of their activities.[16]

On July 12th, 1643, the ministers of Anstruther Easter, Elie, Kingsbarns and St. Andrews were '. . . appointed to goe to Craill on Thursday and speake some witches apprehended ther'. In August there is a reference to the execution of 'some witches' in Anstruther. Some ministers were only too eager to resort to faggot and stake, as a chilling entry for August 16th makes clear: 'It is thought fitting that ministers within this Presbyterie doe advertise the Presbyterie befor any witches with them be put to execution'.

On the same day Messrs. Wilkie and Wood, together with Mr. Monro of Kilconquhar (then including St. Monans), were sent to Anstruther Wester '. . . to sie the execution of some witches ther; and that they goe to Anstruther-Easter and Craill to speake with some quho are apprehended for witches'. On August 23rd comes a mention of executions in St. Andrews, and on the 30th it is the turn of Isobell Dairsie in Anstruther to be arrested. On September 6th a further two women in Crail are taken into custody, and on the 13th Helen Schevis is apprehended. On November 15th Mr. Blair, Mr. Adam, Mr. Traill and Mr. Wood are 'appointed to goe to Craill . . . and attend the execution of some witches', and also to examine charges against others. On January 11th, 1644, a total of six ministers and three elders met with judges at Pittenweem to discuss charges levelled at 'Christane Dote (Dott) in St. Minnance', and three colleagues witnessed the execution of Isabell Dairsie at Anstruther.

Up till now Robert Bennett's witchhunting activities had been confined to his colleagues' parishes, but that was about to change: 'February 7th., 1644 – The Presbyterie doe appoint the Moderator, Mr. Arthur Myrton, David Monro, Johne Heart, Robert Bennett and Johne Melvill, James Lentron, Johne Alexander, Johne Livingstone, to meitt at Silverdyke with a quorum of the Judges, and considder of the dilations against Margret Myrton (i.e. Martin) concerning charmeing and consulteing with witches, and give ther advyse quhat course to take with her. As also to meitt at Pittenweeme and give ther advyse concerning the watching (i.e. guarding) of Christane Dote, and her dyett of sleepe, bed, meate and drinke.'

'February 21st., 1644 – These quho had commission given to considder the dilations against Margaret Myrton in Silverdyke, concerning consulteing with witches and charmers, declared that they fand her to be deiplie guiltie of these, yea likelie to be guiltie of witchcraft in diverse particulars, quherupon they did advyse the Judges to apprehend and try her; quherin they are approvin.'

It is probably Margaret Myrton who is referred to in an entry for June 12th:

'Mr. Robert Bennett shew that one in his paroch apprehended for a witch, quho is now burnt for that fact, did a short tyme after her apprehending (before shee confest herselfe a witch) confesse that shee had committed adulterie with Alexander Beaton; and thereafter said that her committing of that adulterie was the first cause of that wickednes of witchcraft wherein shee hes fallen; quho (i.e. Beaton) being accused therof, both in private and befor the Session, denyes the same; yea, quhen he was desired to stay to be confronted with her for clearing himselfe, promised to doe so, bot notwithstanding went over to Edinburgh and stayed ther till shee was brunt.'

Later that year Alexander Beaton was named by another 'confessing witche', Bessie Mason, in terms which echo Margaret Myrton's testimony.[17] To the judges, however, such confessions – far from moving them to leniency – only served to emphasise the moral turpitude of the accused women, and to guarantee them the stake. For men, of course, the situation was different, and there is no indication that the mysterious seducer was ever brought to book. Was he one of the band of depraved individuals who acted the warlock's part at midnight covens, and had carnal intercourse with his credulous followers? More prosaically, he may be identical with the Alexander Beaton who petitioned, along with his brother skippers, for a lighthouse on the May Island, and who by 1634 was a member of the town council of Kilrenny.

Some years later came the turn of Isbell Smith 'in Kylrinnie paroch, quho confest shee used charmeing wordes, and being altogether ignorant is discharged to use those wordes and appointed to make publicke acknowledgement of that sinne befor the Congregation thrie dayes'. It would appear from this that the authorities distinguished between women known to be merely superstitious and, presumably, harmless, and those believed to have real power to do evil.

Not only witches and warlocks came under clerical scrutiny at this time. Ironically, the very fanaticism of the clergy in rooting out 'wickedness', and their faithful recording of their findings, reveal to future generations what they would probably have preferred to conceal: namely, the surprising degree to which both pagan and pre-Reformation practices had survived into the seventeenth century. On June 26th, 1644, for instance, all ministers within the Presbytery of St. Andrews were instructed to find out who in their parish had been guilty of lighting Midsummer bonfires, a complaint which recurs more than once in subsequent years. Another relic of the 'Popish' past had been ventilated on March 20th:

'The Presbyterie, considdering of the great abuses and manifold disorders that are frequentlie at night wakeings of the dead and burialls . . . doe appoint that people at these tymes when the dead are in the house hold there doores close as at other tymes, and that they give no entrance to the confused multitude quho frequent such occasions . . . and they are to remember that it is not a tyme of eating or drinking, or making merrie after a wordlie (i.e. worldly) maner, bot to carie themselves christianlie as becomes persones professing godlines. As also they appoint and ordaine that that heathnish custome, under a popish name, of drinking dirgies after the corpes are interred, be utterlie abolished.'

A lighter note, at least for the modern reader, is struck by two entries in April of that year:

'April 2nd – This day it was shewn to the Presbyterie that Thomas Bonar, servand to Sir James Sandielands younger of St. Minnance, being drinking in Kylrinnie, they did sing a malignant song, and drinke drinkes to James Grahame, sometymes Montrois, and others.'

'April 30th – These quho were appointed to try concerning Thomas Bonar declared that they found it verified by thrie witnesses that he did sing these wordes:

> Bobo Finla did command
> The valiant Grahame and the Irish band
> To beate the rebells out of the land.

and that he dranke a health to Bobo Finla. Both which he did thereafter confesse, alledging he knew not quhat Bobo Finla meant, bot that he had heard diverse of note (i.e. various important or well-known people) sing that song, and drinke that drinke in Edinburgh a twelvemonth since.'

'Bobo Finla' was presumably a secret way of referring to King Charles I, allegiance to whom was by now strictly forbidden; and the Marquis of Montrose, with his wild bands of Catholic and Episcopalian Highlanders and Irishmen, was a name to strike terror into Lowland Presbyterian ears: although the excellent memory of three separate witnesses for the words of this jaunty little ditty suggests it was not entirely unknown in Kilrenny! Thomas Bonar was sentenced to make public repentance at Kilrenny, where the offence was committed, and at Kilconquhar, the mother-church of the St. Monance people, and then to appear before the General Assembly.

Of course, for the ordinary Dyker who was neither witch nor malignant rebel, life went on pretty much as before; and the first independent parish registers of Kilrenny, commencing in 1647, provide a welcome antidote to sorcery and sensationalism. Their mundane lists of marriages and births, interspersed with routine kirk-session business, testify to the continuity of everyday life in the burgh; and there are just sufficient appearances before the kirk-session to reassure us that the populace was not wholly cowed by the discipline of the Kirk. In 1647 Alexander Young, John Adamsone and John Watsone were 'cited for hauling their netts on the Sabbath', and Grizzall Hutton was 'dilatit for scolding her mother'. Meetings of the kirk-session regularly opened with the minister inquiring of the elders 'anent drunkennesse, banning (i.e. cursing) and swearing and breach of the sabbath', but on most occasions the clerk recorded the prudent response 'No answer made'. The elders were in theory the moral eyes and ears of the community, but in a parish where everyone was related to everyone else, or near enough, it was dangerous to 'clype' on one's neighbours. One never knew what interesting stories they might have themselves for the minister's ear!

On April 1st, 1649, the ever-simmering feud between Kilrenny and Anstruther found its way into the session-records. In those momentous weeks, as the nation reeled from the shock of Charles I's execution at Whitehall, the parish clerk of Kilrenny lamented '... how that the inhabitants of the landis of Anstruther, being an part of the parish of kilrinny, hath absented themselves thro long tym bygon from the Church of kilrinny ... notwithstanding they have been compleaned of to ther maisters be the minister'. But this time Mr. Bennett was fighting a losing battle. On the positive side, the minister and kirk-session were well-pleased with their new schoolmaster, whose predecessor, Robert Rough, was ordered to desist from trying to win back his former pupils. Indeed this particular kirk-session minute deserves to be quoted from at length, so clear an insight does it give into the educational facilities available in the parish at that time. The elders, justifiably proud of the school they have set up in Kilrenny, are determined to stamp out the various free-enterprise 'adventure' schools which have sprung up in recent years, and which are creaming off pupils whose fees should by rights be contributing to the upkeep of the parish schoolmaster:

May 27th., 1649.
The Session ... have gott a schoole established at the kirke and Towne of kilrynny & planted with a schoolmaster of whom none can iustly complean; and finding him greatly preiudged by others undertaking to teach barns w^{t}in the parish, especiallie Robt Rough late Schoolmaster in ye parish, and also thorow the unwillingness of some to put their children to the schoole, wherby ye schoolm^r. is greatly preiudged ... doe y^{r}for ordaine y^t ye s^d Robert Rough nor any other q^{t}somever shal not undertake to teach any of ye children of this parish w^{t}out a tollerance from the sessione; and ordains also that al those whom god hath blessed w^t children, doe put y^r children to the schoole at kilrynny how soon they be able to travell, and that upon no pretext they be w^{t}holdin.

The session's confidence in Mr. Harry Page was soon shaken, however, for before the year was out he had been suspended from his post for fornication; and only after a suitably contrite appearance before the St. Andrews Presbytery was he conditionally reinstated as session-clerk and schoolmaster. The Dykers proved no more willing as the years passed to force their children to trudge through the mire to the schoolhouse in Kilrenny, for fully five years later, on January 10th, 1654, the session met to consider the schoolmaster's complaint that 'thair came not a boy out of the whole town of Sillerdykes to the school ... but (the Dykers) does, contrare to the acts of the session, send them to intruders, both men and women, that have no call to teach'. The centralisation of church and school in the village of Kilrenny, when the bulk of the population lived down by the shore in Cellardyke, was to be a bone of contention for several centuries.

Even when a child *did* attend Kilrenny school, the parents were not always satisfied that his time there was well spent:

January 27th., 1657.
Margaret Strang in Sellerdykes spouse to Robert Unston (Ovenstone) was appoynted to be cited the nixt dyet for falsly calumniating the schoolmaster in saying her sone had not got a Lesson for a month.

At the next meeting of the session the mother apologised, and was 'rebuked for her temerity and rashness'. Modern-day teachers might well envy this degree of back-up from a local education authority! Not that the master was necessarily blameless here, for two years later he would be admonished to spend more time with his scholars, and 'to let them play but on y^r ordinar play days'. Nevertheless, however many failings we may attribute to these early Kilrenny schoolmasters, it was an achievement merely to keep such a school going in a rural backwater of East Fife. Indeed, in the troubled period from 1660 to 1690, only Kilrenny and three other parishes in the county seem to have managed to maintain a full-time schoolmaster, and – in Kilrenny's case – to pay him relatively well for his services (see J. M. Beale, *A History of the Burgh and Parochial Schools of Fife*, p. 99. The other three parishes were Elie, Kemback and Leuchars).

So much for educational facilities in our parish. But what other momentous events are recorded for posterity in the kirk-session minutes? In 1659, as the various political factions in the nation wheeled and dealt over the restoration of the monarchy, 'the session met, and it was represented to the magistratis of the town of Sillerdyks of the iniquitie of not paying the annualrent of the 400 mark owing be them to the kirk'. (Kirk-session funds were often lent to needy borrowers at a low rate of interest – the session acting as bankers for the parish.) James Cunningham younger was ordered to apologise to Bailie Thomas Peacock for some unspecified offence against him, and, in their self-appointed role as marriage-guidance counsellors, the elders rebuked David Craigie and Elspeth Thomson for their 'scandalous marriage'. A neighbour, on entering the house, had found Elspeth 'sleeping upon a kist before his bed side; quhilk thai both confest but denyd they had misbehaved thamselves'. Whatever the cause of the rift between the couple, such unnatural behaviour could not be tolerated: a wife belonged in her husband's bed. Vigorous vituperation and name-calling were also much in evidence, and Mr. and Mrs. Robert Cook and Mr. and Mrs. Thomas Cunningham were reprimanded for resorting to such epithets as 'hanging loun' and 'barren bitch' (applied by Mrs. Cook to Mrs. Cunningham); while Robert Howieson objected to Cathrin Millar calling him 'false old Carle'. In such a society, where neighbours and relatives could in a trice turn into spies and informers, and such relatively minor sins as drunkenness, swearing and quarrelling in public incurred the censure and punishment of the Kirk, it is not surprising that periodic outbursts of witchhunting were necessary as an outlet for pent-up frustrations and hatreds. To scream abuse at a neighbour in the street was an offence; to denounce her as a witch was commendable public-spiritedness.

The Restoration of Charles II in 1660 may have gone some way towards easing the oppressive moral atmosphere of the times, but it did nothing to improve the economic climate in the former 'Golden Fringe', for Kilrenny, along with her sister burghs of Anstruther Easter and Wester and Crail, was reduced to petitioning Parliament for exemption from public taxation on account of their poverty, '. . . which was occasioned be the Inglisch plundering of thair burghis and away taking of thair whol schippis (i.e. of all their ships) and barkis and boatis,

the meanes of thair subsistence'.[18] This was perhaps a slight exaggeration, for the *Aberdeen Shore Work Accounts* for 1662 reveal the arrival
there, on November 17th, of two Kilrenny vessels whose masters were
James Brown and William King respectively.[19] However, the penur-
ious situation of the burgh might have cancelled out the usefulness of
a measure enacted by Parliament in 1661, whereby the fishers of Crail,
Kilrenny, Anstruther Easter and Pittenweem were to have preference
over 'foreigners' from Hamburg and Lübeck in the Shetland fisheries.
The prime mover here was an Edinburgh merchant, Gideon Murray,
who had at his own expense fitted out two 'busses' for the Northern
fisheries and crewed them, one presumes, with mariners from the East
Neuk. Later, Gideon Murray would acquire the lands of Pitkierie, in
Kilrenny parish, and would represent the burgh in Parliament and at the
Convention of Royal Burghs.

The latter institution had by now become more of a hindrance than a
help to the ancient royal burghs, whose privileges were being steadily
eroded by vigorously expanding burghs of regality and barony, many of
which had powerful patrons, such as the Duke of Hamilton at Bo'ness,
and the Earl of Lauderdale at Musselburgh. In 1672 the blow fell. The
'unfree' burghs were at last granted the legal right to retail, export and
import more or less whatever they wanted, and the only privilege left
to the royal burghs was the doubtful one of contributing to burghal
taxation: a distinction which their rivals were only too happy to grant
them. No longer would the merchants of the unfree burghs have to arm
themselves for a visit to the coast; no more would they have to bribe an
unscrupulous skipper in Anstruther or Pittenweem to take a little parcel
of goods to Rotterdam or the Baltic and pass it off as his own. There was
no longer any point in clinging onto the status of a royal burgh – a status
which in Kilrenny's case was not even historically justified – and in
August 1672 the following petition was presented to the Scottish parliament by Gideon Murray of Pitkierie, acting on behalf of the councillors
and burgesses of Kilrenny:

TO His Grace His Majesties high Commissioner and the Lords of Articles The
humble petition of the Inhabitants of Kilrinnie
     Sheweth
THAT your Petitioners wer never erected in a Burgh Royall by his Majestie without
which no place can be accounted a burgh Royall nor did they ever compt in
Exchecker or make an Aeque as a Burgh Royall, nor in effect are they able to find
persons to be Magistrats nor to bear any burden as a burgh Royall But the truth is
that any priviledge they have is from the Lairds of Balfour upon whose lands their
houses are built and whose burgh of barony they are Likeas though they have been

represented in some late Parliaments yet that was only occasioned by the tumultuariness and rebellion of the late times whereon some factious persons desireing to have Votes Did intise some of our inhabitants to come and sitt in Parliament, And the present inhabitants being young men and new intrants, and till of late, yea within thir twenty dayes last never haveing considered their predicessors rights bot continued the course of these who formerly lived on these bounds; And since wee neither wer, nor are yet able to continue a burgh Royall and since wee have no erection to that effect

May it therefor please your Grace and Lordships To Declare, that wee shall no more be burdened as a Burgh Royall nor be obleidged to attend Parliaments and publict conventions as such.

Robert Howesone	baylle	William Smyth	
Will: Wallace	Counsellor	James Duncan	bailie
Wiliam Layell	Counselleor	Alexander Watson	
Thomas Halsone	Cownselleire	Allexander Allexander	Coounseller
Dawed Dwdingston			

The petition was granted, but only on condition that the burgh agree to pay its share of the latest round of royal taxation for which it had just been assessed. Then, as now, death and taxes were the only certain things in an uncertain world.

Only four years earlier the burgh had been in danger of losing its fishing population altogether, as we learn from a petition addressed to the Privy Council of Scotland in 1668 by the town council of Kilrenny. For the past thirteen years they had not even had a harbour for their boats, since in the great inundation and storm of December 1655, 'the harbour of the said brugh (i.e. burgh) of Kilrinnie (which was the greatest mean of subsistence and the onlie comon good of the same brugh) was totallie demolished and rased to the ground and yet continowes unrepaired throw their inabilitie to help the same'. If the harbour is not rebuilt soon, the petitioners continue, 'it is impossible to them to continow and subsist longer as a brugh, but will certanly fall to utter ruine; for the two pairt and more of the haill inhabitants consisting of seafairing and fisher men not having a harbour to lay their barkes or boates but necessitat to goe to other places, as they have done this tyme bygone, wil certanly remove and doeth declare that they will remove themselves and families to other pairtes, and thereby the said burgh will undoubtedlie be altogether redacted and brought to utter ruine and miserie'.[20]

The Lords of Privy Council seem to have grasped the seriousness of the situation, for they immediately granted the petitioners permission to carry out a nationwide fund-raising exercise for a new harbour at Cellardyke. It was by no means the last time that such a parlous situation would arise for the fishermen of Cellardyke.

There is little left to tell of our burgh in the seventeenth century, except for the 'short and simple annals of the poor'. James Watson and his wife had a son, William. George Tarvet and Janet Anderson were married. Gilbert Kaye and Isobel Hamilton had a son, William, and John Murray and Isoble Young an unnamed child. Henry Watson and Girzall Lidsdale had a daughter, Margaret, and the session paid for a coffin to Helen Broun, Thomas Fowler's wife. Alexander Broun and Elspeth Salter had a daughter, Janet, and the witnesses were Thomas and James Salter. Thomas Fouler and Elspeth Hay, and John Reid and Effie Spindie, were married, and David Kay and Janet Anderson contracted: witness, Thomas Salter, 'his maister'.

On March 24th, 1692, there was a meeting of the town council, consisting of 'James Peacock ballie (Wm Smyth being dead and William Andersone ye other ballie being at sea) . . . together with James Duncan, Tho. Peacock, James Davidsone, Andrew Louthian, Alex^r. Layng, Alex^r. Millar, John Young and Andrew Wayd (councillors)'. They agreed to admit John Reid, James Stivensone, Andrew Murray and John Lessels burgesses and freemen of Kilrenny. The following year Olipher Watsone was also admitted to these privileges. Though most burgesses were fishers or mariners, there is mention too of Thomas Louthian, 'maltman'; Thomas Scott, 'tallyer' (tailor); David Reid, 'land-labourer'; Mr. James Lumsdaine, 'doctor of medicine', and others. The townspeople are summoned regularly 'by tuck of drum' to 'inbring the stent', or pay their taxes, and James Cunningham, fisher and town-officer, receives £2 12s. 'out of the town box, his due'. In 1695, one of James's tasks was to lodge an official complaint against Thomas Young, burgess, and Margaret Gilbert, for breach of the peace. Margaret Gilbert's fault had been 'praying imprecatiouns on Young, & that her malisone should come on him', whereupon the offended burgess had struck her. Thomas Young was fined, and Margaret Gilbert, who failed to appear at the hearing, was sentenced to be arrested and set in the 'jougs'.

For a detailed list of the inhabitants of the burgh at this time we can turn to the first official census of Kilrenny and Cellardyke, in the shape of the Hearth-Tax list of 1691, a copy of which survives in the Scottish Record Office.[21] Every householder in the land was to be taxed according to the number of hearths in his house, and the Kilrenny list gives us an insight into the stratified community of the 1690s (see Appendix 2). Sir Philip Anstruther's 25 hearths easily outnumber the 17 belonging to his fellow-laird of Scotstarvet, to say nothing of Innergelly's 12 or the laird of Balfour's mere 8. The 'relict' or widow of Captain Murray, the late M.P. for the parish, has 6 hearths, which implies a fair-sized house, and a relatively large number of householders can boast of 2 – although the extra one, as in the case of David Ramsay the smith, may often have been for occupational purposes. Only the heads of households feature in this list, and many other inhabitants were probably too poor to qualify for assessment, but the Kilrenny Hearth-Tax nevertheless provides fascinating evidence of the geographical distribution and relative wealth of the townspeople in the late 1690s.

As the glorious Revolution gave way to the appalling series of famines remembered later as 'King William's Ill Years', the burgesses of Kilrenny continued stolidly with their everyday tasks, and the burgh records speak only of the 'rouping' of anchorages and shore dues, the collection of 'stents' (local taxes), and the admission of new burgesses: an increasing number of whom are outsiders, such as David Drummond, 'merchant in Dundee', and Alexander Fergusone, 'merchant'; Alexander Finlay and John Scott, skippers; and Robert Ranold and John Coutts, bailies, all of Montrose. This John Coutts was the ancestor of the great trading family whose interests would eventually span the Atlantic, and who today are represented by the famous London merchant bank of that name.[22]

Although control of their own destiny was visibly slipping out of their hands, as it was in so many of their sister burghs along the Forth,[23] and although successive town councils continued to wriggle out of their financial commitments to the Convention of Royal Burghs, the old habit of exclusiveness died hard. As late as 1693 Alexander Murray, William Doig and John Donaldson could still be fined and jailed for allowing the packing and selling of fish by 'unfree' traders; an anachronistic attitude on the part of the town fathers. The ancient royal burghs of the East Neuk had had their day, and it was now the age of upstarts such as Montrose, Bo'ness, Musselburgh, Kilmarnock, and the mushrooming giant in the West which would soon overtake Edinburgh in size and wealth among Scottish cities. But it was with their eyes fixed firmly on the past that the burgesses of Kilrenny slipped quietly into the eighteenth century.

4

The Eighteenth Century:
People and Politics in the Post-Union Period

In his *The History, Ancient and Modern, of the Sheriffdoms of Fife and Kinross*, published in 1710, Sir Robert Sibbald wrote of Anstruther Easter: 'This is a pretty large royal burgh, well built and populous, and of great trade. ... They have good magazines and cellars for trade, and are provided with all accommodations for making and curing of herrings; which is the staple commoditie of this town, and of all the towns in this east coast of Fife. And this town sends about twenty-four boats to the fishing of herring, formerly they sent yearly about thirty boats to the fishing of herring at the Lewis: and at the same time they had twenty-four ships belonging to them'.[1]

On the subject of Cellardyke he was scarcely less informative: 'Very near to the east-end of Anstruther-Easter is Cellar-dyke, a royal burgh, commonly called Kilrinny. (These three burghs seem to be but one town.) It holds of the laird of Balfour as superiour. It consists of one street, and hath ten boats with six men in each, that fish all the year over for white fish; but in the season for fishing herring they set out twenty boats with seven men in each: it hath a little harbour'.[2]

Thanks to a little document preserved among the Leven and Melville papers in the Scottish Record Office, we can put names to eighteen skippers of Cellardyke herring-boats at the turn of the eighteenth century; and despite the archaic spellings we can easily recognise such familiar Cellardyke surnames as Watson, Cunningham, Reid, Muir and Doig:

List of the Dreave Boattes in ye Shire of Fife Anno 1702
Killreney
Alex^r. Halsone
Ro^bt. Andersone
James Cuninghame
James Wattsone
David Reade
John Pride

George Alexander
Thomas Smith Elder
Thomas Smith yr.
William Dog
John Spence
William Moore
Jo. Miller
William Wattsone
John Andersone
Alex^r. Morttone
W^m. Morttone
William Layell (S.R.O., GD26/XII./16)

Cellardyke's 'one street' – that narrow, winding thoroughfare from Caddies Burn past the old Tolbooth to the harbour of Skinfasthaven – seems nevertheless to have housed a community of fishermen almost as large as that of the neighbouring burgh. Nor were herring and the commoner white fish the only sea-creatures known to the East Neuk men, for elsewhere in his book Sibbald lists the local names for a wide variety of species, such as the 'turbot flook' (halibut), 'stone-fish' (blenny), 'podly' (pollack) and 'spout' (razor-fish). The mature cod is a 'keeling', the young one a 'codling'. The crab family includes the 'partan' (males are 'carle crabs', females 'baulster crabs'), the 'keavie' (cleanser crab), 'pelns' (shear crabs) and 'sand-lowpers' (*cancer locusta*). Then, as later, there were fish which the fishermen would eat with relish themselves, and others they would not touch. Many flat fish, including the 'gunner flook' or turbot, fell into the latter category, and Sibbald's nineteenth-century editor adds, in a footnote: 'There are living, or were very lately, in one of the coast-towns, several poor people who were wont to derive great part of their subsistence from the turbots which the fishermen threw away on the beach, because nobody could be found to purchase them. . . . Indeed there seems to have been a prejudice against several kinds of flat fish; for it is not many years since skate and thornbacks came to be used by any class of people, especially on the coast'.[3]

For the herring was undisputed king. A series of Acts of Parliament had attempted to regulate the curing and export of herring from the royal burghs, and in the first decade of the eighteenth century a further act was passed compelling each fisher-town to appoint a 'visitor' who would inspect both herrings intended for the export market and the casks in which they were to be packed. Casks which were found 'sufficient' were to be marked with the town seal.[4] This new concern with quality can be interpreted as part of a drive to take over the export market to the

Continent which in the previous century had been the monopoly of the
Dutch and the Germans, and these foreign rivals were dealt a further
blow in 1712 when a levy was placed on all foreign salt – a commodity
vital for the curing process – and British nationals were awarded a
bounty for curing with British salt.

In 1707 Andrew Gooland or Gullane, merchant burgess of Kilrenny,
was appointed official 'visitor' in Cellardyke, while his brother John,
a cooper, undertook to cast an expert eye over the casks which his
colleagues in the trade were turning out hand over fist. As early as
1701 the Burgh Records contain an admonition to the 'horse-men' of
Cellardyke who have been guilty of descending *en masse* on one or two
boats, especially those of 'strangers', to help with unloading them. In
future they are to divide themselves fairly among all the boats so that
everyone, and especially the town's own burgesses, may be served alike.[5]

The general impression, then, is one of bustling activity, although this
is the period in which the Act of Union was passed: that measure which
later generations of east-coast fishermen would look back on as the
death-knell of their trade. Incidentally, a misunderstanding at this time
reinstated Kilrenny as a royal burgh, and along with her neighbours
from Crail to Pittenweem she became entitled to representation at
Westminster in the new parliament of Great Britain. The records of the
time sound an optimistic note, and fishermen are still well to the fore in
the ranks of townsmen admitted to be burgesses. In the months of June
and July 1709, for example, Thomas Watson, George Smyth, Alexander
Cleatoun, Thomas Louson, John Bett, David Wood, William Boyter,
John Reid, John Anderson, William Watt, James Cunningham and John
Dinnes were among those seamen granted burgess tickets. Members of
the council at this time included Thomas Stewart, David Reid and
Stephen Williamson, and in the following year an interesting account of
Kilrenny's 'sett' or method of electing the council appears in the records
of the Convention of Royal Burghs:

Sett of the Burgh of Kilrenny.

By the sett of the toun of Kilrenny the toun council consists of fifteen persons,
viz., three baillies, the treasurer and eleven burgesses. The election proceeds after
this manner:—Three days before the third Thursday of September, which is the day
prefixt for the said election, the baillies cause their toun officer by touck of drum
make intimation to the haill inhabitants, requiring all the habile burgesses within the
burgh to repare to the tolbuith upon the prefixt day and there give their respective
votes in the election of baillies and treasurer for the ensueing year (it being the
custome of the said toun, ever since its erectione into a royal burgh, to elect their
baillies by a vote of the haill burgesses that will qualifie in the terms of law.) In

obedience to which intimatione, the haill burgesses convene accordingly about nine a clock in the morning. But before electione the old baillies and council conveen within the council house and take in the treasurer his accompts of intromission with the touns patrimony that year; which being done and he discharged, they immediately nominat a new council for the year ensueing, and thereafter ordain all the burgesses that are to vote to qualifie themselves according to law, which being alse done they proceed to elect. And, first, the baillies give in their leit of nine persons, whereof they themselves are always three, out of which they are to choise the three baillies for the year ensueing, and the treasurer gives in his leit of three persons, whereof he himself is always one, out of which they are to elect their treasurer for said year; which being read over in presence of the council and approven of by them, the same is read publicly in audience of the haill burgesses that are to vote. This being done the clerk is appointed to sitt within the council and mark the votes (there being alwayes one of the council appointed to oversee his right marking) and accordingly first the baillies, then the council, and thereafter the haill qualified burgesses, one by one, give their several votes for the baillies and treasurer for the said ensueing year; and the persons chosen by plurality of votes, together with the new council, immediately conveen within the council house and accept of their respective offices and give their oaths *de fideli administratione*, the same being tendered to the three baillies by the clerk and by them first to the treasurer and then to the council, which being done they adjourn.

This forme and manner of electione hath alwayes been practised and made use of within the said toun of Kilrenny, ever since the erectione thereof in a royal burgh, as will appear by the records of council thereof.

Extracted forth of the saids records, upon the fifth day of September one thousand seven hundred and ten years, by me.

Sic subscribitur: Jo. Paton, Clerk.[6]

The parish registers for the years 1696 to 1711 have not survived, but in 1712 a new set appear and the records of births, marriages and deaths are continuous from that year until 1855, when the state took over such responsibilities. Among baptisms recorded in the year 1713 are those of daughters named Helen to Thomas Watson and Isobel Inglis (Wit. William Watson & James Wade); Elizabeth, to James Murray & Mary Harrow (Wit. Andrew Murray & William Watson), and Ann, to John Murray and Isobel Young (Wit. Andrew Murray & James Murray). James Cunningham and Isobel Smith, and Thomas Sater (Salter) and Agnes Lessels were also blessed with children that year. The following year James Watson and Elizabeth Finlay, Henry Watson and Girzel Lidsdale and Olipher Watson and Agnes Smith are numbered among the proud parents.

For a more intimate picture of life in the town we can turn to the registers of the Kilrenny kirk-session, which also commence an unbroken run in the year 1712. The reason for opening a new register on August 4th, 1712 was the induction of a new minister, the Rev. Alexander Anderson. A graduate of St. Andrews University, Mr. Anderson was then aged about 30, and his path to the ministry of Kilrenny had been smoothed by his marriage to Margaret Cleland, the daughter of his predecessor. George Gourlay describes him (with what authority he does not say!) as 'a thin little man, with high cheekbones and grey, restless eyes, very nervous and excitable'.[7] No doubt we should allow for a degree of poetic licence here, but Gourlay's pen-portrait may be based retrospectively on the unfortunate minister's experiences during his short pastorate at Kilrenny (he was to die an early death only nine years later).

But at the first meeting of the session after his ordination Mr. Anderson was in brisk mood. Enquiring, as holders of his office traditionally did, whether there were any 'unpurged scandals' in the parish, he was informed of two (perhaps the elders of the session were also on their toes and eager to show their diligence, at least until they got the measure of the new man): 'Thomas Anderson Seaman in Nether Kilrenny (was) guilty of Adultery with Helen Muire his own servant, which both the parties had already confessed. The Session understanding that the Man had fled the Countrey did not see any present step they could make with respect to him: But the Woman having been already beffore the presbytry, and by them refferred back to the Session to be censured according to the Discipline of the Church, the officiar was appointed to summon her to the next Diet.

'Also William Bett was delated as guilty of Fornication with Agnes Scot. The Session found that the man had been taken up for a Recruit to yᵉ army, but they appointed the woman to be summoned to their next meeting.'

On September 15th Helen Muire appeared before the session and acknowledged her guilt with Thomas Anderson. She was appointed to make public repentance before the congregation, but thanks to a benefactor this punishment was delayed:

'The Reason of Delaying her publick appearance was a petition from an Honest man in Anstruther, to whom she is just now nursing a Child, earnestly desiring the Session would be pleased to forbear her a little till his Child was weaned, fearing danger to the Infant from her breast if she should be obliged to undergo the Censure of the Church while giving suck.'

Thomas Anderson seemed to have made good his escape, but God was not mocked. Three years later he returned to Cellardyke, only to be pounced on by the session as if his crime had been committed yesterday.

The process of public censure was set in motion on October 3rd, 1715, but on February 13th, 1716 we find the session-clerk ruefully recording that '. . . he has since gone off to the sea, when we could not take notice of him because of the Confusion of the Countrey occasioned by the Late rebellion'. We shall return to this latter topic in a moment, but first a more gruesome event claims our attention.

On April 27th, 1714, the Reverend Anderson electrified the session with the news that a dead child had been found 'in an old Coalpit upon the Confines of this parish, supposed to have been murdered'. The 'child' was a new-born baby, and inevitably the culprit was assumed to be a young unmarried woman. Drastic measures were called for. The minister informed the session that he had enlisted some old women 'to search the breasts of the several unmarried women that lived near that place', and as a result the finger of suspicion pointed at Isobel Morris, the daughter of a ploughman at Frithfield. The girl was immediately apprehended and 'laid up with the dead Child in the prison of Sellardyke, till she be further examined'.

The subsequent trial and ordeal of Isobel Morris occupies several pages in the session records, and makes unpleasant reading. A brief summary of the main points will suffice. Isobel admitted that the child was hers, and named the father as James Small, a married man at Frithfield. The birth had occurred last St. Monans market day, while her father was 'at the plough', and she had neither told anyone of her condition nor called for help. The baby had been born dead, and from fear of her sinfulness being discovered she had wrapped it in a cloth and hidden it by her bed, '. . . where it lay a fortnight till the smell of the Corpse began to be nauseous to her neighbours when they came into the House'. She had then hit upon the idea of dropping the corpse into the water-filled disused coalpit on 'Airdrie Lees'.

As for her lover, he had wanted her to induce an abortion with herbs specially culled for that purpose, but she would have none of that. Then – and there is a touch of pathos at this point – she describes how 'he did several times urge her to leave her house and go alongst with him to some distant place of the Countrey, where they might live together as Husband and wife unknown, and that when she objected her weakness and Inability to travel, he offered her a horse'. But she would not go.

Isobel Morris was tried for murder, her former lover, like Thomas Anderson and William Bett before him, having 'fled the Countrey'. By some miracle of mercy she was acquitted and set free. James Small returned to the parish a few weeks later, claiming that he had not 'fled' but had only gone to visit his brother at Newburgh. He was sentenced to the usual punishment of public censure in church for several Sabbaths in succession, but by October 25th the session were in agreement that '. . . his Stupid Carriage in publick did but increase and heighten instead of removing the people's offence'. His case was referred to the presbytery in St. Andrews, who found him 'grossly ignorant and insensible of his sin', and he was discharged from further appearances before the congregation. He is an unattractive character, this James Small, and it comes as no surprise to find him before the session again only three years later, when he is named as the seducer of Euphan Miller.

At one time, such kirk-session records as these we have looked at here were pillaged by local historians eager to establish the ignorance and immorality of past ages (in contrast, presumably, to the unimpeachable moral purity of the Victorian Age!). This attitude does a grave disservice to our ancestors. The true value of these records is twofold: almost alone among the written monuments of the past, they give a vivid picture of the life and conditions of the humbler members of society; and secondly, on rare occasions, they allow them to speak in their own voices – so that for a brief moment the dry bones of history live again. Two more examples must suffice for the present.

In March 1720 Christian Black, a young unmarried woman in Carnbee and 'late servitrix to the Lady Balhouffie in Sellardyke', was discovered to be pregnant. Under questioning she gave Mr. David Lesly, merchant in Anstruther, as the father of her child. In the minutes which were taken of her trial before the elders of Kilrenny kirk-session we see the whole sorry tale unfold before our eyes: '. . . Being further asked when and where the Child was begotten? She answered . . . in the old Lady Balhouffies House in Sellardyke: And as to the time she said Mr Lesly had frequently offered violence to her before he actually committed uncleanness with her; but the first time, as she can mind, that he wronged her, was upon a night about the time of the Herring Fishing last year, after they had been employed in carrying some goods, which came home in John Finlay's ship, up to a high room in the foresaid house'.

David Lesly vehemently denied the allegation, whereupon Christian called to mind another occasion of sin '. . . when a man from Crail came to the Lady Balhouffies house seeking whalebone'; and again, '. . . in the east room of the foresaid house, when there was none of the family within but another servant woman'. Mr. Lesly persisted in his haughty denials, '. . . whereupon she replied with some warmth, Sir, do you not mind the soap, do you not remember the whalebone? He answered it is all false woman, and I know what to do with you for slandering me: and then turning to the session, he added, I never knew her, I know her indeed to be a woman, but no more –'.

The session, in despair, referred the matter to the presbytery, who suspended the whole proceedings until the girl 'should be brought to bed'. When her time came Christian was 'very narrowly examined' by the Carnbee midwife and her assistants, who 'refused to lay their hand upon her till she should declare who was the true Father of her Child'. Despite this brutal treatment Christian adhered to her former statement, and with a sigh of relief the Kilrenny elders handed over the onus of punishing the guilty parties to their colleagues at Carnbee and Anstruther Easter respectively.

A few years later Christian Spence in Cellardyke was in similar straits when a 'flagrant report' went round that she had borne an illegitimate child which had since 'disappeared'. Margaret Brigs, the Cellardyke midwife, reported back to the Kilrenny kirk-session that '. . . she milked her Breasts, and says further that she was making a shirt for a new born Infant at that very instant she came into her house'. Marjorie Alison and John and Jean Lawson bore witness to this. Shortly afterwards Margaret Fortune, midwife in Kilrenny, reported that '. . . she milked her breast and found Yellow Milk in the same upon the fourteenth of October'. Jean Lawson and Alexander Millar were witnesses to this 'milking'. When the session, still not satisfied, ordered yet another such humiliating ordeal, the unfortunate girl fled the parish.

So much for the public scandals and private griefs of the people. We now move onto the national stage, for only a few years before these events the parish had been convulsed by matters of graver import. First, the historical background.

When Queen Anne died in 1714 and George I ascended the throne of Great Britain, there were those among the Scottish nobility who opposed the Hanoverian succession out of loyalty to the 'King across the water', and there were those who, though perhaps only lukewarm for the new ruling house, were nevertheless prepared to show themselves willing and eager to serve it if thereby they might preserve the positions of power to which they had become accustomed. One of the latter sort was John Erskine, Earl of Mar, known derisively to his contemporaries as 'Bobbing John', who was Secretary of State for Scotland at the time of Anne's death. In an attempt to hold on to this influential position, Mar addressed a flattering letter to the new king in the late summer of 1715. The response was a frosty command to surrender his seals of office to his successor. The king did not trust him. Stung by this rebuff, Mar stormed out of the court, and the following day, travelling in disguise under the name of Maule and in the company of his friend General Hamilton, he embarked in a humble coal-bark bound for Newcastle.

There he hired another skipper to take him to the East Neuk of Fife, where he knew he would find like-minded gentlemen who would give him a sympathetic hearing.

On landing at Elie the conspirators consulted briefly with a local laird, Malcolm of Grange, before setting out for Kilrenny and the home of General Hamilton's son-in-law, James Bethune of Balfour. The laird of Kilrenny was widely regarded as the leading man among the Jacobites of Fife, and it was in his mansion-house, in the August of 1715, that the Jacobite Rising of that year was born. On September 6th the Stuart standard was hoisted on the Braes of Mar.

According to the Master of Sinclair, whose *Memoirs of the Insurrection in Scotland in 1715* paint a bitterly sarcastic picture of the whole misconceived enterprise, Mar and Hamilton presented themselves to the Fife lairds as 'the forerunners of a very good thing'.[8] To the burgesses of the East Neuk who were soon to find themselves victualling and paying for the Highland host, it must have seemed a very bad thing indeed; and to none more so than to the skippers of Cellardyke and the neighbouring towns who on the nights of October 12th and 13th were forced to carry the host in their open boats across the Firth to North Berwick, from where they intended to attack Edinburgh. Although each crew was promised a reward of £20 sterling (which never materialised) for its efforts, it was the threats of the grizzled veteran 'Brigadier' Mackintosh of Borlum and his heavily-armed clansmen, rather than the lure of monetary gain, which made the fishermen carry out this distasteful duty. But the laird of Kilrenny was not the only Jacobite in the parish. For the full story we turn once again to the kirk-session records:

July 17th 1716.
Hora quarta post meridiem (4 p.m.)
The Minister acquainted the Session, that in pursuance of an Act of the Late Synod at Couper, whereby Presbytries and Kirksessions are appointed to enquire into the Conduct and behaviour of Elders, schoolmasters etc. within their bounds that had any accession to the late unnatural Rebellion, or were guilty of Rebellious practises on that occasion: In obedience to the said act he had drawn up some Articles of Information against Mr Robert Wilson present schoolmaster in this parish. Whereupon Mr Wilson leaving his place as Session Clerk, William Taylor Elder was chosen Clerk pro tempore. Thereafter, the sd Mr Wilson being present, the Information was read, as follows.

'Articles of Complaint and Information to the Session of Kilrenny by Mr Alexander Anderson Minister against Mr Robert Wilson present schoolmaster there.
1mo   It is of Verity that when the Late Earl of Mar his Order for raising a General Cess imposed upon this province came to the sd Mr Wilsons hand, about the Beginning of October Last, he went through the parish on the Munday thereafter, and Intimated the Rebellious order to the Heritors and Tenents.

2do That when Strathmore passed by Kilrenny with his party upon the second or third Sabbath of the sd month of October last, on their way from Crail to Auchterardour, Mr Wilson was standing on the Highway ready to meet with them, he came in Messenger from the Rebels to the Ministers house, and called him out to go and speak with Strathmore and these that were in Company with him. As also that in the very time the sd Strathmore and others were urging and threatening the Minister to desist praying in publick for our only rightfull soveraign King George, he, Mr Wilson, Spoke to the Minister pretty audibly, saying, Sir Leith and Edinburgh were taken in by the Highlanders yesternight, adding, that they, viz. the Rebels present had got certain Information of it. The telling thir unseasonable News in such a juncture of time the Minister could construct to be nothing but a wicked design in Mr Wilson to put him in Confusion, and cause him betray himself into a Compliance with the Rebels demand, contrary to his Conscience and Duty.

3° That the sd Mr Robert Wilson went along with the Rebels and attended them through the several Towns upon the Coast side when and where they proclaimed the pretender as King of Britain and Ireland with Sound of trumpet. This was on the seventh day of October Last.

4to That the sd Mr Robert Wilson used to keep Company and converse with the Rebels when they Quartered in this Countrey, particularly with Stonniwood and the officers of his party which lay at Anstruther In November and December last; about which time he was frequently with the foresaid persons in M^r Le Blanc's house, where they met ordinarily, and had their Consultations with people about that favoured their Interest.

As also that the sd Mr Wilson did upon a Sabbath in December last at night sit in his Schoolhouse with two or three of the Rebels, of which George S^t clair, late Gager at Anstruther was one, the whole time that the Minister was preaching to a good Number of the people of the parish in Rennihils house. They sent the sd Mr Wilsons servantmaid twice to a Change-house in the Town for ale. The people as they came to and went from the Exercise saw the Horses sadled, having pistols and other furniture of that Kind upon them, standing at Mr Wilsons door, as they did also the Light shining in the school, where they were drinking. The Congregations wanting publick worship that day is no small aggravation of Mr Wilsons mispending & profaning the Sabbath evening, as has been said, especially when he might have had sermon at his door.'

Mr. Wilson's attempts to defend his conduct were feeble in the extreme, and the session were not impressed. He was relieved of his duties as teacher, precentor and session-clerk, and the session appointed Mr. John Webster, chaplain to the Lady Drumrack in Crail, as his successor.

A student of social life in eighteenth-century Scotland would find much of interest in these old kirk-session records, quite apart from the occasional scandals and uproars we have mentioned. Collection and 'contract' money, for instance, was kept in special boxes variously labelled the 'town-', 'landward-' and 'mid-boxes', and the distribution of money to the deserving poor gives an insight into the elders' priorities and the needs of the scattered population of the parish. For his services as session-clerk Mr. Wilson received one crown per year; while the kirk-officer received five pounds Scots as house-rent, in addition to one pound sixteen shillings with which to buy shoes: all this from the town- and landward boxes equally. In May 1713 the poor of the town, named as Isobel Kellock, Agnes Taylor, Elizabeth Davidson, Helen Spindie, Andrew Walker, Elizabeth Dryburgh, William Watson, Jean Brown, Margery Kinloch, Thomas Campbell, Isobel Boyter, Janet Edie, George Bett, Margery Stevenson, George Wilson and Christian Robertson, received twenty-six pounds between them. The poor of the landward parish – David Mores (Morris), Agnes Craig, Margaret Black, John Jamison, Helen Laing and Ann Taylor – received fourteen pounds ten shillings. On June 29th new elders were elected, and their ordination was speedily arranged to take place 'before the Herring Fishing come on' – an indication of how important an event this was in the fishing year.

What *was* the exact state of the fishing at this time? Many years later the old Kilrenny minister William Beat or Bett, who was born in Cellar-dyke in or around 1711, could look back nostalgically to this period and compare it favourably with the time at which he was writing (1791): 'The incumbent was born, and has spent the greatest part of his life, in this parish; and within his remembrance vast quantities of large cod, ling, haddocks, herrings, holibut, turbot and mackerel have been caught here; but the fisheries are now miserably decayed. He can remember, when he was a young man, that he numbered no less than 50 large fishing boats, that required 6 men each, belonging to the town of Cellardikes, all employed in the herring fishery in the summer season. ... He has seen 10 or 12 large boats come into the harbour in one day, swimming to the brim with large cod, besides 30, 40 or 50 strung upon a rope fastened to the stern, which they took in tow; and, what will hardly be credited, many a large cod's head lying for dung on the land. ... At that time he remembered no less than 24 small brewers in the town of Cellardikes ... but now they are reduced to two or three, owing to the decay of the fishery'.[9]

But the townspeople's energies were not solely devoted to the catching of fish, even in Cellardyke. An entry in the Burgh Records for 1708 mentions duty to be paid on every web of green cloth carried out of the town, and weavers figure prominently in the lists of burgesses, alongside maltsters, brewsters, land-labourers and (once) a gardener. James Millar and William Boyter are appointed 'to visit the length, breadth and thickness of the Town Cloth', and David Ramsay 'to visit the waulkers and washers'. Nor were municipal improvements neglected. Also in 1708 those Dykers living 'betwixt the Tolbooth Wynd and the end of the

Town' were granted permission to dig a well in the Urquhart Wynd, 'in regard they are very much in want of water'; the only drawback being that they had to pay for it themselves. Anyone who was 'obstriporous' and refused to pay his share was to be 'debarred from any benefit therefrom'. And for the benefit of those whose hearts were set on a flesh market, a 'Flesh Shambles' was to be built at the north end of the Tolbooth, and it was ordained that 'in the summer ensuing the Common way above the Braes be helped where it is most needed, in regard the Inhabitants nor no other person can pass that way'.

The market cross at this date still stood facing the Tolbooth on its stair in the middle of the street – that street which had not yet been graced with the names of James, John and George, and which straggled eastwards to the original nucleus of the 'Shore' or harbour area, in the narrow strip between braefoot and foreshore. It was in this period too that most of the old fishermen's cottages took on their present appearance, and although many of the great outside stairs have vanished in the course of time, enough still remain in John Street and George Street to give us some idea of the days when approaching packhorse and sledge forced the pedestrian to duck into the safety of the nearest doorway. George Gourlay has left us a graphic description of the average fisherman's living quarters at this time: 'Looking back . . . you find the fisher home usually little other than a narrow smoke-begrimed cot – the walls rough and unplastered as the low roof, across which the rafters are seen exactly as they were left at the last stroke of the carpenter's axe. You stumbled over the earthen floor, perhaps more damp and broken than the footpath on the other side of the threshold, as you step to the 'creepie', serving for a chair at the ingle side, or to the sea chest under the little window, filled with mysterious green glass, through which the sunshine, so bright and joyous in the outer world, comes struggling and dimly, as through the folds of a curtain, scarce lifting the shadows that all but hide the curious recess or the close bed, and the big wooden press, not forgetting the corner shelf, with its long array of brown dishes and antique Riga ornaments, brought home by the head of the house in the voyage to retrieve the fortunes of net and line'.[10]

Of course, more exotic goods than brown dishes and antique ornaments came back from some of these trips, and not all of them were unloaded in broad daylight at Cellardyke or Anstruther harbour. No account of eighteenth-century Fife would be complete without a mention of 'the pernicious and distractive trade of smuggling', as it is described in a minute of Kilrenny town council dated July 28th, 1744. How the bailies and councillors managed to keep a straight face on that occasion is a mystery, for if ever there was such a thing as a 'democratic' crime, involving all classes of society, this was it.

Merchant seamen were the first link in the chain, bringing back wines and spirits from Portugal, Spain and France, tobacco from the Americas, tea and silks from Amsterdam and Rotterdam, and timber and iron from the Baltic countries. Cargoes destined to avoid the hated Customs duties were transferred near the shore to local fishing-boats, which ran them ashore in convenient bays and creeks. From there they were conveyed to local merchants, who sold them – openly or otherwise – to minister, laird and nobleman. Sometimes the gentry took a more active part, as we shall see in a moment, and often the excisemen themselves were hand in glove with the local smugglers. In this they might simply be acting from a sense of self-preservation, for it was easier to join the smugglers than to beat them. The Customs officials had after all to live with their families in the very midst of the smuggling communities, and a successful 'seizure' all too often culminated with mob vengeance being taken on the officers responsible. The surviving Customs & Excise records at West Register House in Edinburgh bear witness to many such 'deforcements', but their number is dwarfed by the amount of references to officials censured or dismissed for corruption and/or negligence.

Who *were* the officials of the Customs service in the early eighteenth century? On the lowest rung of the ladder was the 'tidewaiter' or 'tidesman', whose duty it was to inspect the cargoes of ships entering harbour. If a ship was carrying the type of cargo favoured by smugglers, such as tea or brandy, several tidesmen might be stationed aboard her with strict orders to ensure that nothing was carried ashore without payment of duty. A favourite excuse of masters putting in unexpectedly to an east-coast port was that their ship had been blown off course while bound for Norway, and this feeble excuse rebounded on the master of the *Friendship* of Crail in the summer of 1726 when his vessel was discovered in Lunan Bay, near Montrose, her hold stuffed with wine and brandy. The *Friendship* was taken under escort to Montrose, where two tidesmen were sent aboard to enjoy a free trip to Bergen. There was no doubling back on that trip to one of the myriad little coves or creeks on the Angus coastline.[11]

Above the tidesman in the pecking order was the 'landwaiter', whose job it was to check inward and outward cargoes, and to search suspect houses for smuggled goods. Both tidesman and landwaiter took their orders from the 'surveyor', who led the flying squads of officers into action when tipped-off that a cargo was actually being run ashore. The surveyor also kept the keys to the King's Warehouse, and to the cellars where imported foreign salt for curing was kept under bond. Senior to the surveyor was the 'comptroller', who coped with financial matters, book-keeping and public sales or 'roups' of seized goods; then, at the top of the tree, was the 'collector'. The seas were patrolled by a number of fast sloops manned by Customs & Excise personnel, including the *Princess Mary, Princess Caroline, Prince William* and *Royal Charlotte.* Their Hanoverian names would not have added to their popularity with the many Jacobite sympathisers among the smuggling fraternity.

We have already noted that corruption was not exactly unknown in the ranks of the Customs & Excise, and regrettably even the highest ranks of officialdom were not immune to temptation. In 1729 the Commissioners of Excise in Edinburgh were scandalised to learn that Hercules Smith, collector at Kirkcaldy, had not only converted the local salt office into a bedchamber, but was actually retailing wine from the former salt warehouse. His son in addition was busily distilling spirits from confiscated wine and selling them from his father's house. Both men were dismissed the service, and Kirkcaldy's tipplers had to find another 'local'.

More scandalous still was an incident in February, 1742, when a band of excisemen from Kirkcaldy under Mr. James Stark raided Cambo House, Kingsbarns, home of Sir Charles Erskine. The Erskines' involvement with local smugglers is well attested, for only four years previously the laird's brothers, Thomas and William, had been 'principal Actors' in a mob which had assaulted the crew of a Customs sloop in the East Neuk.[12] On this occasion the excisemen, bursting into Sir Charles's drawing-room, were taken aback to find the three Erskine brothers convivially quaffing smuggled brandy with none other than David Row, Comptroller of Customs at Anstruther! Enraged and embarrassed by this discovery, Row shook his cane at the officers, and – according to the report James Stark forwarded to his superiors in Edinburgh – 'gave the Serjeant who Commanded the Party of Soldiers and himself very opprobrious and abusive Language, tending to Animate the Servants & People then in the House of S[r]. Charles Erskine to Rescue the said Seizure'.[13]

It says much for the composure of the raiding party that they proceeded, despite the attitude of their superior officer and the hostile atmosphere of the Erskine household, to remove the contraband spirits to the safety of the King's Warehouse in Anstruther. But they had underestimated the criminal cunning of the disgraced comptroller. Mr. Row, who lived next door to the King's Warehouse, had taken the precaution of knocking a hole in his cellar wall for easier access, and the first time anyone thought to check on the Cambo House seizure, the whole consignment had vanished. David Row was tried before a tribunal in Edinburgh, found guilty, and thrown out of the Customs service. Like many another malcontent and black sheep at this period, he found a congenial niche in the ranks of the Jacobite forces, and paid the penalty for his lack of judgement when he was hanged at Carlisle after the fiasco of the '45. At his trial he admitted to being in charge of the Prince's baggage-train at the Battle of Prestonpans, but what damned him in the judges' eyes was the revelation that he had once been an officer of the Customs House at Anstruther. There was no mercy shown to civil servants who turned traitor.[14]

Corruption on such a grand scale was hardly possible for the humble tidesman, whose main failings were timidity and laziness. Thomas Nairn, who in 1729 succeeded the late William Watson as tidesman at Anstruther, was more than once rebuked by his superiors; and in 1732 Elias Ross and John Cunningham were judged unfit for service through age, Cunningham also being charged with neglect of duty. Yet two years later he was still at his post. It was an unenviable job, and there would have been few takers for the vacant position. The dangers are well illustrated by the following story from Pittenweem, recorded in the Customs & Excise minute-book for Monday, April 14th, 1740: 'The board having received an Account of a Mobb at Pittenweem on Saturday night last between the Hours of 11 & 12 who forcibly Enter'd the Princess Anne Sloop under the command of Mr. Hay, And the Ship the Margaret & Christian of Pittenweem pretending to be bound with a Cargo of Tea & Spirits from Amsterdam to Norway but brought into that Harbour by the said Mr Hay, together with the Precognition of Robert Watson, Alexander Baxter & Robert Gilchrist, now in custody, on board the said Sloop, taken before the Baillies of Pittenweem; Order'd That Mr Hay do come forthwith to Leith with the three Persons & the ship Margaret & Christian abovemention'd, And that Mr Armour do then take further Precognitions more particularly, & lay the same before the Board'.

Among others who pillaged the *Margaret & Christian* were William Grieve, tidesman at Pittenweem, who made off with 6 pieces of silk and 10 pounds of rhubarb! Found guilty, he was dismissed the service.

Less than a year later the threat of mob violence at Pittenweem was enough to daunt another pair of tidesmen, who came to the conclusion that discretion was the better part of valour: 'The Collector & Comptroller of Kirkcaldy having represented that David Smith & Andrew Paul Tidewaiters there, were boarded on the Ship Speedwell to see her off the Coast, and that they left their Station & went on Shoar at Pittenweem, whereby an opportunity was given to run the Cargo out of the Vessel, and moreover that they have Confessed that they afterwards Concealed themselves one day at home, that they might not be put on Duty; Ordered that they be Suspended'.

There is no mention of Cellardyke in these early Customs records, despite frequent references to 'considerable Seizures' at Anstruther and Fifeness. Perhaps the Dykers were too fly even for the most vigilant of excisemen. We do however have one notable tale of smuggling at Cellardyke, beside which our other anecdotes pale into insignificance. The incident in question took place in the early part of 1736, and its gory aftermath is well captured by Sir Walter Scott in his novel *The Heart of Midlothian*. Other useful sources are Matthew Conolly's *Fifiana* and Walter Wood's *The East Neuk of Fife*, but for a detailed account of the Cellardyke connection we turn to an article in the *East Fife Observer* of August 9th, 1945.

One night at the beginning of January, 1736, a large consignment of brandy was run ashore at the foot of 'Wullie Gray's Dyke', between Cellardyke and Caiplie, from where it was transported the few hundred yards to Bailie Andrew Waddell's store in Cellardyke. Later it was moved, again under cover of darkness, to James Wilson's tavern in the High Street of Anstruther, known locally as the 'Smuggler's Howff' (next to Gray & Pringle's hardware store). Here the story might have ended, like the others we have related, for Customs officers were lying in wait, and the whole consignment was seized. Jubilant at this stroke of good fortune, exciseman James Stark made preparations to sell the contraband goods by public roup, as was the custom.

For Andrew Wilson, king of the Fife smugglers, this was the last straw. A native of Pathhead in the parish of Dysart, Wilson was a baker to trade, but his more adventurous nocturnal activities had made him a folk-hero up and down the Fife coast. Lately, however, the Customs service seemed to have advance knowledge of his every move, and this latest setback left him a ruined man. But he was not beaten yet. By the 8th of January Wilson was in Edinburgh recruiting a pair of accomplices named Hall and Robertson to help him carry out a daring plan to 'recover his own'. The following day the three men crossed the Forth to Kinghorn, hired horses from one Patrick Galloway there, and accompanied by Galloway's son John made their separate ways to Anstruther. By nightfall they had stabled their horses at James Wilson's tavern.

But they were too late. The brandy had been sold, and the excisemen were on their way back to Kirkcaldy with the money. Yet all was not lost, for the excisemen planned to spend the night at Widow Fowler's inn in Pittenweem's Marygate. There were inns and taverns aplenty in

Anstruther itself, but without exception they were notorious haunts of smugglers. The hostelry of Mrs. Fowler, an exciseman's widow, seemed a better bet for a good night's rest.

The remainder of the story is well known. Later that night the three desperadoes, Wilson, Hall and Robertson, mounted an assault on the little hostelry in Pittenweem, so terrifying the three Customs officials that they leapt out of their second-storey bedroom windows, leaving behind the money they had collected. While James Stark and his assist-ant William Geddes hid in a field, the third exciseman, Alexander Clark, ran barefoot and in his shirt-tails to Anstruther to alert the military. Before long the villains were caught red-handed with the stolen money, and taken to Edinburgh to stand trial. Hall was let off with a prison sentence, but Wilson and Robertson were condemned to be hanged on the 14th of April in the Grassmarket.

It almost never came to that. The two men found themselves sharing a prison cell with a couple of horse-thieves from Arbroath called Ratcliff and Stewart, who with the aid of a spring-saw had sawn through the bars of their window. They offered to share their escape route with the two smugglers, and Robertson, the younger and slimmer of the two, thought he might just squeeze through. But he did not get the chance, for his heavily-built accomplice insisted on going first – and stuck fast. From then on the two men were placed under stricter guard.

If the failed escape attempt was galling for Robertson, it was all the more so for Andrew Wilson, whose conscience told him that he had selfishly stood between his young friend and freedom. Not until Sunday, 11th April, did he have an opportunity to make amends. It was the custom for men about to be hanged to spend their last Sunday on earth in the Tolbooth Church, hearing the 'condemned sermon', a soldier guard-ing them on either side. On that particular Sunday, as the congregation solemnly rose to their feet at the conclusion of the sermon and benedic-tion, Wilson suddenly seized the two soldiers standing beside him, and shouting 'Run, Geordie, run!', sank his teeth into the shoulder of one of Robertson's guards. Left with only one soldier to grapple with, the dumbstruck Robertson shook himself awake and leapt to freedom over the pews, while grinning well-wishers in the congregation took up the chant of 'Run, Geordie, run!'

There was no hope for Wilson after that. The following Wednesday he was taken from prison to the Grassmarket, shackled so tightly to Captain Porteous of the City Guard that he was in considerable pain. Porteous was no favourite of the Edinburgh citizenry, and his callous treatment of Wilson, accompanied by heartless jibes at the unfortunate man's predicament, only served to heighten their sympathy for the victim. This feeling grew to fever pitch when Wilson's body finally dangled from the gibbet, and stones were thrown. Incensed by this display of lawlessness, Porteous ordered his men to fire into the crowd, and set them an example by himself shooting an onlooker dead on the spot. Six or seven people were killed in all, and a great many more wounded.

The affray in the Grassmarket became a national scandal, and even the Edinburgh city council could not deny that Porteous was to a large degree personally responsible for the mayhem. Further outbreaks of rioting were only prevented by his swift trial and subsequent death sentence for wanton murder. The date of execution was fixed for September 8th, 1736.

But Porteous was not without friends in high places, and petitions were addressed to the Queen herself on his behalf. The outcome was a stay of execution until October 20th. Was this the prelude to a free pardon? Not if Porteous's enemies in Edinburgh could help it. Rumour had it the captain would be despatched on September 8th, come what may, but in fact it was on the night of September 7th that the Porteous Mob swung into action.

That night, while the city slept, a group of conspirators secured the 'ports' or gates, and invaded the Tolbooth, dragging the object of their anger into what must have seemed like a waking nightmare. Only minutes before Porteous had been celebrating his imminent release with a band of friends. Down the West Bow they carried him, into the Grassmarket, where a dyer's pole had to serve as an impromptu gallows. A coil of rope was taken from Mrs. Jeffray's booth in the West Bow, and to show that they were no common thieves but honest men in search of justice, a golden guinea was left behind to pay for the coarse hemp. And so, crudely but effectively, Captain Porteous was lynched in the Grassmarket by a carnival crowd disguised, we are told, in sailor's uniform and 'women's attire'.

The repercussions in government circles were tremendous, and bills were introduced into Parliament to censure the Lord Provost of Edinburgh and punish the people of Scotland. But despite threats, cajolings and promises of reward, no information was ever forthcoming as to the identity of the ringleaders of the 'Porteous Mob'. The east-coast Scot is a tight-lipped specimen at the best of times, and it seems not to have leaked across the Forth that the man who threw down the golden guinea in Mrs. Jeffray's shop in the West Bow was Sandy Bruce, barber, smuggler and town-councillor in Anstruther Easter. Many local worthies have carried the story down to us by word of mouth, including the highly-respected mother of the Anstruther sailors Rear-Admiral William and Captain James Black, R.N. As a young girl, so Mrs. Black told Matthew Conolly, the author of *Fifiana*, she had imbibed the story from the lips of old Smuggler Bruce himself. Thus ended a gruesome episode in Scottish history which had begun humbly enough, with the running ashore – one chilly January night in 1736 – of a cargo of spirits in the douce little parish of Kilrenny.

In the wake of the Porteous affair municipal councils throughout the land drew up resolutions against smuggling, but to little effect. In one incident almost twenty years later the *Isobel and Mary*, stuffed with contraband and guarded by four tidesmen, was boarded at Pittenweem by a mob who removed the cargo, locked the officials in the cabin and cut the ship's cables, with the express intention of letting her founder on the nearby rocks. Only the timely intervention of some well-disposed persons prevented the four excisemen being drowned. One of the perpetrators of that particular stroke of villainy was James Johnston, town-councillor and treasurer of Anstruther Easter. As long as men like Johnston, Sandy Bruce and Andrew Waddell held sway in the council chambers of the East Neuk burghs there was little hope that the 'pernicious trade' of smuggling would soon be rooted out.

Due to irritating omissions in the Kilrenny burgh records it is hard to judge the effect on the town of the 1745 Rising, but the following entry for March 26th, 1744, no doubt expressed the sentiments of most of the townspeople: '(The council) unanimously resolved to address his Majesty upon account of a design of an Invasion supported by the tyrannical power of France, the common Disturber of the peace and tranquillity of Europe'.

A list of rebels in St. Andrews district drawn up in 1746 reveals only one Dyker: Mr. Andrew Lothian, 'Brewer & Precentor to the Unqualified Meetinghouse', who 'pay'd the whole of his own duty & demanded & received the Revenue from others liable therein, which he also pay'd to the Rebels whom he caused use severities on the people, he pray'd for the prosperity of the Rebels & shews himself upon all occasions to be disaffected'. The informers who gave Andrew Lothian away were 'James Simpson, Town Treasurer of Cellardyke, Marjory Alison his Spouse, Marjory Alison their Servt & Thomas Anderson Brewer there'. But even Andrew Lothian was not in the same league as Anstruther Easter's Charles Wightman, who, according to the same document, 'Went with his Wife & waited on the Pretender's son, Entertained the Rebels, had a man in pay in their Service at his own Expense, is said to be factor for the Earl of Kelly, Collected the Excise for him, had the assurance to ask the Excise Officer how he liv'd under his Governm^t & has alwayes been known for a dissaffected person'[15] (the Earl of Kellie was a colonel in the Rebel army).

He is a sinister figure, this Factor Wightman, in his rambling old house beside the ruins of Dreel Castle, ancient stronghold of the Anstruther family. A 'Black Lady' was said to haunt the house, her glance alone sufficing to drive men mad, but the evidence suggests that she was an invention of the factor himself – a clever ploy to dissuade his superstitious fellow-townsmen from prying too closely into his affairs after nightfall: 'Charles Wightman was the prince of plotters, but this is unmistakably his masterpiece. The Guard House was within a musket shot, but not a single keg of gin or a chest of tea of the hundred cargoes run to his stair foot was ever taken by the officers. Yes, and it was in this guest room that Comptroller Row, hanged at Carlisle, feasted and drank with the French colonels in the Rising of '45. It was also to the little door in the wynd, there to this day, that the fugitives skulked after Culloden Moor. "Wild men frae the hills wi' staring een, and haffits wae tae see", as Peggy Millar said, yet who, one and all, lay in safe hiding, with the "Black Lady" on the watch – the clansmen in the big barn and the chieftains in the secret stair – till, by-and-bye, the smugglers gave them a safe passage to France'.[16]

But this is Anstruther history, and the 'wild men frae the hills' were less welcome in Cellardyke, where the fishers had not forgotten their epic voyage across the Forth with the Highland host during the '15.

Much more interesting to the ordinary man than the chancy business of insurrection was the equally exciting and almost equally violent business of political elections; and what political animals our ancestors were! For if the kirk-session records are preoccupied with fornication and finance, the burgh records are almost wholly devoted to elections: elections of townsmen to be burgesses; elections of burgesses to be delegates to the General Assembly or the Convention of Royal Burghs, or to the caucuses which chose the local member of parliament; and most absorbing of all, the elections of the M.P.s themselves, with all the attendant bribery, corruption and intimidation that entailed.[17]

The method of election, from the time of the Union in 1707, was as follows. The five burghs of Crail, Pittenweem, Anstruther Easter, Anstruther Wester and Kilrenny – the latter included among its betters by some oversight, since it was no longer officially a royal burgh – jointly elected a member or 'commissioner' to represent them in the Westminster parliament. In each burgh a writ signed by the sheriff was forwarded to the senior baillie, who then ordered the town officer to summon the councillors to a meeting in three days' time. The purpose of this meeting was to choose a delegate to go forward to a final meeting with the delegates of the other four burghs, so that together they could choose the member of parliament. Each town took it in turn to be the returning burgh. In the first election after the Treaty of Union, on May 26th, 1708, the unanimous choice of all five delegates was Sir John Anstruther, who held the seat until 1715, when he retired to make way for his cousin, Colonel Philip Anstruther of Airdrie. But just as this office seemed about to become hereditary in the Anstruther family, a dangerous rival appeared on the scene.

The Scots of Scotstarvit were relative newcomers to the East Neuk of Fife, having arrived first in 1611 when Sir John Scot of Knightspottie, director of Chancery, purchased the lands of Caiplie and Easter Pitcorthie. Later he was to add to these Inglis-Tarvit, Wester Pitcorthie and Third-part, and it was on this last-named estate on the fringes of Kilrenny parish that the family seat was erected. By the time our story takes place the estate had passed to Sir John's great-grandson David Scot of Scotstarvit, an ambitious young advocate who had set his sights on winning a parliamentary seat.

No expense was spared by either side, that spring of 1722, to ensure the 'right' result on election day, but when the time came it emerged that the two Anstruthers were solidly behind General (formerly Colonel) Anstruther, while Crail and Pittenweem were equally staunch for his rival, and so Kilrenny – which was also the returning burgh that year – held the balance. A delegate in the shape of Baillie Robert Waddell was chosen to represent the burgh, and entrusted with the sheriff's writ and a signed and sealed commission to vote for General Anstruther; but no sooner had this fact been announced than the good baillie disappeared off the face of the earth! Rumours spread like wildfire through the town. The baillie had yielded to pressure from the opposition and switched sides, reneging against his colleagues on the council. He had been seen at an upper window of Cambo House, home of Scotstarvit's crony Sir Alexander Erskine. Not until the day of the election itself, when Robert Waddell reappeared as if by magic at the old Tolbooth of Cellardyke, did the full story emerge. Having been lured up to Innergelly House on a false pretext, Mr. Waddell had been pounced on in the tree-lined avenue, bundled into a chaise and driven off at speed to a place of confinement. There he had been visited by a masked figure using a disguised voice, but bearing an uncanny resemblance to the Laird of Scotstarvit, who had tried to persuade him of the crying need to break the stranglehold of the Anstruther family on the five burghs.

Once back in the familiar surroundings of Cellardyke, and in the encouraging company of his friends, the baillie regained his courage and cast his vote for the Anstruther interest. Emboldened by this example the Pittenweem delegate, James Melville, adroitly changed horses in midstream, and what had begun as a daring, if unscrupulous ploy, ended in near-farce. David Scot had another ten years to wait before the more pliable burgesses of Montrose gave him his ticket to Westminster.

Almost two decades passed before the Anstruther hegemony was challenged again. This was in 1741, and the challenger this time was Captain John Stewart, the dashing younger son of the Earl of Moray. The fickle Pittenweemers and Crailers were won over immediately, and even the Anstruther burghs wavered, for their General had gravely offended them by his pro-Government stance on the hanging of the smuggler Andrew Wilson, an admired folk-hero on the Fife coast. Only the fishers of Cellardyke were solidly behind General Anstruther, for had he not fought hard throughout the last parliamentary session to save them from the hated press-gangs? Yet the moral support of unenfranchised fishermen was hardly enough to secure victory against such overwhelming odds. In a fit of sheer aristocratic bravado which perhaps owed not a little to Scotstarvit's earlier example, eight Anstruther councillors were lured to Airdrie House, where they were detained for almost three weeks and plied with the best of food and drink, the stateroom of the old mansion even being turned into a temporary theatre where the captives were treated to performances by imported stars of the London stage. Armed patrols deterred curious or anxious relatives from invading the grounds, and not even the death of Councillor Watson's mother could procure his release from his indulgent captor.

On the other side, Captain Stewart had the backing of the wealthy Edinburgh merchant John Wilson, whose moneybags are supposed to have swayed at least nine councillors. After a heated pre-election campaign during which rival mobs of supporters came to blows in the streets of Anstruther, the fatal day dawned; and General Anstruther lost the election on a technicality. What happened was this. It was the custom, at the election of a delegate, for those present to take an oath against bribery and corruption. On this occasion, however, the Kilrenny delegate – Sir Philip Anstruther of Balcaskie – had, not surprisingly, refused to take the oath. When revealed at the final election, this was enough to ruin his cousin's chances, and the Anstruther family left the council chamber in high dudgeon, leaving Captain Stewart's supporters to celebrate his victory with a magnificent bonfire at the Billowness.

The new M.P. was to represent the constituency for only six years before handing it back to its former owner, who lost it again in the following decade to Sir Harry Erskine. Allegations of bribery and corruption abound in the burgh records, as for instance in 1765, when Andrew Boyter, 'eldest bailie' in Kilrenny, alleged that Robert Fall, the provost of Dunbar and uncrowned king of the east-coast fisheries, had bribed his wife and threatened himself with violence in order to influence his vote. Even the hold of the Anstruther family began to slip badly, and a detailed account of their alleged shortcomings appears in the burgh records of 1784, when they are accused of enforcing 'thraldom' on their dependants and of 'gradually sapping the fundamental Constitution of these Towns'. The petition is signed by seventy Kilrenny burgesses, who also take the opportunity to slate their elected councillors for being willing tools of the Anstruther family. There is a new note of defiance here which reminds us that the French Revolution is only five years away. But long before this it had been remarked by a critical observer that the town councils of Kilrenny, West Anstruther and Pittenweem, 'and of Kilrenny in particular, were composed of low indigent persons incapable to resist any money temptation. And it is proved against them, that they were unanimously resolved not to neglect the opportunity of the ensuing election to sell themselves to the highest bidder'.[18]

As we have already implied, these violent political controversies did little to bridge the yawning chasm of the Caddies Burn, and the animosity between Dyker fisherman and Anstruther merchant was still as alive as ever in these years. The most telling case in point that has come down to us occurred in 1755, when the Cellardyke skippers James Watt, William Powrie, Thomas Watson, James Millar, William Dryburgh, Thomas Scott, John Anderson, George Lothian and William Young were charged with not paying teinds to the laird of Anstruther for fish landed by them at Anstruther harbour. By this time the teinds were no longer collected by the laird himself but were sold for a lump sum to a local merchant, who collected them in as best he could. But the effrontery of the old cooper James McDougal and his accomplices among the Anstruther magistrates was dashed when the laird of Kilrenny, Mr. Henry Bethune (Beaton), produced the charter granted by the Cardinal to his ancestor in 1543 exempting the Kilrenny men from paying any dues at Anstruther. This incident only served to deepen the mutual hostility between the two communities.[19]

If laird and councillor could no longer rely on unquestioning support from the burgesses, the church was in no better case. As the eighteenth century wore on, the fierce Presbyterianism which had been so marked a feature of the Kirk in the previous century began to abate somewhat, and national fasts and witchcraft trials became as much a thing of the past as hillside conventicles. In some parishes, though not yet awhile in Kilrenny, public humiliation on the stool of repentance was gradually commuted to a money fine. Most importantly, the Patronage Act of 1712 reasserted the right of lairds rather than congregations to appoint ministers, and inevitably the ministers so appointed tended, like their colleagues in the Church of England, to share the attitudes and interests of the gentry. In many parts of Scotland those who disagreed with the new order of things broke away from the Kirk to form their own exclusive sects. In the records of Kilrenny parish such dissent surfaces only when a particular individual's conscience forces him to defend his ideological position before the kirk-session. In August 1762, for example, Simon Couper was asked to explain why, for the past year and a half, he had absented himself from the kirk and from his duties as an elder. Simon's answer was that he and his fellow-elders were robbed of their privilege of choosing their own pastor, 'which he looked on as a Divine Right'. The session's attitude is interesting here. Simon Couper was evidently a well-respected man in their eyes, and their attempts to win him back to the fold and to turn a blind eye to his absences from church are conciliatory in the extreme. When he persists in his refusal to hear their pleas William Salter and Robert Gilchrist are sent out into the churchyard to entreat with him there, but in vain. Only with the greatest reluctance do the session finally agree to delete his name from the church roll and the list of elders.

Much more typical of the average parishioner than Simon Couper are the delinquents who still appear regularly before the session accused of a multitude of sins, and who submit, with a greater or lesser degree of ill-will, to that body's censures. Thus on March 24th, 1765, William Watson appeared before the minister and elders after prayer and acknowledged that he was guilty before marriage with his young Largo bride Margaret Imrie, 'and promised that both himself and his wife should make Satisfaction as soon as the session shall judge it proper to call them thereto'.[20] More colourful by far than this, though, is the young serving-man Alexander Swine, who flits artfully in and out of the records at this period like some mischievous spirit of misrule. When he is accused by Helen Miles in Kilrenny of coming upon her suddenly in the South Whin Park where she was keeping her cattle, he neatly turns the tables on her with a tale straight out of the Garden of Eden: 'He further declar'd that when he was sleeping at the Green Dam beside some horse teithered there, and which he had been keeping, she came and awoke him, gave him an Apple out of her pocket, dallied with him, & so drew him into the snare'.

Whatever the truth of the matter, Alexander Swine took care soon afterwards to distance himself from his temptress by betaking himself to the parish of St. Vigeans, near Arbroath, from where however he was forced to return only a year later to answer to charges made against him by one Janet Skirvine, servant to Baillie Millar in Cellardyke. Being questioned as to whether he could remember any occasion of guilt with Janet Skirvine which could have led to her present condition, Alexander could remember only the night when Baillie Millar's servant-girls' bed collapsed. The story deserves re-telling. Janet Skirvine and her fellow-servants Mary Crabie and Sarah Tait shared a bed in Baillie Millar's house in Cellardyke. One night, 'the bottom of it fell down', and who better to call in to mend it for them than Alexander Swine? (Quite how he gained this reputation as a handyman is unclear.) In any event, Alexander was asked to mend the bed, '. . . which he accordingly did, & in a sort of Daffing, as he called it, lay down upon the foreside of their Bed with his Cloths on and fell asleep'. Nothing indecent had occurred, he assured the elders, and with wide-eyed innocence the three girls also testified that indeed nothing untoward had taken place, at least on *this* occasion. Mortified by this evidence of the younger generation's immodesty, the session passed the case on to the Presbytery for their judgement. In his dealings with the female sex Alexander Swine is reminiscent of his eighteenth-century contemporaries Tom Jones and Robert Burns.

Meanwhile, an even more heinous crime was becoming commonplace along the coast, as more and more young couples shrugged off the conventions of their day and sailed off to Edinburgh for a so-called 'irregular' or 'clandestine' marriage without banns or payment of 'contract money'. These marriages were most often performed by 'non-juring' clergymen who had not taken the oath of allegiance to the royal house of Hanover, and here was another reason for the wrath of the Kirk. In 1764, for example, William Moncrieff and Anne Ramsay admitted to an irregular marriage in Edinburgh by Mr. Peter Wilson, while Robert Tervit and Janet Hodge confessed to a similar sin on April 27th and followed this with an admission of their antenuptial fornication on November 18th. Most abandoned of all, if we believe the testimony of George Gourlay in *Our Old Neighbours*, were the twenty-seven couples who squeezed aboard Michael Doig's new boat, the *Thrifty Lass*, one July morning in 1764 to tie the marriage knot in Edinburgh – a miracle of compression if the story is true! Repeated warnings from the pulpit had little or no effect, and the nuptials of Thomas Cunningham and Janet Wilson in November 1775 seem to have been the last straw: for only weeks later the following minute was inserted in the session-register:

December 10th 1775

Whereas the irregular Practice of Clandestine Marriages is become so frequent in this Parish, and some pretend that they did not know they were lyable to a fine for such Practice, The Session have unanimously resolved to insist upon the Fine for the future and to give publick advertisement of it from the Letteron (lectern) next Lord's Day that none may pretend Ignorance any more.

As the eighteenth century entered its last quarter, the modern world was taking shape. First the American War of Independence set that mighty giant free; then the French Revolution and subsequent Napoleonic wars redrew the political map of Europe. Against this background, the fragments we can recover of our ancestors' lives are more poignant than ever: and always the sea is there in the background. The Cellardyke fishing-fleet swims into view on Monday, August 7th, 1778, and is captured for all time in the report of David Loch, Inspector of Fisheries:

> A good fishing is carried on here (at Cellardyke). The people are very industrious. ... On Monday, the 7th., I visited the fishers and all concerned in the fishing trade, who were in high spirits on account of their success, very considerable quantities of herrings having been taken.[21]

The buccaneer John Paul Jones slips unnoticed into the Firth and badly shakes up the douce burghers of the coast, before resuming his fabulous career in more exotic waters.[22] But many Cellardyke men are serving in exotic parts themselves by now, for the thirst of the armed services for able men shows no signs of abating; and the increasing references to foreign parts by the session-clerk are a sign of the times:

> Lent Alex^r. Mentiplay who is now in America, and whose Wife died lately, for the Support of his Children, till it please God that he return from his Majesties Service, Thirty shillings sterling equally out of the 3 Boxes.
> This day the Town and Landward Elders lent to David Reid's Wife, in her Husband's absence, serving his Majesty in the Navie, six pounds scots.

In discipline cases the absent lover is as often as not out of the country too: as when Margaret Hodge became pregnant by George Corstorphine, 'mariner belonging to Cellardike and presently Serving on board his Majesties frigate the Iris' (Dec. 29th, 1793); or when Molly Moncrieff bore a child to Robert Frazer, 'now a Soldier in his Majesties Service in the West Indies' (Jan. 8th, 1797). One can only feel sympathy for the aged minister and his faithful body of elders as they struggled to cope with the demands made on them by the conditions of the times, and

The Rev. William Beat, minister of Kilrenny from 1760 to 1797, from Kay's *Original Portraits* ('Beat' is probably a variant of 'Bett': still a common surname in Anstruther and Cellardyke).

sought to accommodate unprecedented needs on the part of their parishioners. Their attempts to alleviate the poverty and starvation caused by a series of calamities occupy much space in the contemporary records, and not all the heritors and landowners of the parish shared the concern of General Scot of Scotstarvit's widow for the poor. In 1783 that lady donated £20 to buy victual for the poor, giving as her reason that 'The very near concern my children & self have with the Parish of Kilrenny occasions me commiserating the poor upon that Spot as there may be many Sufferers among them owing to the present Deplorable State of Scarcity which renders the necessaries of Life very difficult to procure from the exorbitant Market prices'. Others of her station were less mindful of their obligations.

In wartime it is notoriously difficult to maintain pre-war standards of morality, and it must have become increasingly obvious to the Kilrenny elders that the age-old bogey of the stool of repentance was an anachronism now. On July 10th, 1791, they decided to go with the current of the times: 'The Session . . . Considering, That in Several parishes around it was now become customary to absolve Persons Guilty of Antenuptial Fornication with a private rebuke before the Session, Agreed that, for the future, (as an Encouragement to Marriage) all Persons guilty of Antenuptial Fornication in this Parish Should not publickly compear before the Congregation, but be rebuked in private before the Session'.

One of the last victims of the old dispensation was Catherine Tarvit, who in the months following the storming of the Bastille in Paris was interrogated regarding the paternity of her child, thus inaugurating a discipline case which was to drag on for over two years. There is little to distinguish this case from the many others we have noticed, apart from the length of time needed to bring the 'culprit' to book, and the significance of the unfortunate Catherine for the author's family-tree![23]

Catherine's initial explanation was a colourful one, and yet again there is a nautical flavour to the anecdote. Her misfortune, so she informed the session, occurred in the course of a visit to her sister at Abernyte, in the Carse of Gowrie, when '. . . she was mett be a man between Abernite and Dundee in a Sailor's habit who flew upon her and threatened her with Murder if she hindered him Satisfying his Wicked intentions'. The session, with the weary resignation of men who have heard it all before, sent the girl away with an injunction to think the matter over, then return and tell them what had *really* happened.

A week later a chastened Catherine made her second appearance in the session-house and admitted that the father of her child was John Gosman, a married man and the tenant of Kilrenny Mill farm. The remaining two years during which the 'unpurged scandal' was on the session's agenda were occupied with attempts to make the unrepentant Mr. Gosman do his repentance before the congregation. Gone were the days when the people had followed their ministers with more or less unquestioning obedience. When the old minister William Beat or Bett died on December 21st, 1797, in his 87th year, it was almost like an epitaph for the century.[24]

Lastly, we close the tale of another century with yet another catalogue of disasters, for thanks to parish schoolmaster Mr. John Orphat, who also officiated as parish- and session-clerk, we now have names to put to the anonymous statistics of death at sea. Mr. Orphat was blessed with a fine sense of the dramatic allied to not inconsiderable artistic talent, and the burials register he inaugurated in 1791, headed *Burials in Kilrennie* in fine Gothic script, bears the following apposite texts on its first page:

– It is appointed unto Men Once to Die, – Rev:IX.27.

– Blessed are the dead which die in the Lord from henceforth; Yea, Saith the Spirit, that they may rest from their labours; and their works do follow them. Rev:XIV.13.

– Blessed and holy is he that hath part in the first Resurrection; on Such the Second death hath no power. Rev:XX.6.

One who 'died in the Lord' was David Brown, who perished within hailing-distance of the shore near the rocky islet known as the 'Basket', when the string of a creel entwined round a jacket-button pulled him into the depths. So little might stand between life and death. Another was the worthy old wright Alexander Wood, whose death – along with four comrades – in 1793 prompted the following account from the eloquent pen of Mr. Orphat:

> Alexander Wood, Wright and Boat builder in Cellardike, also one of the Elders of this parish; with Bailie John Tarvitt Weaver in Cellardike, and David Donaldson Wright and Sawyer in Cellardike, having been lost in a boat in going out of Cellardike harbour in the drave, on Monday morning being the 23.^{d} Septr. were all buried here at the same hour on the 25th. of said month, An. Dom. 1793.
>
> Also lost in Said Boat and at Same time, William Bauldie Weaver in Anstruther-easter, and John Gardiner (tho' pick'd up) lived only a few days. All much and Justly Regretted: Married persons, and left large families.
> *Quis talia fando temperet a Lachrymis.* (Who, in reporting such things, could refrain from tears?).

Only one survivor, James Martin, succeeded in clawing his way to the safety of the Craw Skellie. This disaster, and many others like it, are graphically portrayed in Gourlay's *Fisher Life*, and for convenience we shall refer to that work in later pages.

Other men found an even chillier death in the Greenland whalers which plied from Dunbar, Leith and Dundee, and which took their crews from the pick of the East Neuk mariners. But worst of all, in the final decade of the century, were the Royal Navy frigates and men-of-war which skulked behind islands and in sheltered creeks, or stole into quiet harbours under cover of night to impress men for His Majesty's service. Not Highland clansmen nor even Customs officials, nor any other oppressors of the poor fisherfolk, were so universally hated and feared as the thuggish pressgangs, and many are the tales told of houses with secret connecting passages, trapdoors hidden by 'sea-kists', or other stratagems to outwit them. Yet there were still those who, like young John Moncrieff – the son of William Moncrieff and Anne Ramsay – were seized and bludgeoned into submission within sight of the shore, never to see their families again. Others returned to their homes only after years of confinement in French prisons. Sometimes a whole crew would fail to return home, and their wives and relatives would be left in agonising suspense. Had they perished in a storm, or had they fallen prey to the press-gang?

James Anderson, Sailor in Cellardike (but now amissing being either lost or Taken at Sea) and Margaret Millar his Spouse had a lawful Daughter born Octr. 22nd. 1797 and baptised on the 24th. of Same month, named Andrea.

The clerk obviously felt it incumbent upon him to explain to future generations the choice of such an outlandish name: 'N.B. She was named after Andrew Anderson, Supposed to be lost also'.

The agonies of civil war were long forgotten, and 'Jacobite' was a word long out of fashion, but an even bloodier conflict was now sucking in the lives of men. At home there were other battles to fight, not least the battle against disease of all kinds, with smallpox a particularly virulent scourge in the bad years of 1796 and 1797. John Reid, 'son to Adam Reid, sailor in Cellardyke', and the two children of Thomas Crichton were only three of the pathetic little victims of that 'auld enemy'. And if the herring fishing was set to reach a new peak of prosperity, the ancient staple of the white fishery had failed entirely for years in a row. If the Lord gave, he also seemed to take away in equal measure. Life was never entirely fair.

5

The Nineteenth Century, Part I: The Pre-Victorian Era

The nineteenth century blew into Cellardyke with gale-force winds which brought tragedy in their wake. On the morning of February 24th, 1800, one of the seven Cellardyke boats then engaged in the 'keeling' or great-line fishery was making its way back to harbour in the teeth of a rising south-easterly gale when it was hit by a giant wave and swept towards the reef known as the 'Skellie Point'. The crowd on the pier could only watch helplessly as the boat was crushed on the rocks, and the crew, one by one, disappeared into the sea. 'I see't the noo', cried an eyewitness sixty years later. 'The cry's in my lug yet', wept another, even later. Only one man escaped that terrible maelstrom:

'And so the death scene closes on one and all, save the solitary swimmer, William Watson, whose escape is one of the most romantic incidents of the coast. His companions had disappeared in the recoiling waves, but anticipating this danger he bade them all farewell and divesting himself of his big jacket, plunged into the sea. "I felt as if I walked on the water", he told his friends, and so it almost seemed to others, so strangely was he borne on the great billow that swept him to the shore. Here another thrilling scene occurred. His devoted wife, Mary Galloway, had been one of the spectators of the fatal scene, and now in the heroism of woman's love, and with a strength that was not to be resisted by those around her, she rushed in to his rescue, and clasped him to her bosom, with no thought but the overflowing joy of the moment. Singular as it may appear, he stepped almost on the very spot of the Craw Skellie on which his townsman James Martin had landed as the single survivor seven years before.

'William Watson, 'Water Willie', as he was usually called after his extraordinary escape, was a fine specimen of a Scottish fisherman, one whose courage and endurance was as conspicuous as his strength and activity.'[1]

A 'romantic incident' indeed, and it is perhaps fitting that the present writer – his great-great-great-grandson – should preserve the memory of it for posterity. Those who lost their lives in this tragedy were Philip Anderson, Leslie Brown, William Muir, Thomas Fowler, Thomas Smith, Andrew Robertson and Thomas Crichton, flax-dresser and part-time fisherman (not Thomas *Christie*, as Gourlay mistakenly asserts in *Fisher Life*).

'Water Willie' was born in 1774 to William Watson and Margaret Imrie, and was the younger brother of that Thomas Watson whose even more romantic exploits at sea have figured in a work of local history, a news-paper article and a collection of short stories set in the East Neuk.[2] The following account has been pieced together from the first two sources.

Legend tells us that Thomas Watson was married twice, and that his first wife died at a young age. Perhaps he is the same Thomas Watson, 'Son of William Watson Mariner', who was called before the Kilrenny kirk-session on January 15th, 1786, to account for the fact that his sweetheart had been found to be pregnant. The girl was Margaret Thomson, daughter of George Thomson, 'Miller in Cellar-Dykes'. On being asked whether or not their future plans included marriage, the girl proved to be decidedly more starry-eyed than her reluctant suitor: 'She declared that she was willing to Marry Thomas Watson, and he said, that he *might* marry Margaret Thomson, but not just now'. Despite these unromantic beginnings, the couple were married later that year, and Margaret was to bear her husband five children in rapid succession before dying of a consumption.

As for Thomas Watson's second wife, Mary Buick, we are told only that she was a native of Dundee; and it is possible that Thomas was one of the band of East Neuk mariners who sailed from that port to the 'whalefishing' in the Davis Strait. Like many another Cellardyke sailor, Thomas Watson was the object of the pressgang's unwelcome attentions, but unlike most of his fellow-townsmen he seems to have been expert at eluding them. Such was their determination to have him, however, that he was eventually caught. According to *Our Old Neighbours*, it was only after nine days of hiding out among the whin bushes of Kingsmuir and the coal pits of Lochty that Thomas Watson was driven to risk a visit to his cousin Annie at the Cunzie Burn in Anstruther. Annie Watson was married to the Anstruther merchant Alexander Tennant, whose barn would have afforded a dry, if temporary, refuge. There, just after twelve that night, he was taken. Incidentally the Tennants' younger son, William, was a boy of thirteen at the time, and it must be a matter of regret that the future Professor of Oriental Languages at St. Andrews University and author of *Anster Fair* never saw fit to exercise his poetic talents on the theme of that fateful night!

So distraught was Thomas's wife at the news of his capture – or so we are told – that she contrived to be taken on as a nurse on board her husband's ship: a not uncommon role for women at this time, when the

Royal Navy was more flexible in its attitude towards women at sea. And so it came about that Thomas and Mary Watson were serving together aboard H.M.S. *Ardent* in the spring of 1801 when she was ordered to join in the historic attack on Copenhagen under Admiral Sir Hyde Parker and his second-in-command, Vice-Admiral Lord Nelson. On April 2nd, at about half-past ten in the morning, there began what Nelson himself, dodging flying splinters on the quarter-deck of the *Elephant*, summed up as the most terrific of all the 103 engagements he had been in. On being told of Parker's signal to cease action and withdraw Nelson jokingly put his telescope to his blind eye, and entered the realm of popular mythology.

Other commanders were equally eager for a brilliant victory. Next to the *Ardent* in line of battle was the *Glatton*, whose master William Bligh was obsessed with the need to erase the ignominy of the mutiny on the *Bounty*, a blot on his career for the past dozen years. (After acquitting himself with honour at Copenhagen, Bligh would ask an embarrassed Nelson for a written testimonial.)

When the smoke of battle cleared, about three o'clock that afternoon, the *Ardent*'s losses totalled 31 men killed and 68 wounded. Only the *Monarch* had a higher casualty list. Three ships had gone aground and missed the battle altogether, leaving the others to bear the brunt of the fighting. Incredibly, as the shore batteries in the Kattegat pounded the old warship's wooden sides, Mary Watson went into labour and gave birth to a baby daughter, Mary Watson junior. (Fifty years later during the 1851 Census of Kilrenny, little Mary Watson – now Mrs John Campbell of John Street, Cellardyke – would give her 'Place of birth' as 'Aboard H.M.S. *Ardent*, 64-gun ship, at sea'.)

Later, the little family were transferred to Nelson's new flagship, the *Victory*, just in time to take part in the battle of Trafalgar. While Thomas Watson took charge of a guncrew, and his wife tended to the wounded and dying, little Mary Watson was sent below in the care of another Cellardyke man, Malcolm McRuvie; and when Nelson succumbed to his fatal wound it was Thomas Watson's wife Mary Buick who was called on to help prepare the corpse for the embalmers.

Thomas Watson obtained his discharge from the navy after Trafalgar, and with his bounties and prize-money returned to his native town to open a public-house by the Shore, opposite the old bulwark. Here the veterans of many a bloody naval engagement would gather to relive their experiences for the benefit of a more pampered generation, as George Gourlay well recalled:

'At this time many an old face had returned to the bulwarks that had been a stranger for many a year. These were the sailors who had been so

The headstone of Thomas Watson and Mary Buick in Kilrenny churchyard.

ruthlessly dragged away by the press-gang, but who, nevertheless, had done their duty with the bravest, whether in the battle or the storm; who had seen Nelson's glorious watchword, and sent back an answering cheer in the thunder of Trafalgar; or who had also fought and bled in the thousand conflicts which had made the "meteor flag" the tenor and glory of the seas. It was a proud privilege to be a listener by the old pier in these days'.[3]

Before those peaceful days arrived, however, there were to be more demands made on the patriotism and seamanship of the Cellardyke fishermen, as for example on the June evening in 1807 when the Admiral of the Forth appeared in person at the fishyard where drill-master Vilant was drilling the Volunteers. With typical naval brusqueness those present were given forty-eight hours to prepare themselves for active service in the expedition led by Admiral Gambier to seize the Danish fleet at Copenhagen. 'We are kindly received by the officers, let us try to deserve it', wrote Michael Doig at the time, and before long the Cellardyke men were being handpicked to land the future Duke of Wellington, Sir Arthur Wellesley, and his men on the shore. Only weeks later, having assisted in the capture of 17 line-of-battle ships, 11 frigates, 14 brigs and 25 gunboats, Michael Doig, Tam Boyter, Alexander Watson, David Reid and Alexander Pratt were safely home again in the bosom of their families, Alexander Pratt having in the meantime singlehandedly saved a squadron of five battleships from destruction on the Goodwin Sands during a gale.[4]

If life at sea was fraught with peril in those early years of the century, life ashore imposed rigours of its own. So disastrous were the harvests of 1799 and 1800 that in 1801, when a spell of better weather led at last to 'an abundant Crop', the synod of Fife ordained a day of thanksgiving. Schoolmaster and session-clerk Mr. John Orphat, so contentious and cantankerous in his dealings with his fellow-men (in particular with his sworn enemy the kirk-officer), was nevertheless a conscientious chronicler of the life of the parish; and it is to his careful jottings in the kirk-session minute-book that we are indebted for the following pages.

'For the information of Posterity', wrote Mr. Orphat on November 5th, 1801, 'the following Remarks, and prices of grain, meal and other necessaries of life, are Subjoined.' There follow detailed lists of the exorbitant prices charged for wheat, barley, pease, oats and other commodities in 1800 and early in 1801, followed by the more 'normal' prices of November 1801. Wheat, having gone as high as £3, 10s. per boll, has sunk again to between £1, 2s. and £1, 4s. Barley, having hit a ceiling of £2, 15s., is down to between 18/– and £1. Potatoes which, though of bad quality, had been retailing at 13/– to £1 a boll, are down to between 5/– and 6/–. A wheaten quarter-loaf, formerly 1/3d. to 1/8d., now costs only 10d. to 11d; and so on. But the encouraging downward trend in prices is likely to be reversed at the New Year, when the distilleries recommence operations.

So much for Mr. Orphat, the economist. A few years later, it is the antiquarian who comes to the fore. On November 9th, 1806, we learn that as a consequence of a 'couple baulk' having dropped off the west end of the roof, the old kirk of Kilrenny has been shut up until further notice. Shortly afterwards, the decision is taken to demolish the building and build a new, more commodious kirk. Thus a vital part of the parish's history disappears for ever, with only the curious pen of the session-clerk to record its passing. Only now do we learn of 'the West Loft or Sea-Box Society', 'the East Loft or Trades Society', 'the Weavers' Seat' and the patch of ground to the north and east of the churchyard called the 'Pottersfield'. During the rebuilding, 'almost a cartload of bones' is taken from under the east gable, including 'a Scull having a considerable hole in it, over which was stitched a piece of leather, all remarkably fresh'. For a brief moment these twittering ghosts return to the bright light of day, before their callous removal to the rubbish dump. In an age when the minister energetically asserted the right to graze his beasts on the churchyard grass, little else could be expected.

On September 18th, 1808, the new kirk was opened, but the old minister did not survive to officiate there. His successor was the Reverend Joseph Duncan of Kemback. Respect for the rules of the church does

The whale's jawbone erected by Captain William Smith of the *William and Anne* and *Caledonia* at the end of his garden in George Street, facing the east end of East Forth Street. The building on the extreme left, at the top of Shore Wynd, is an old gear-loft.

not seem to have increased in the new century, and two couples – David Watson and Elspeth Salter, and Henry Stevenson and Euphame Watson – were severely rebuked for having their babies baptised by the Anstruther Wester minister after being denied the sacrament at Kilrenny on account of their antenuptial fornication.[5] For those who were more conventionally pious, the communion service for 1812 was moved forward to the second Sabbath in July, 'in order to accommodate the Fishermen who go to the Caithness fishery. ... The which was Agreed to, as the Fishermen generally go off about that time'.

As well as the great summer herring rendezvous at Wick, which attracted the bulk of Cellardyke's fishermen at this time, the Greenland 'whale-fishing' still exerted a powerful attraction. On that memorable day when the first steamship seen in the Forth rounded the Carr, and the local inhabitants rushed out to see the 'ship on fire', no fewer than seventy East Neuk men were on board, having booked their passage at Aberdeen.[6] Perhaps the most outstanding of Cellardyke's whaling-skippers was Captain William Smith, who earned the distinction of having killed the largest whale ever found in Arctic waters: a monster whose jawbone still stands at the foot of his garden in Cellardyke, towering over George Street. Yet for most of the men involved, this was a temporary, money-making expedient – rather like the North Sea oil-rigs of the present day: 'A good Greenland voyage . . . was that day the joy of the shore. "It just turned oor hand", said the honest goodwife, in all ages the Chancellor of the Exchequer in the fisher home, and many a time and oft it replenished the 'ways and means' for the new fishing tackle, if not for the last year's rent'.[7]

While adventurous spirits like William Smith, Henry Bett and George Boyter followed the Greenland whale, and others of their fellow-townsmen like Thomas Cunningham of the *Jennet* went to the drave at Wick, yet others were exploring the possibilities of their home waters. One February night in 1827 the old skipper of the *Box Harry*, Alexander Cunningham, was persuaded by the activity near the surface of the water to shoot his nets between Cellardyke and the May. Even his own son mocked at his presumption – for this was not a recognised herring ground – but the groaning nets that resulted from this lucky shot led to a new spring herring fishery in the Forth, with upwards of 150 boats resorting to Cellardyke and Anstruther in the season.

As always, in return for the riches it yielded the sea demanded recompense. In June 1805 the *Nancy* foundered off Crail, with the loss of the brothers Alexander and Thomas Scott, together with James Morris, David Rhynd, David Wilson and James Watson. Then it was the turn of the *Brothers*, when the unfortunate Leslie Brown followed his father and grandfather before him to a watery grave. A few years later David and George Rodger and Thomas Watson suffered the same fate, although of David Rodger's five remaining sons – David, Alexander, James, Thomas and Robert – the last four all grew up to be masters of foreign-going vessels.

In 1819 the *Flora*, skipper Alexander Parker, went to the bottom with the loss of only one young man, Alexander Watson, but in 1826 the loss of the *Victory* left seven men dead. Two years later Andrew Crawford, James Budge, Peter Watson and John Philp were drowned in Largo Bay, and only months later the *Olive* came to grief after rounding Fife Ness in a gale, taking with her skipper John Davidson, his son James, and his nephews William and Andrew Davidson. Saddest of all was the appalling fate of John Sutherland's drave boat, the *Johns*, on July 1st, 1837, when no fewer than sixty-five souls crowded on to the 36-foot-long boat for a pleasure-trip to the May island: a not uncommon excursion at that period. No sooner had the vessel touched at the landing-stage of Kirkonhaven than, trapped in the surging eddy, she was driven onto a sharp skerry. In the panic that ensued among the women and children on board, thirteen lives were lost, including a girl of thirteen, one aged twelve, nine-year-old Euphemia Anderson and a baby boy of only nine weeks.

The luckless skipper was tried for manslaughter at the High Court in Edinburgh on March 15th, 1838, but the testimony of his crewmen and fellow-skippers helped secure his acquittal. Robert Davidson told the court that Sutherland's own wife and three or four of their children were on board at the time, so the skipper had every reason to take good care. When the accident occurred he had shouted to his crew 'never to mind the boat – to let the boat go', as long as the people were saved. Alexander Wood, skipper of the *Briton* – known in Cellardyke as 'Briton Sandy' – testified that he had known Sutherland since he was a boy, and the skipper was 'a steady good seaman'. The pleasure trip to the May, he added, '. . . has been a practice from time immemorial'.

In a gesture rarely seen in the High Court, the prosecuting counsel, Mr. Shaw Stewart, intimated that it was not his intention to press the case further. The evidence showed that skipper Sutherland could not be held responsible for the events of that sad day. Lord Meadowbank, the Presiding Judge, then dismissed the prisoner, remarking – according to the newspaper account – 'that he retired from the bar with a character as good as it was before; and from the evidence it appeared that no better character could be maintained in his profession'. It was a glowing tribute for any working man, let alone a fisherman, to receive from a High Court judge at a period when rough justice and savage sentencing were the order of the day.[8]

The trip to the May never regained its old status as an enjoyable annual ritual for the Dykers, although even today there are regular trips in the summer for visitors, subject to demand. What did endure was a folk memory of that dreadful day, and of individual acts of heroism which helped reduce the death toll: acts like that of Alexander Murray, who 'soomed a lassie ashore alow his oxter'.[9]

Even before the herring returned to the Forth, the cod and ling fishery had grown to such an extent that the 'prince of Scottish fish-curers', James Methuen, christened Cellardyke 'the cod emporium of Scotland'.[10] As fish landings increased, so the coopers of Cellardyke sweated to keep pace, and curing-sheds and smoke-houses sprang up all along the shore. Glasgow had now overtaken Edinburgh as the main home market, but during the season of Lent thousands of barrels of pickled cod were freighted to the insatiable London market. It was a time for throwing caution to the winds and taking risks. Once the cooper Andrew Innes had wormed the secret of the English 'bloater' out of an acquaintance at Peterhead, he lost no time in buying up all the herring he could find at the unheard-of price of twenty-five shillings a barrel. His master, Baillie George Darsie, cried that he had lost his senses, but the same herrings in the form of bloaters fetched forty-seven shillings a barrel at Billingsgate.[11]

As the implications of the potential bonanza sank in, the Kilrenny weaver left his loom, the Anstruther tailor his bench, and one and all sank what little savings they could muster into barrels and salt, the indispensable tools of the curer. A case in point was the Kilrenny weaver John Salter, father-in-law of the Cellardyke fisherman David Watson. A humble weaver at the time of his marriage to Elspith Grieve, on November 29th, 1783, John Salter – by the time of his death in 1826 – had become a 'Feuar, Tennant, Weaver, Innkeeper & Fishcurer': a resounding success story by eighteenth-century standards.[12]

The only obstacle to the enterprise of the fishermen, and a frustrating one at that, was the state of their cramped and dangerous little harbour. In 1825 a petition was addressed to the commissioners for the herring fisheries, and so informative is it about the contemporary state of the town that it repays quoting at some length:

'THE PETITION of the Magistrates and Town Council of the Burgh of Kilrenny, the fish-curers connected therewith, and the whole body of fishermen belonging thereto,

'Humbly sheweth,

'That Cellardyke is the Eastmost Haven, except one, on the North side of the Frith of Forth, and now one of the first Fishing Stations in Great Britain, there being upwards of thirty boats proceeding to sea therefrom every day, manned by upwards of 200 Fishermen. It is from this place that the Edinburgh and Glasgow markets are for the most part supplied with Fish, as well as London, during the season of Lent:– Indeed, so great celebrity has it now acquired, that the Cellardyke brand is earnestly sought after, and obtains a preference to any other in the London market, which can be attributed to nothing else but the superiority of its fish – the extent of its supply – and the clean and beautiful mode of curing.

'From its local situation, so near the entrance into the Frith of Forth, the inhabitants of Cellardyke, who consist chiefly of industrious fisher-men, are enabled to proceed a much longer way to sea, and consequently to catch much finer fish, than those of other towns situated farther up the Frith; and accordingly it is not uncommon for them to go as far as Marr's Bank to fish for Cod, a distance of 38 miles, when they are sometimes absent 30 hours. It not unfrequently happens too, that although it is fine weather when they go away, a storm arises while they are at sea; and if the wind is blowing strong from the north-east, or south-east, it throws such a tremendous surf into the haven, and at the entrance to it, that no boat could live in it for a moment: at these times, the boats must therefore proceed to Anstruther, Elie, or such other place as they can take; for they dare not approach Cellardyke. The most melancholy disasters have accordingly taken place here, owing to the badness of the Harbour.

'In the year 1793, a boat's crew perished at the very entrance to the Harbour, in presence of their wives and families, leaving five widows, and in all seventeen helpless children. Another dreadful catastrophe of the same kind happened in the year 1800, when seven men were drowned at the same fatal spot, within a few yards of the shore, all leaving widows, and thirty-three children in whole, to bewail their loss.

'Besides the dangerousness of the entrance to Cellardyke Haven, it is far too small to contain the boats belonging to it. At present there are two chains extended across the Harbour, to which they moor their boats, as they come in; but as these chains are not capable of holding nearly the whole of the boats belonging to the place, owing to the want of room in the harbour, those that come in last, must lie off these chains altogether; – hence quarrels are apt to arise, – and various poor families are in danger of being thrown destitute, from their unmoored boats being dashed to pieces against each other, during a storm, or broken in fragments upon the beach.

'The improvement of the Harbour of Cellardyke is then not only an object of great solicitude to the Petitioners, but from its being (it may be said) the first Fishing Station in the Island, its enlargement may almost be reckoned a national advantage; and it is very capable of being improved, for if the rocks which obstruct its entrance to the westward were cleared away, and the South Pier extended as far west as the Beacon Rocks, with the Little Pier or Jetty removed west an equal distance, so as in some degree to lock the Harbour, it would not only render the Harbour safer to take in storms, and prevent a recurrence of the dreadful calamities before alluded to, – keep out the surf or swell which at present is thrown in so violently by north east and south easterly gales, and which renders the safety even of the boats lying moored therein doubtful, but it would afford a roomy Harbour, capable of accommodating the numerous boats belonging to the town, as well as the many stranger boats which constantly frequent this place; and in fine, it would inspire a degree of life and spirit to the fishing trade in general, for which no other place almost offers equal facilities.'[13]

The petition concludes with the signatures of 132 Cellardyke fishermen, 13 curers and the 11 magistrates and councillors of the burgh. The fishermen resolved to raise £500 by their own efforts, and the commissioners bound themselves to contribute three guineas for every one raised in this way. Furthermore, Gilbert Bethune of Balfour, concerned like his ancestor John Beaton for the welfare of his lieges, agreed to waive for a period of four years his entitlement to thirty pounds annual tack-duty from the fishers of the parish – the modern equivalent of the old teinds – so that the money could be applied to the harbour fund. This latter document was drawn up for the skippers of Cellardyke, who signed themselves James Anderson, David Watson, Robert Watson, James Smith Jun[r]., William Watson, Alexander Cunningham, David Morris, John Carstairs, Adam Reid, William Watson, Alexander Keay, Robert Cunningham, David Rodger, Peter Murray, Alexander Pratt, James Murray, William Davidson, Alexander Watson, James Smith, David Taylor, Thomas Watson, John Sutherland, John Parker, John Moncrieff, John Davidson, George Smith, Henry Stevenson and William Wood.[14]

Only three days previously the Justices of the Peace for Fife had met at Anstruther, where their support for the project had been energetically canvassed. The Earl of Kellie chaired the meeting, which ended by concluding that Cellardyke was now 'a place of such importance as to deserve the best encouragement of the proper authorities, and they accordingly hereby recommend it in the strongest manner to the protection and liberality of the Honorable Board of Fisheries'.[15]

A letter from James Reid of the office for the herring fishery at Anstruther to James Dunsmure Esq. in Edinburgh, dated October 3rd, 1826, is more vividly phrased, and arrived with the pungent accompaniment of two dozen red herrings – an earnest of the local curers' expertise. The letter is preserved at West Register House in Edinburgh; the fish, fortunately, have not survived. The writer is an unashamed, if ungrammatical, propagandist for his townsmen and their objectives: 'I may safely say there is not 50 Boats with such active Crews belonging to any port in the Kingdoms. I do not know what the Town of Edinburgh would do for fresh Fish were it not for this place, – they speak of the Town being supplyed with fresh Fish from the Deep Sea by Smacks, this is mere nonsense, how often has these Smacks in the Winter Season to take shelter under the high land at the head of the Firth when the Boats here are going out and in to the Fishing as if it were a summer day'.

As to the accompanying delicacies, the curer from whom they were bought 'recommends boiling the Herrings it takes away all the smocked taste and gives them a fine flavour'.[16]

Three years later the harbour area was surveyed by a competent engineer, Mr. Joseph Mitchell, whose report is of considerable technical interest:

'I found', he wrote 'that the position of the present Harbour lay in a direction E.N.E. and W.S.W., and that the Storms which bear with greatest violence on it range from E.N.E. to S.S.E. – I also understand that the general effect of the sea, during storms from that quarter, was to run along the back of the present Pier, with a heavy swell, turning in the direction of its outer head upon a ridge of Rocks on the Western side of the Harbour – From these the sea recoiled into the interior, creating great commotion and frequently occasioning considerable damage, so that it is generally a custom among the Fishermen, on the approach of a storm, to remove their Boats into the Shipping Harbour of Anstruther – Another defect in the present Harbour is the Want of sufficient accommodation for the Boats belonging to the place –

'To obviate these defects, and make this Harbour safe and commodious, I propose that the present Main Pier should be extended nearly in the same direction for a distance of 126 feet, with a short Return Head towards the N.W. – By these means, the sea will be carried past the Ridge of Rocks, from which it at present recoils; but in case that should not be sufficient, and in order to afford greater protection, another Pier or Breakwater should be extended, from the Street or Road of Approach to the Harbour on the Western side, for a distance of 176 feet – leaving a clear opening of about 48 feet at the entrance – This Pier is so formed that should any recoil from the Rocks come upon it, the sea will be thrown out in a Southerly direction, – thus passing the entrance of the Harbour, and of course preserving it from any commotion within –

'It is proposed that the Rocks within these Piers are to be excavated, and partly used in their construction; so that a greater extent of accommodation than is afforded by the present Harbour will be thus attained.'

With scrupulous exactitude Mr. Mitchell calculated the expense of the work at £2,499, 13s, 4½d![17]

His report was, by and large, well received by the skippers of Cellardyke; but they did have some misgivings. The West Pier, as proposed by Joseph Mitchell, was from 10 to 15 feet too long, and slightly too far to the westward. It would narrow the entrance to the harbour, for, as James Reid pointed out in a letter of February 11th, 1829: 'They require full room for their oars to ply between the Pier heads, besides a good allowance must be given for the Boat falling to leeward when taken by the Sea that comes around the East or Main Pier head, so as she may not be dashed against the head of the West Quay; – By thus making the West Pier so much shorter, not only widens the mouth of the Harbour, but gives room for the heavy seas that comes round the East Pier head to waste themselves to the westward of the Breakwater, and so prevents a heavy run from coming in to the Harbour, as is the case in Anstruther, their west Pier is too long which casts in a heavy sea and makes a very unsafe Harbour in a storm'.[18]

The revised plans were put into effect at the lower than estimated cost of £1,700, but, sad to say, the result of all this endeavour was to diminish rather than increase the harbour's usefulness. In the words of the Report of the Commissioners of Municipal Corporations in Scotland of 1833, the new quays 'have not been judicially (sic) placed, and the harbour is said to have been rather injured than improved by their erection'.[19] Paradoxically, the long-desired improvements were only to hasten the day when the Cellardyke fleet would remove once and for all to Anstruther.

It is also sad to relate that the Kirk was no more in tune with its hard-living parishioners now than it had been in the past. On the front page of his neatly-kept Marriages Register, Mr. Orphat had made no bones about his and the Kirk's attitude to human sexuality:

'Marriage is honourable in all, and the Bed undefiled.' Heb:XIII.4.

'To avoid Fornication, let every Man have his own Wife, and let every Woman have her Own husband.' 1st Cor:VII.2.

'I will therefore that the Younger Women marry, bear Children, guide the house, &c.' 1st Tim:V.14.

But the kirk-session minute-books for the 1820s and 1830s are a depressing testament to the yawning gulf between pastor and flock. Now that the stool of repentance, and with it the public humiliation of offenders, have receded into history, the session are more desperate than ever to find a cure for sin. Couples guilty of antenuptial fornication are refused all the sacraments, including baptism for the fruits of their union, until nine months after their marriage. Communion tokens are withheld from those whose normal behaviour is a scandal, including an elderly publican who comes drunk to the kirk and 'is troublesome to women in the same seat with him or near him'. Instead of marrying fornicators in their own homes or at the manse, the minister conducts the ceremony in the school-room at Kilrenny, calculating that the stigma of such 'school-marriages' will prevent sexual lapses. But Fallen Man was not so easily restored to grace.

One person whose 'hardened and impenitent conduct' is frequently singled out for comment is Isobel Wilson, who in 1817 bore a child to 'George Sorelie, farm-servant in Kilrenny Miln': brazenly denying, until 24 hours before her delivery, that she was even pregnant. A few years later her name is coupled with that of the Trafalgar veteran Malcolm McRuvie, widower of Cecilia Jack, and shortly afterwards the two were married. Isobel was only one of the many townspeople whose connection with organised religion was almost non-existent: the whalers being particularly notable in this respect. In 1829 George Boyter admitted to having no connection with any church in the area, ostensibly because of his frequent absences at the whaling. Robert Brown, about to depart for the northern fishery but detained on an antenuptial fornication charge, was found to be illiterate and 'very ignorant'. John Wilson, an old bachelor sailor in Cellardyke, 'died suddenly from excessive drinking of Spirituous liquors on New-Year day, and was buried Jan^r. 4th., 1828'.

'Spirituous liquors' also figure in a smuggling story recorded in the Customs & Excise Book of Seizures for 1821. On the afternoon of Friday, January 15th, skipper Alexander Keay of Cellardyke informed the Acting Comptroller of Customs at Anstruther that he had 'picked up' three kegs of gin at sea, but that his crew had opened one of them and were busy drinking its contents. Another skipper, James Smith, reported having two kegs on board. The Comptroller promptly instructed a tidesurveyor called Hodge to turn out his crew, sending half of them to Cellardyke and half to Anstruther to intercept the rest of the fishing fleet as they returned to harbour.

Meanwhile, out on the open sea, a number of crews had been indulging freely, and on Peter Murray's boat several crewmen were quarrelling bitterly with their skipper over his stated intention to report his liquid cargo on arrival. Instead of making for Cellardyke, Murray put into Anstruther harbour, and lost no time in informing Mr. George Keay, Acting Land-Surveyor, that he had picked up thirteen kegs. Mr. Keay 'immediately repaired to the Spot', meeting on the way skipper Alexander Pratt, who reported three kegs (Pratt's boat was later found to contain five kegs).

Back at Cellardyke, things were not going so smoothly:

> Before Keays Kegs could be got ashore one of them was emptied. The officers being on the spot before the arrival of any of the other Boats, there was no opportunity of landing any part of the Spirits picked up, but the greater part of the different crews being much in Liquor, it was with considerable difficulty the officers got the Spirits conveyed to a place of Safety, not only from the obstruction they met with from the Fishermen that were drunk, but also from the Women who usually meet waiting the arrival of the Boats.

These were the same women who, ferocious in defence of their menfolk, had more than once repelled the press-gangs with hails of stones and curses.

By evening, thirty-six kegs of gin had been lodged in the Customs warehouse at Anstruther. After posting guards at both local harbours, the customs officers assembled at the Watch-house to plan their tactics for the night; for it was not unknown for casks to be submerged, like anchored nets, along the shoreline, to be retrieved after dark. Mr. Keay

resolved to ride to the westward as far as St. Monans, while Mr. Hodge
headed east to Cellardyke.

This latter trip was not a wasted one, for no fewer than eight kegs were
found lashed together and 'driving ashore among the Rocks, east of
Cellardyke harbour, which had been put out of one of the Boats with an
intention to Smuggle them away'. They were brought to the warehouse
in Anstruther 'with some difficulty', which implies some degree of
resistance on the part of the locals. In the meantime Mr. Keay's party
had returned from the westward with a further fourteen kegs, of which
three had been obtained from Lock Horsburgh at Pittenweem, while
John Hutt in St. Monans had been relieved of eleven. Neither skipper,
the writer comments darkly, had previously reported having any gin.

The officials must have been relieved to be back among their colleagues at headquarters, for they had 'received great obstruction from
the Mobs at both these Creeks, particularly at St. Monance, where they
were followed above a mile from the Town, & had great difficulty in
keeping possession of the Spirits'.

This whole episode illustrates how the smuggling trade, itself a direct
consequence of the iniquitous taxes on such 'sweeteners of existence' as
tea and spirits, could criminalise its practitioners: encouraging the forces
of law and order to regard the hardworking fishermen as villains to be
outwitted and brought to justice. It also vividly demonstrates the sim-
mering violence which lay just beneath the surface of the fishing
communities.

Sometimes that violence flared into life, as for example in 1830 when
a group of Dykers were convicted of 'drunkenness and rioting' at
Kingsmuir market. One man, dead drunk, lay out in the fields all night,
while another – Alexander Robertson – was tried at the sheriff court for
stabbing a fellow-rioter. James Forrester Watson was rebuked for heavy
drinking and 'gross impropriety in Speech & behaviour'; denied baptism
for his latest child, he resorted to the saintly old Bishop Low in Pittenweem.[20] Andrew Boyter broke into his brother's house on the New
Year's Eve of 1831, 'striking and maltreating him and family'. The
whaler Alexander McRuvie, whom the session found 'very lame in the
knowledge of Christian principles', assaulted his wife in a drunken fury
when she was barely recovered from childbirth. Finally, in what was
probably the major scandal of the decade, John Orphat junior fathered a
child on Margaret Davidson in Kilrenny. Shortly afterwards his father
tendered his resignation, after forty-eight years' service, from the posts
of parish schoolteacher and parish- and session-clerk.

Of course, it would be foolish to regard these individuals as wholly
representative of their thousand-odd fellow-townspeople: yet there

seems to have been a new strain of brutality in the fishertown which had been less marked in earlier days, and which seems to have been absent from the more tranquil landward part of the parish. Was this perhaps a reflection of the neurotic 'gold-rush' conditions under which the fishers now laboured to earn a living? Here is a near-contemporary account of Wick, the centre of the 'Northern Fishery' and, for a time, the herring capital of the western world: 'At all seasons of the year, whisky is drunk in considerable quantities, but during the fishing season enormous potations are indulged in. . . . Snuffing is almost universal among the men, and both it and smoking are very common among the women'. (Care was taken to increase the take of herrings, but) '. . . no care was taken of the 10,000 young strangers of both sexes who were crowded together with the inhabitants within the narrow limits of Wick during the six principal weeks of the fishing, exposed to drink and numerous other temptations'.[21]

Raw whisky and snuffing women were a potent mix; yet 'the life style rendered stimulants almost indispensable: 'All around the atmosphere is humid; the sailors are dripping, the herring-gutters and packers are dripping, and every thing and person appears wet and comfortless. . . . Men are rushing wildly about with note-books, making mysterious-looking entries. Carts are being filled with dripping nets ready to hurry them off to the fields to dry. The screeching of saws among billet-wood, and the plashing of the neighbouring water-wheel, add to the great babel of sound that deafens you on every side. Flying about, blood-bespattered and hideously picturesque, we observe the gutters; and on all hands we may note thousands of herring-barrels, and piles of billet-wood ready to convert into staves. At first sight every person looks mad. . . .'[22]

As for the whalers, it takes little imagination to picture the daily round of men who sailed in old wooden vessels to the Arctic Circle. Even a successful trip might bring scurvy, frostbite or an injury which would send a fit young man home a helpless cripple. Or if the captain was a poor judge of weather or greedy for profit, the ship could become a frozen tomb in the encroaching ice: as in the winter of 1836 when the old *Thomas* of Dundee was 'beset by the sea'. Neither William Davidson nor the cousins John and William Muir came home from that voyage.[23]

Nor did the home fishermen fare much better. The very act of re-entering their own harbour was fraught with peril, as we have seen, and they might even be marooned for days, unbearably, within sight of their homes: like the 500 individuals who in the winter of 1833–4 were 'detained on the Island of May . . . and could get no provisions of any sort that were fit for human food, and for a number of days . . . were compelled to gather shell fish and dig rabbits from their holes, in order to support existence'.[24]

For this appalling mode of existence the kirk-session seems to have had scant sympathy. Even the pasting on the kirk-gate of 'Advertisements of Roups, Sales of Merchandize, &c.' was banned with effect from November 1831, for the number of such advertisements 'had now come to an alarming height, and still increasing, whereby not only much time was mis-spent in the reading & conversation thereon, but also tended to abstract the attention of the People from the proper exercises of the Lord's day'. No latitude was allowed for human frailty, and it does not seem to have occurred to the session that there was little hope of reforming sinners as long as the punishment for their lapses continued to be total exclusion from all the sacraments of the church: a policy which could only confirm and strengthen them in their ignorance of basic Christian principles.

To give them credit, the session were the mainstay of the parish when dearth and disease threatened. The same minute which records their disapproval of advertising also demonstrates their disquiet at the approach of a far deadlier distraction, 'that mortal malady called *Cholera Morbus*', which now is 'making such extensive ravages among the human race in the Empire of Russia, and other places on the Continent'. Disease being a more palpable foe than sin, there are definite practical measures that can be taken. 'Nuisances and putrid Substances' can be taken off the streets, the poor can be furnished with lime-water with which to white-wash their houses, supplies of clothing and food can be got together for the neediest – those whose resistance to infection would be lowest. The heritors and kirk-session hold a joint meeting, and consider a report that '(with the exception of hooping-cough, and 5 or 6 individuals labouring under temporary disease,) all in Nether Kilrenny alias Cellardyke, were in a healthy state, but from the last & present year's unsuccessful fishing at home, – in the North Country, and also at Greenland, 15 families and 49 Individuals (old men, widows, &c.) in Cellardyke, were in a very necessitous state, some needing supplies of Bed and body clothes, and shoes in particular, – others, of coals, soap & cordials'.

The heritors assessed themselves 'in the sum of £50', and handed the money over to the session for distribution; but despite the best efforts of minister and elders, the dread disease finally arrived in Cellardyke the following year, and the deaths register for 1832 is a grisly catalogue of victims 'buried speedily' the very day of their deaths. Yet at least the session had done their best to stave off catastrophe. Whether or not this was appreciated by the 'delinquents' of the parish is another matter, however, and all the signs are that not even the kirk's charitable work could reconcile them to its harsher aspects. All things considered, it is hardly surprising that when a religious revival really *did* take the town by storm, as was to happen later in the century, it was spearheaded not by ministers of the Established Church but by a new breed of evangelist preaching the seductive doctrine of individual salvation in the Lord – a gospel tailor-made for sinners.

So far we have concentrated almost exclusively on the life of the fisher-community, as it was in Cellardyke that the bulk of Kilrenny's population lived, and it is their doings which occupy most space in the written records of the parish. Yet only a few hundred yards inland from Skinfasthaven the weavers and farm-servants of Kilrenny were going about their own very different, and perhaps more peaceable, pursuits. There is nothing of this in George Gourlay's *Fisher Life*, and conversely there is not the slightest tang of sea-air in David Lumsden's *Reminiscences of Kilrenny*, published in Edinburgh in 1911. Mr. Lumsden, who became a watchmaker and town-councillor in Anstruther Easter, where he died in 1909, was born in Kilrenny in 1827, and his earliest recollections commence with the agitation surrounding the passing of the Reform Bill of 1832. The old councillor remembered being sent, as a little boy, to fetch the latest *Scotsman*, and how the journey was fraught with imaginary perils: 'To a youngster it was no pleasant duty to execute the order in the dark winter evenings, for in those days the belief in ghosts and apparitions was still prevalent, and, our home being located on the outskirts of the village, we had to traverse a path that led through a clump of large trees, and it required no great effort of the imagination to convert an old grizzled-looking elm tree into something uncanny'.[25]

Not even George Gourlay could have claimed much actual 'beauty' for the seatown of Cellardyke, but David Lumsden's Kilrenny was a rural hamlet of great natural charm, much of which still survives today. The 'Smiddy Brae' is now the busy main road to Crail, but one still looks over the little Gellie burn to the ancient churchyard, with the farm-cottages of Cornceres in the foreground and the mansion-house of Innergellie beyond. To David Lumsden the manse, with its fine sloping garden to the east of the path leading down to the sea (the 'Din', in local parlance), was 'one of the most attractive features of the sweet scenery around'.[26]

But most vivid of all to an old man's memory were the pawky characters who inhabited his childhood world – 'old Sandy Forbes, Gow Grieve, Willie Corstorphine and his donkey, and other members of the group of worthies to whom, in fancy, we assigned an existence coeval with the old elms that adorned the banks of the Gellie'.[27] Of an evening the worthies would gather in the weaver's shop, where matters of common interest would be debated. Like the tradesmen and merchants of Anstruther, the Kilrenny villagers had sufficient intellectual curiosity to found a debating society and clubs such as the Newspaper Club, where

The milk-cart stops outside the smithy at Kilrenny. Cornceres farm cottages are on the left. Undated, ?early 20th century.

the 'village laureate', James McGill, would regale the company with a new ditty of his own composition, attended with much fiery gesticulation and flinging of manuscript sheets into the air.[28]

Less convivial was the park-keeper on the Innergellie estate, James Paterson, whose stern bearing together with the attentions of his collie Betty ensured the respect of the local youth. But little respect was paid to half-blind old Willie Corstorphine, who dispensed a variety of groceries from two capacious panniers slung across the back of his faithful ass. Although outwardly simple and easily deceived, the old packman had an attractive vein of sly humour in his dealings with his customers: 'If a guidwife remarked: "I'll no' be needin' onything till ye come back again," Willie would call next door, and immediately repeat his previous visit, saying loudly: "I'm back again, Jenny!" The humorous ruse often resulted in a sale. At one time Willie tried an addition to his company on the road, someone having presented him with a small dog, whose acquaintance was much sought after by the rising generation. On Willie being pressed to divulge its name, he replied to the youngsters, "Askum" (Ask him). The urchins were sorely puzzled to know why the dog never looked up nor wagged his tail when saluted with a shower of "Askums". Further interrogations of Willie on the subject were useless'.[29]

Kilrenny at the turn of the century.

When a public clock was placed in the church tower, and 'the flight of time was publicly announced to the villagers', the event was deemed worthy of commemoration by the local bard:

> Kilrenny folk are proud and vain,
> They've got a timepiece o' their ain;
> When first the hammer struck the bell,
> Like music thro' the air it fell,
> Auld Eppie ran to Betty Broon,
> And Betty hirpled thro' the toon;
> She left her rock and pickle tow
> And cared na' tho' they'd gane alow,
> But wi' the bairnes took the play,
> And span nae mair that lee-lang day.[30]

And then, one magical morning, the children of the village were summoned by drum and shepherd's reed to a circus which had drawn up on the Common. All too briefly the monotony of everyday life was transformed by fat lady and giant, until finally 'old Ginger was reyoked, and crawled out of the village, while the youngsters, who had paid their first visit to Wonderland, escorted the troupe for some distance on their journey westward'.[31] It is pleasant to have this testimony that the young, even at this period, could have some occasional respite from the hardships of existence before being caught up in the rougher practicalities of daily life in the first half of the nineteenth century.

6

The Nineteenth Century, Part II: The Middle Years

On the night of June 7th, 1841, the first detailed door-to-door census of Kilrenny parish was carried out; and the enumerators' transcript books, preserved in Register House, Edinburgh, provide a wealth of information about the inhabitants of the town at the beginning of the Victorian Age. There *were* defects in this census which had to be corrected in later surveys – people's ages were rounded down to the nearest five years, relationships of individuals in a household were not given, the exact place of birth was not specified – but these details can usually be checked in later censuses or in the Old Parish Registers.

The census begins with Enumeration District No. 1, defined as 'That part of the Royal Burgh of Kilrenny extending from the Stream called Caldies Burn at the West end to Urquhart's Wynd, including the west side of said Wynd, and bounded on the North by Mr Bethune's Lands and on the South by the Firth of Forth'. We commence, in other words, at the west end of the present James Street, where the first house is occupied by John Galloway, carpenter, and his wife Janet, spirit dealer; together with George Young, shoemaker, his wife Margaret, and their children Barbara (a dressmaker), Elisabeth, Alexander and Robert. All members of both families were born in Fife.

Next door lived George Marr, cabinetmaker, with his wife Janet and their sons Charles and Thomas, and next to them were William Rhind, hairdresser, and family, together with Agnes Lindsay, aged 76, 'pauper', Margaret Malcolm, 73, 'independent', Margaret and Isabella Morris, and Margaret Boyter, aged 12, 'female servant'. Not only the rich had servants at this period, and a female servant – often very young and frequently a relative – was a common feature of even the poorer fisher-homes, as we shall see.

The majority of fisher-families, however, lived further east than James Street in 1841, and the next few houses were occupied by agricultural labourers, coopers, bakers, and elderly ladies of independent means, including Elspeth Williamson and Barbara Philip, aunts of the future M.P. Stephen Williamson. Then comes one of Cellardyke's most gifted sons, the schoolteacher Alexander Moncrieff, who deserves more than a passing mention.

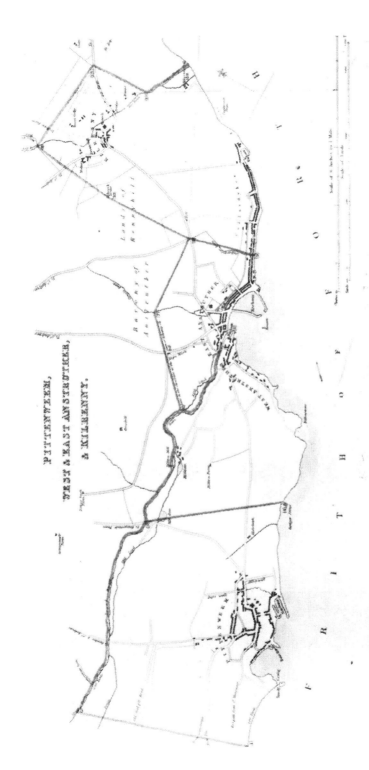

A map of the late 1830's showing Kilrenny and Cellardyke in relation to the two Anstruthers. 'Cellardykes burn' was actually known as 'Caddies burn'.

99

Born in 1790, one of the twin sons of John Moncrieff and Agnes Myles, Alexander Moncrieff was never destined for the sea like his father. A weak constitution, allied to a fine intelligence, pointed instead to the schoolroom, yet this sickly landlubber was to coach more master mariners through their Marine Board examinations than any other teacher on the Scottish coast. How was it done? The answer is an intriguing one. As a young man Alexander Moncrieff befriended an old sea-captain, Robert Lothian, who in old age became sadly prone to attacks of mental instability. During the long watches of the night it was Dominie Moncrieff who, more than any other, watched over the old man and tended him in his suffering. Out of gratitude for this care, and during his more lucid spells, Captain Lothian conferred all his knowledge of navigation and his experience of the sea on the younger man; and thus it was that generations of Cellardyke mariners began their study of the art of navigation by calculating the latitude and longitude of the honeysuckle in Mr. Moncrieff's garden![1]

The Moncrieff household in 1841 consisted of Alexander, aged 51, his wife Elspeth Marr, 52, their children Margaret and John, and Elspeth's sister Ann Marr, then 57.

Next door to the Moncrieffs lived a much larger household in the shape of fisherman James Forrester Watson with his wife and seven children; Hugh Calder, cooper, and family; Hugh's apprentice James Morris, aged 15; Mary Ann Wallace and her two-year-old son Robert, and Helen McFie, female servant. Such multiple households were the rule rather than the exception in a Cellardyke where space was at a premium and the 'Braes' above Main Street had not yet been fully exploited for overspill housing.

After the homes of Andrew Young, David Scott and James Imrie, agricultural labourers, we come to David Wilson, fisherman, with his wife and eight children. David Wilson is only the second fisherman we have encountered so far, and unlike most of his fellow-mariners to the east of the Tolbooth he was not even a native of Cellardyke: yet few of his contemporaries could have boasted of a more eventful career at sea. Born in 1792 at Brownhills, near St. Andrews, where his father was farm foreman, David had left home at the age of 12 to be cabin-boy on a Kirkcaldy smack – the *Maggie Lauder*; from where he moved on later to a Dunbar brig. Despite the rigours of the life (once he fell from a top-gallant yard and was over an hour in the water) he kept his love of the sea, and eventually he found his way onto the old Dundee whaling-vessel the *Advice*.

It was during this spell of duty that David Wilson met the sternest test of his manhood, for one September day, as the old whaler was returning from a Greenland voyage, she was intercepted by the war brig H.M.S *Pickle* and ordered to round to. No set of mariners were more in demand for His Majesty's service than the whalers, as the crew of the *Advice* well knew, so turning a deaf ear to the shouted orders they sped on their way, David Wilson meanwhile taking the wheel. To spare their captain the consequences of being seen to disobey naval orders, David Wilson's shipmates hit upon the ruse of staging a mutiny, and went through the motions of locking Captain Adamson in his cabin. The brig responded with gunfire, and eventually the reluctant conscripts were forced to heave to. For his part in the act of insubordination David Wilson was confined below decks in the brig, a six-foot long iron bar across his legs and his hands rivetted to the ring bolts. Later, at his trial in London, he succeeded in establishing his innocence only at the cost of agreeing to join the crew of his erstwhile prison-ship.

Eventually, David succeeded in escaping from the *Pickle*, but his troubles were not yet over, for his next ship, a trading packet, was captured by French privateers in the Bay of Biscay, and David and his new shipmates were carried off to France and imprisonment in an inland citadel. Not until Wellington's victory over Napoleon at the Battle of Waterloo in 1815 was David Wilson free to return to his family, who by now were living in Pittenweem; but even then he was scarcely a free man, being a known deserter from the Royal Navy. It was only after his marriage to a Cellardyke girl that he was persuaded to make that town his home, and it was there that he spent the remainder of his long life, dying in 1875 at the age of 83.[2]

After David Wilson and his family comes Maria Wattling – possibly the only English-born inhabitant of Cellardyke, and also the town's only recognized midwife. In its laconic way the 1841 census gives only 'E' for England as Maria's birthplace, and there is no indication of her marital status. However, she shares her house with twelve-year-old Elisabeth Wattling, together with Janet Redpath (24), Isabella Jones (6) and Janet Taylor (3). A shoemaker, George Smith, follows, then comes James Nicol, aged 50, teacher. Like Alexander Moncrieff, James Nicol had come from humble beginnings, having commenced a study of astronomy while still a herd-boy on the braes of Kenly Water. His wife was Agnes Wilson, daughter of James Wilson, who had once been a farm-servant at Barnsmuir.

As we move further east towards the old Tolbooth, the number of fisher-households increases (the names include Pratt, Martin, Millar, Dick, Salter and Watson); but these are interspersed with builders, shoemakers, a tin-plate worker (Alexander Davidson), two weavers (Andrew McGill and John Dick), an army pensioner (James Broderick)

Tolbooth Wynd, Cellardyke, which separates James Street (bottom right) from John Street (bottom left).

and the Crail-born ship's carpenter James Horsburgh, who would later take Dominie Nicol's eldest daughter as his second wife. There are also Elspith Lothian, grocer, and John Reekie, 'meal man', along with old Malcolm and Isabella McRuvie and their children Mary, Isabella, Cecilia and Duncan. Malcolm McRuvie was to live another twenty years, and later censuses reveal him to have been a native of Campbeltown, in Argyll. The son of a groom (his parents were Duncan McRuvie and Mary McKenzie), he may have been one of that band of Highlanders who first came to Cellardyke as 'half-dealsmen' at the turn of the century.

In Tolbooth Wynd itself there were only three houses, inhabited by five families of Martins, Pratts, Boyters, Browns and Wilsons, then the census sweeps round the corner and back into Main Street (i.e. the west end of John Street). Here the first name is Wallace, followed by Henderson, then another Henderson and another Wallace, and we are now in the old fishing-village of Cellardyke proper, where almost all the adult males are fishermen (exceptions are 80-year-old baker James Hutchinson and spirit-dealer George Morris). Ancillary trades are represented by cooper John Campbell (husband of the Mary Watson of Copenhagen and Trafalgar), and curer Andrew Crawford, but they are heavily outnumbered by fishermen.

Interesting sociological conclusions can be drawn from the evidence of the census. Relatives tend to cluster together, and many houses contain a staggering number of individuals. John Wilson, George and Alexander Watson (sons of 'Water Willie') and James McRuvie are the four heads of household in a house with nineteen inhabitants; and nineteen Woods – divided into three households – inhabit a nearby dwelling. Nine other Woods live two doors away in a house of twenty-one souls, but even these are outclassed by twenty-three Boyters, Smiths, Murrays, Robertsons and Horsburghs under one roof nearby. The old fisher-surnames have different 'regional' concentrations, for Watsons, Muirs and Fowlers increase in frequency as we near Urquhart Wynd. Elizabeth Watson, 'beer-dealer', appears along with her daughters Janet and Grace, while next door are Robert and Mary Watson with Elesabeth, Robert, James and Thomas. Next door again is the oldest Dyker we have yet encountered, 'Grace' or Grizel Watson, the 82-year-old widow of David Watson. Cunninghams and Reids are yet to come, clustered together further 'ist the toon'.

In the Urquhart Wynd there are four houses and five families, headed by Thomas Fowler (54), Margaret Pratt (59), Thomas Muir (25), Isabella Hodge (53) and Robert Fowler (50),[3] all the men being fishermen; then the census enumerator moves up the wynd to the Braehead, where the first house is the Female and Infant School. The only residents are 25-year-old Grace Michael (i.e. Mitchell), 'Female Teacher'; Margaret Taylor (39), 'infant school teacher', and Margaret Taylor – presumably the latter's daughter – aged 14.

From the Female School to Caddies Burn – the whole length of the present East and West Forth Streets – there are only ten houses listed in the census, and not a single fisherman in any of them. Agricultural labourers predominate, and their surnames – Ireland, Duff, Lindsay, Fairbairn, Money – are conspicuously different from those of their seafaring townsmen a few yards away down the brae. On the site of the future Martin's factory lived the builder George Taylor, and at the west end of West Forth Street we find the fishery officer George Smith; but the prize for an unusual trade must surely go to James Lindsay, the 40-year-old son of old Lowe Lindsay (formerly a farm-servant at Caiplie), who describes himself as 'Experimental Assistant to a Natural Philosopher'. This is the 'old herring fisher', according to George Gourlay, who was 'so famous in Edinburgh University as Sir John Leslie's man', and who was known to his neighbours in 'Braehead Street' as 'the philosopher'.[4] For 58 years, from 1814 until 1872, James Lindsay served Professor Leslie and his successor Professor Tait in the 'Natural Philosophy' or Physics department at Edinburgh University, although on

John Street, *c.* 1904.

Gourlay's evidence he was also a crewman on Baillie Crawford's herring-boat. No doubt the university's long summer vacation gave him ample opportunity to attend the drave.

For one unlikely student of physics during Professor Tait's regime the reminiscences of 'old Lindsay' were far more enthralling than the dry revelations of science: and in 1886, in an essay entitled 'College Memories', Robert Louis Stevenson penned this affectionate tribute to the old worthy:

At the near end of the platform, Lindsay senior was airing his robust old age. It is possible my successors may have never even heard of Old Lindsay; but when he went, a link snapped with the last century. He had something of a rustic air, sturdy and fresh and plain; he spoke with a ripe east-country accent, which I used to admire; his reminiscences were all of journeys on foot or highways busy with post-chaises – a Scotland before steam; he had seen the coal fire on the Isle of May, and he regaled me with tales of my own grandfather. Thus he was for me a mirror of things perished; it was only in his memory that I could see the huge shock of flames of the

An old marriage lintel at 22 John Street.

Urquhart Wynd, Cellardyke, which runs between John Street and George Street (bottom left).

May beacon stream to leeward, and the watchers, as they fed the fire, lay hold unscorched of the windward bars of the furnace; it was only thus that I could see my grandfather driving swiftly in a gig along the seaboard road from Pittenweem to Crail, and for all his business hurry, drawing up to speak good-humouredly with those he met. And now, in his turn, Lindsay is gone also; inhabits only the memories of other men, till these shall follow him; and figures in my reminiscences as my grandfather figured in his.[5]

At the age of 16 young Thomas Lindsay – still unborn in 1841 – was enlisted as assistant to his father. Twelve years later, in 1872, he inherited the post of chief assistant, a position he was to fill for the next 46 years: so that father and son between them achieved a staggering 116 years of service to the University of Edinburgh. Like his father, Thomas was a favourite with the young students, and he was to be immortalized in his turn by another Edinburgh graduate in the shape of J. M. Barrie, of 'Peter Pan' fame:

I had forgotten Lindsay; 'the mother may forget her child'. As I write he has slipped back into his chair on the Professor's right, and I could photograph him now in his brown suit. Lindsay was the imperturbable man who assisted Tait in his experiments, and his father held the post before him. When there were many of us together, we could applaud Lindsay with burlesque exaggeration, and he treated us good-humouredly, as making something considerable between us. But I once had to face Lindsay alone, in quest of my certificate; and suddenly he towered above me, as a waiter may grow tall when you find that you have not money enough to pay the bill. He treated me most kindly; did not reply, of course, but got the certificate, and handed it to me as a cashier contemptuously shovels you your pile of gold. . . . Lindsay was an inscrutable man, and I shall not dare to say that he even half-wished to see Tait fail. He only looked on, ready for any emergency; but if the experiment would not come off, he was as quick to go to the Professor's assistance as a member of Parliament is to begin when he has caught the Speaker's eye. Perhaps Tait would have none of his aid, or pushed the mechanism for the experiment from him – an intimation to Lindsay to carry it quickly to the ante-room. Do you think Lindsay read the instructions so? Let me tell you that your mind fails to seize hold of Lindsay. He marched the machine out of Tait's vicinity as a mother may push her erring boy away from his father's arms, to take him to her heart as soon as the door is closed. Lindsay took the machine to his seat, and laid it before him on the desk with well-concealed apathy. Tait would flash his eye to the right to see what Lindsay was after, and there was Lindsay sitting with his arms folded. The Professor's lecture resumed its way, and then out went Lindsay's hands to the machine. Here he tried a wheel; again he turned a screw; in time he had the machine ready for another trial. No one was looking his way, when suddenly there was a whizz – bang, bang. All eyes were turned upon Lindsay, the Professor's among them. A cheer broke out as we realised that Lindsay had done the experiment. Was he flushed with triumph? Not a bit of it; he was again sitting with his arms folded. . . . While the Professor eyed him and the students deliriously beat the floor, Lindsay quietly gathered the mechanism together and carried it to the ante-room. His head was not flung back nor his chest forward, like one who walked to music. In his hour of triumph he was still imperturbable. I lie back in my chair to-day, after the lapse of years, and ask myself again, How did Lindsay behave after he entered the ante-room, shutting the door behind him? Did he give way? There is no one to say. When he returned to the classroom he wore his familiar face; a man to ponder over.[6]

It was done like a true Dyker. In 1918 Thomas handed over the reins to his son James, who promptly died of a rapid consumption, and thus the line of succession was broken.

Returning to the 1841 census, we move on now to Enumeration District No. 2, which commences at Upper Kilrenny. Here we meet David Ritchie, shoemaker; George Wilson, blacksmith; William Wilson, baker; David Stobbie and John Motion, agricultural labourers – all married men – and Margaret Mays (70) and Margaret King (38); then we turn seawards again and re-enter Cellardyke at the south side of the future George Street. Between here and Sharp's Wynd there are eleven houses (one uninhabited), containing almost twenty fishermen, two grocers, a cooper, a handloom-weaver and an ironmonger's apprentice, along with some female net-menders; and in Sharp's Wynd itself, where the heads of household are Wilson Brunton, Thomas Boyter, Donald Henderson and Philip Scott, there are six fishermen, and, in the person of 12-year-old Thomas Boyter junior, one sailmaker's apprentice. Boyter is the commonest name at this end of the town, although there is also a twelve-strong family of Doigs. Donald Henderson's 10-year-old son Andrew would later be 'king fisher' of the town.[7]

Back in Main Street the corner house is occupied by George Barclay, also in his day the 'king fisher' of Cellardyke. Several houses further on (now No. 57) live Elspeth Watson (Salter), widow of David Watson, with her son David and his family, together with Anne Davidson (51), Anne Brown (75) and David McRuvie (24), David's wife Christian (24) and their son David (6 months). Elspeth's younger son John Watson and his wife Elspeth Anderson live immediately to the west, and next door to the east is David Melville. It was to this old worthy, in years to come, that an important task was to be entrusted: namely, the firing of the fog cannon; and it is worth quoting here the reminiscences of 'Auld Wull' Smith in the *East Fife Observer* some seventy years later: 'In foggy weather the fog signal for Cellardyke was a cannon fired every twenty minutes. It was stopped with old nets and anything to make a sound. Some powder was put on the touch hole and a red hot poker was applied to it and off it went, giving a loud report. It was in charge of an old fisherman named David Melville. He used to let us boys get the task of setting off the gun. We got the poker, and having applied it to the powder, ran back as hard as we could, for the gun was a putter and ran back on its wheels. It was fired at his back door which was a little to the west of the little pier'.[8]

57 George Street, Cellardyke, once the home of the author's great-great-grandparents David Watson (1808–73) and Elizabeth Murray (1803–89)

Next to David Melville are Thomas and Elisa Cunningham, then two households of Muirs. Further along are another Thomas and Elisa Cunningham – this Thomas being a merchant-seaman – who share their house with Peter Gellatly and Grace Reid, and their children Margaret and David, together with Mary Don. Wilson Birrell, George Morris, James Smith and Elisa Cunningham (aged 71) are the heads of household in the adjacent house, and the census enumerator with his list of questions arrived at an awkward moment here, for the Smith household contained a one-hour-old baby boy! The next two houses are occupied by families named Carstairs, then comes Margaret Morris, 'inn-keeper', and finally James Fowler, grocer, with his wife Rae and their eight children.

The same names occur on the north side of George Street, and here the first individual to claim our attention is 55-year-old Thomas Smith, who in 1841 lived in the eighth house along with his second wife Euphemia Boyter, and their children Janet, Thomas, James, David, John, Euphemia, Robert and Andrew. As a boy of 14 Thomas Smith was one of the witnesses to the tragedy in which seven men drowned within hail of Cellardyke pier, only 'Water Willie' Watson escaping. One of the less fortunate sailors was Thomas's father. Six years later, he was himself the

Sloping gardens at the back of the houses in George Street.

sole survivor from a Leith smack which went aground near Stonehaven, and on that occasion he owed his life to a young woman who passed by the beach on which he had been washed up the following morning, and found his seemingly lifeless body. Nor was this to be his last brush with death. On the last day of December, 1814, David Rodger's drave boat was fishing for herring off Burntisland when it was capsized by a sudden squall. The only survivor of that disaster was Thomas Smith. No more is recorded of his eventful life until the morning, in his sixty-eighth year, when he awoke to find his second wife dead in the bed beside him. Despite all the vicissitudes of his life, and against all the odds, he would survive to be the oldest fisherman in Cellardyke, dying on March 19th, 1869, in his eighty-fifth year.

Next door to Thomas Smith lived David Brown, son of that Leslie Brown who also perished in the disaster of 1800, and then follow a succession of Davidsons and Doigs. William Watson and Euphemia Reid share their home with William's mother, Anne Cunningham, and their neighbours to the east are four families of Murrays. Then come the William Smiths, father and son: redoubtable seamen whose fame has long outlived them. William senior, the captain of a number of Leith whaling-vessels, including the *Caledonia* and the *William and Ann*, was the proud owner of the whale's jawbone mentioned earlier. As for

The east end of George Street, looking towards Shore Street and the harbour area. The author's Cunningham ancestors lived at No. 50 (white house on left), with the Meldrums and Gellatlys next door at No. 52 (on corner with Toft Terrace).

William junior, his personality is captured for us in the affectionate portrait of him painted by Frank T. Bullen, one of his former cabin-boys, in a book of reminiscences entitled *The Log of a Sea-Waif*: 'Captain Smith, our chief, was a jolly, easy-going Scotchman of about sixty, always good-tempered, and disinclined to worry about anything. He had his wife and daughter with him, the latter a plain young lady of about twenty-two. Both of them shared the skipper's good qualities, and the ship was certainly more comfortable for their presence'.[9]

The next three householders are all Moncrieffs, then the names are Fleming, Cunningham, Keay, Hodge and Sutherland. This John Sutherland is probably the skipper of that name who, only four years previously, had faced a manslaughter charge in the High Court of Edinburgh. John Sutherland's neighbours are Robert Cunningham and Janet Fowler, with their children Robert, Alexander and Janet. Robert senior, the son of Thomas Cunningham and Janet Wilson, and skipper of the *Friends*, would live to the ripe old age of 88, dying in 1874. His son Alexander would later marry Janet (Jessie) Horsburgh, daughter of the Pittenweem whaler Lock Horsburgh, and although Janet would die

Shore Wynd, looking towards Cellardyke harbour. The car on the left is at the entrance to Dove Street. The house at the bottom was the home of the author's great-great-great-grandparents 'Water Willie' Watson (1774–1850) and Mary Galloway.

an early death at the age of 25, Alexander was to take a second wife (Agnes Pratt) and survive into the twentieth century. Robert's great-granddaughter would still be living at 50 George Street a century later.

In the next house to Robert Cunningham lived David Gellatly, a native of the Carse of Gowrie, and his wife Catherine Tarvit, whose exploits in the year of the French Revolution we reviewed in an earlier chapter. Apart from their servant, Jane Sutherland, the elderly couple also shared their house with their daughter Anne, her husband John Meldrum (the son of John Meldrum and Christian Keay) and five grandchildren, ranging in age from four-month-old Peter to six-year-old Catherine. (Anne Gellatly's brother Peter lived, as we have seen, just across the road.) There follow Muirs, Davidsons, Smiths, Bruces, Stewarts, Henry and Elisa Bett with their family of six, and finally William and Janet Moncrieff (Davidson) and their unmarried daughter Lucy.

Shore Wynd has only one house, shared at this date by the families of David Corstorphine and Michael Doig, whose wives were daughters of 'Water Willie' Watson and Mary Galloway; then comes Williamson's Lane: the present Dove Street. Here Robert and Isabella Pratt and their three children enjoy the luxury of a one-family home, but the only other house in the lane is home to no fewer than four families, whose heads are

Thomas Reid (to whose wife, Agnes Birrell, we shall return later), Thomas Watson, Robert Birrell and James Corstorphine.

Robert Pratt, like David Wilson, was an old sea-dog whose colourless statistics in the census belie his adventurous life. In 1800, at the age of 11, Robert had begun life as a cabin-boy in the Excise yacht *Prince of Wales*. Later he served in the Dundee whaler *Mary Ann* and then the Leith and London trader *Hope*, where the press-gang finally caught up with him. Like David Wilson he was a fine sailor whose obvious talents brought him promotion and favour, but like David too his mind was more occupied with thoughts of escape from his bondage. This escape was in fact effected when a gale forced his ship into Kinghorn harbour, but his next berth on a London-bound coasting-schooner led to his recapture. Robert Pratt's next bid for freedom was made at Greenwich, but still later – and here there is another uncanny parallel with David Wilson's story – he was to be one of another ship's company captured by a French privateer. At this point the tale becomes almost incredible, for despite being marched three hundred miles into the interior of France, and imprisoned in a military fortress, Robert Pratt was one of a band of prisoners who contrived to escape and find their way back over the Channel to Falmouth. Soon Robert was back home in Cellardyke, where he took to the whaling again, and where he died in 1870 in his eighty-second year.

Thus we come at last to the Shore, the ancient cluster of houses fronting the harbour; and in the first house – now 6 Shore Street – we find 'Water Willie' Watson, his wife Mary, and the little family of Andrew Robertson (24). Next door lives the widowed Mary Watson (Buick) of Trafalgar fame, with her daughter Euphemia (24) and son Thomas (22), and in the next house again are two families of Moncrieffs and merchant seaman David Gellatly junior. Then, in the old Bishop's Palace – probably the first building erected in Cellardyke, and later replaced by the present 9 and 10 Shore Street – are three families: James Salter, his wife Anne Davidson and son John; James Watson (the son of David Watson and Elspeth Salter) with his wife and cousin Elspeth Salter; and Peter Murray and his wife Elisa, with their children Janet, Margaret, Peter, Mary and Elisa. Then come Stephen and Sophia Barclay, with George (18), Leslie (14), Sophia (12) and Christian (3).

The next house contains two families of Watsons, including William Watson and Margaret Reid, the son and daughter-in-law of 'Water Willie', as well as Margaret's brother Henry Reid and his family. Then after a family of Woods and another of Browns comes Jane Reid (36), grocer, with her six children, and Henry Reid senior (41) with wife Catherine and son William. Next door is Adam Reid (45), then a large household of Flemings, Davidsons, Doigs and Muirs. David Rodger is next, in the family home at 26 Shore Street where a plaque now marks the birthplace of his more famous brother Alexander; then follow Elisa Reid (74) and her two daughters, and finally the large house which shelters Alexander Balfour, 'flax-dresser', John Smith, 'carter', and Chapman Lowrie, fisherman: a total of fifteen individuals.

On the opposite side of the road, East Shore has nine houses which, in addition to their fisher inhabitants, contain fish-curer George Sharp, baker James Donaldson and spirit-dealer John Marr. In the last two houses there are three families of Smiths: James and Lilie Smith (Fowler), Alexander and Binnie, and William and Catherine (Murray), with young James, Peter, Alexander and Thomas. And so we come to the end of the fishing-village of Cellardyke.

Enumeration District 2 concludes with 'Upper Kilrenny', where apparently the modern street-names 'Trades Street' and 'Routine Row' are not yet in use. The first householder, Andrew Young, is a fisherman – a relic of the days when Kilrenny crofters were the original fishermen of the parish – but he is by this time the only representative of that trade in the entire village. In the next cottage lives 70-year-old joiner Robert Malcolm, and further along we find John Brown (67), tailor, and his Crail-born wife Murray Hill. This couple's third son, Thomas – a future inspector of the poor in Kilrenny – was to attain some small fame as a religious poet in years to come.[10]

The variety of trades represented in the little hamlet is a token of the thriving community which Kilrenny then was: a rural village like many another the length and breadth of Scotland, and with the sole exception of Andrew Young bearing no trace of the fishing industry which so dominated its near neighbour by the shore. Aside from the tradesmen just mentioned, there are masons, slaters, handloom-weavers and gardeners here, as well as a grocer (James Lindsay), a baker (Robert Smith), a 'coal-worker' (Robert Pooler), a 'meal-monger' (James Wishart) and two shoemakers (Thomas Gilchrist and Thomas Melville). Not unnaturally, most male heads of household are agricultural labourers, and there is one farmer (Charles Marr). Schoolmaster William Bonthrone, the census inspector himself, brings up the rear. Despite the obvious diversity of the little community, it has an ageing population, for the twenty-nine houses enumerated contain twenty individuals aged 60 or over. The handloom-weaving trade, once such a thriving cottage industry, was by now almost moribund, and it is significant that out of Kilrenny's four practitioners, two – David Greig and Thomas Baldy senior – are aged 63 and 75 respectively, while the two younger men – Thomas Baldy junior (45) and James Baldy (35) – are the latter's sons, still living in their father's house.[11]

Enumeration District 3 in the census schedule is that part of the burgh 'bounded on the North and East by the Lands of Mr. Bethune and

Innergelly and on the South and West by the ancient Royalty'. There are just over a dozen houses here, but they include such mansions as Innergellie House, Rennyhill farmhouse and the minister's manse, where we find the most prominent men of the parish. Rennyhill, formerly a possession of the Lumsdens or Lumsdaines of Innergellie, had passed by the mid-eighteenth century to the Anstruther baillie Andrew Johnston, and at the time of the 1841 census was inhabited by his great-grandson George Johnston. George's brother Andrew was to become M.P. for East Fife.

Next on the list is Kilrenny Manse, whose incumbent – the Rev. George Dickson – had been minister at Pettinain in the presbytery of Lanark before his translation to Kilrenny. At Kilrenny Mains the farmer is George Mackie, and other Mackies are resident at the 'Manse Office house' and at Kilrenny Mill farm.

On the Innergellie estate there are a total of twenty-seven residents, eleven of whom were born outside Fife. The big house itself belongs to William Dick Esq., who maintains a staff of six servants, and in the surrounding cottages live Thomas Poustie, gardener; William Redpath, coalworker; David Lumsden, lime-worker; Anstruther Carstairs (profession not stated), Robert Donaldson, handloom-weaver, and David Donaldson, blacksmith. David Lumsden's 13-year-old son David is the future author of *Reminiscences of Kilrenny*. In one of the two bothies attached to Kilrenny Mill farm live farm-labourers John Bonthrone, Alexander Donaldson and Walter Carmichael; while the other houses the heterogeneous mixture of Janet McKenzie (65), washerwoman; Jane McKenzie (40); Helen Smith (13); Thomas Morris (11); John Cutler (8) and Catherine Lumsden (11).

The fourth and last enumeration district takes in the whole of the landward part of the parish, beginning at Cornceres, to the east of Kilrenny churchyard, then moving down to the seashore to Caiplie. From Caiplie it moves north to Barnsmuir, then swings inland to Thirdpart, Leys, Pitcorthie, Firthfield (i.e. Frithfield), Blacklaws, Balhouffie, Pitkierie, Cauldcoats and Crawhill, finishing at the present Toll Road, Cellardyke. The vast majority of men here are agricultural labourers, and both tradesmen and family servants are very thin on the ground compared with other parts of the parish.

At Cornceres the tenancy was shared at this time by William and David Gray, the latter being also a miller, and the tenant of Kilrenny Mill. At Caiplie, by contrast, there seems to be no resident tenant – only five families of farm labourers named Wilson, Cairns, Jack, Christie and Falls. Barnsmuir is perhaps a more prosperous estate, for here farmer William Fortune rules over a community of twenty-six individuals housed in a farmhouse, a lodge, three cothouses and a bothy. Long gone, by this time, was the lairdly family of Cunningham of Barns whose daughter had so captivated the poet William Drummond of Hawthornden, friend of Ben Jonson and contemporary of Shakespeare. From 1376 until 1743 the estate of Barns belonged to the Cunninghams, before passing to the family of General Scot of Scotstarvit.[12]

To the north-west of Barnsmuir lies the farm of Thirdpart, and here the farmer in 1841 was 46-year-old William Aitken. In the farm's three cothcuses were families named Brown, Thomson and Swan, and in the nearby bothy lived Thomas and George Taylor, aged 15 and 12 respectively. The bothy system of early nineteenth-century Scotland was vehemently criticised at the time by such social critics as the English radical William Cobbett, and this 1841 census of Kilrenny parish shows that here too many young men and boys were forced into this degrading and cheerless form of accommodation, where comfort was unknown and provisions and belongings had often to be protected against the ravages of vermin.

Leys farm, due north of Thirdpart and nearer to Crail than to the village of Kilrenny, has a much more tightly-knit community than these other farms; for here – living together in one house – are only five people: 50-year-old tenant William Black; Martha Black (80); Robert Black (35), joiner; John Clark (20), blacksmith; and Charlotte Robertson (15), female servant. But further west along the present A921 trunk road at East Pitcorthie and Butcherhall it is a different story. Here there are six houses, and thirty-eight individuals named Butcher, Young, Robertson, Bonthron, Dowie, Gilchrist, Lindsay, Wallace and Nicolson. All the men are farm-labourers, but there is no mention of a tenant-farmer, in contrast to neighbouring West Pitcorthie where the tenancy is held by 66-year-old James Band. Similarly, the farms of Firthfield, Blacklaws and Balhouffie are farmed by Robert Wilson, John Laing and Thomas Wilson respectively. West Pitkierie, on the road to Anstruther, belongs to the Gosmans, while East Pitkierie is in the hands of the Russell family. East Pitkierie has a 'wright', James Henderson, and at Mayfield, between the two Pitkieries, lives blacksmith John Brown. 'Coldcoats' (Cauldcots) has a tinsmith, Alexander Philp, and at Crowhill (Crawhill) and Burnside there are two families of Motions.

Lastly, we come to Toll Road, where there are only two houses. The toll-house is in the charge of James Lowden or Lothian (65), whose son John would follow in his footsteps and be known to future generations as 'Toll Johnny'.[13] Next door are John Brown and David Rodger, cabinet-makers; James Brown, carrier; James Storrar, male servant; and Alexander Cathro, aged 10, together with the families of the brothers

Brown. And to round off the entire census William Bonthrone is pleased to report that the town's gaol has had no prisoners 'for upwards of ten years'. This was the parish of Kilrenny on the night of June 7th, 1841.

'The fishers also shall mourn ... and they that spread nets upon the waters shall languish.' (Isaiah 19:8)

The decade or so which followed this census – George Gourlay's 'Black Decade' – was one of the worst periods for disasters at sea in the history of the parish. On Tuesday, March 29th, 1842, Henry Reid's *Lord Melbourne* sank in a westerly gale with the loss of seven men. Two years later came the turn of the *William*, whose skipper, George Smith junior, perished along with his brother James, James's son George Smith, James Forrester Watson, John Sutherland junior, Wilson Brunton, James Salter and Robert Mackay. Two years later again the *Nancy* foundered east of the May Island, and the dead were Thomas Reid, William and Thomas Muir, George Anderson, John and Alexander Wilson and John Boyter. Finally, on November 3rd, 1848, the Cellardyke fleet put to sea on an ominously dark and blustery morning of mist and sleet, and before nightfall one boat, the *Johns and Mary*, had gone down, taking with her John Smith, James, Thomas and John Fleming, Henry Reid, James Dick, David Birrell and James Dickson. The sea, always cruelly impersonal to our human way of thinking at such times, exacted a particularly savage toll that day. Two victims – James Fleming and David Birrell – each left a widow pregnant; Henry Reid's seventh child was born on the very day the father drowned, and young James Dickson, who was unmarried, had been the sole survivor from the *Lord Melbourne* six years before. Twenty-six children were left fatherless by this tragedy, which brought to thirty the total of Cellardyke seamen drowned in that ghastly six-year period.

It was also the beginning of the end for Cellardyke as a viable harbour for the fishing fleet. For some time the Cellardyke fishermen had been petitioning for a new deep-water harbour at Craignoon, behind the present John Street, and in one such petition addressed to the British White Herring Fishery Board they set out their reasons.[14] 'With coarse weather', they pointed out, Cellardyke harbour was positively dangerous, for 'the internal commotion is so great that Boats cannot lie in it with safety; and it can be taken only in moderate weather, and when the Wind blows from certain points'. In any case, the harbour had accommodation for only thirty-five boats, although the local fleet had now risen to a record one hundred and thirty. They were already making extensive use of Anstruther harbour, but even that was not ideal for their

The 'Saurlins' with the Craignoon skelly, from the foot of the Tolbooth Wynd. The house on the left was built on the site of Tam Melville's kippering kiln, once a familiar landmark to fishermen out in the firth.

requirements, as a recent catastrophe clearly indicated: 'On the night of the Sixth Instant, about One hundred and fifty Herring Boats, having their nets on board, rode there at anchor; a heavy gale suddenly arose; your Memorialists (i.e. the petitioners) helplessly looking on, saw their Boats drag their anchors, and drifting against each other, they were crushed and dashed against the Quay. – Several Boats became total wrecks, scarcely any escaped uninjured, and Forty-two Boats will take from Eight to Forty pounds Sterling each to repair them. Competent parties have calculated the loss in Boats and Nets to amount to seven hundred and twenty five pounds'.

Even sitting snug and safe in the haven of his own home, a fisherman could be ruined by the fury of the elements. It was monumentally unfair. The Craignoon project was kept alive for several more years, but was eventually killed off by the decision to build the Union Harbour at Anstruther.

The Kilrenny minister, Mr. Dickson, gives a useful description of the state of the local fisheries at this time in the *New Statistical Account* of 1845. The Cellardyke fishermen, he tells us, are 'active, hardy and enterprising', and in the summer season about a hundred large boats are involved in the herring fishery. As well as its regular local crew, each boat has in addition one or two 'half-dealsmen' – outsiders who contribute no nets of their own but simply assist with the rowing and the hauling-in of the nets. Each skipper has an agreement with a particular curer, generally of the order of 9/– to 11/– a cran, with an allowance of

117

whisky. The white-fishing is prosecuted at other times by up to thirty boats manned by eight men each. In summer the fish are taken to Fisherrow and Newhaven, or Dundee and Perth, but in winter they are brought into harbour and sold to the curers for the Glasgow, Liverpool and London markets, or to the cadgers who carry them round the inland farms in their carts. The main expense to the fishermen, apart from the upkeep and replacement of nets and lines, is the expensive cartloads of mussel-bait from the river Eden near St. Andrews. 'Many of the fisher-men are in respectable circumstances', adds Mr. Dickson, 'and careful in the management of their substance, but it is matter of deep regret that the same cannot be said of all of them.'

The minister's carefully neutral sketch of the parish omits any reference to the very real poverty of many of its inhabitants. For the true picture we must turn to the records of meetings held jointly by the kirk-session and the heritors of the parish, the latter group including members of the Bethune and Anstruther families together with other landed gentry of the area. In the minute-books of these meetings we learn, for instance, that no more than 10/– is to be allowed towards a pauper's coffin, and that the schoolmaster is to be allowed to charge half-fees for poor children attending his school. Those in the direst need may have their house-rent paid for them, or receive a grant to help clothe their children. The widows of the men lost at sea during this decade figure prominently here.

Given the eminence and undoubted wealth of several of the heritors, the financial aid awarded was often less than princely. One young woman who was bedridden, and whose parents were aged and 'unfit for work', was awarded 1/6d. per week. Others, on condition that they could plead their case effectively, might be granted an additional 6d. or 1/– on an existing weekly pension. Coals were bought and distributed to the needy. Janet Anderson Marr was awarded 1/6d. weekly on condition that she returned to her husband. The cause of the marital estrangement is not given.

One issue which bitterly divided the heritors themselves was that of the Female and Infant Schools. First envisaged by Mr. Johnston of Rennyhill in 1834, and generally agreed by the heritors to be an asset to the town, the schools and accompanying schoolhouse had turned out to be more expensive than anticipated – to the indignation of the non-resident majority of the heritors – and these gentlemen were not disposed to agree to the lavish expenditure which had been sanctioned in their absence by Mr. Johnston, Mr. Sandys Lumsdaine of Innergellie and Mr. Drinkwater Bethune. Not only that, but the latter three gentlemen had applied for a government grant. If the schools had been able to pay for themselves that would have been something, but as a minute of April 25th, 1845, pointed out: 'there is at present so much poverty among the population that an adequate Salary cannot be assured to the School-mistresses'. Such candid comments are a salutary corrective to the breezy optimism which pervades George Gourlay's depiction of this period.

On a more jocular note, the *Pittenweem Register* for September 11th, 1847, gives an example of the sly, buccaneering spirit of the Dykers: 'On Friday night, last week, while the fishermen of Crail were off their guard, and lying comfortably in bed, a fleet of Cellardyke boats came and caught from 4 to 40 barrels each, just opposite the harbour. The Dykers are like marine blood-hounds, they follow the herrings by their scent'. Poor recompense for the helpful Crailers who traditionally dispatched a horseman post-haste to warn their Cellardyke neighbours when there were 'herrin' in the Haiks'!

Both at sea and on land the dreaded cholera continued to be a scourge throughout this period, and while the Kilrenny and Cellardyke poor put their trust in lime-water and the Pittenweemers burned coal-tar, the local press carried weekly mortality lists. The disease could be gruesomely sudden in its onset, as at least one Cellardyke fisherman found to his cost:

> The *Pittenweem Register*, No. 242, Saturday, September 29, 1849.
> *Remarkable Fact.–* William Small, fisherman, who died of Cholera last week at Cellardyke, was at sea when the disease came upon him, and said to his companions – 'If there is such a thing as swallowing Cholera, I am afraid I have caught it'. When asked, what made him say so? he said, 'I felt as if something having the feeling of a soft cold potato had forced its way down my throat'. In less than five minutes after he made this curious remark he complained of pain in the stomach, – looseness of the bowels and cramp immediately ensued, and in half an hour after the first attack his countenance altered, and his features assumed the appearance of a dying man.'

The same newssheet carried a poem by another Cellardyke man, Michael Doig, whose gloomy reflections on mortality have an almost mediaeval ring:

> While wand'ring in auld Nature's field,–
> The heart with sorrow pressed;
> A pensive thought the reapers yield,
> As they do glean the harvest store.
>
> While they cut down the golden corn
> That yestermorn did sweetly wave,
> It teaches man he's here forlorn,
> And should prepare him for the grave.

Though he may blithely sport in health,
With pleasure's variegated bowl,
And madly boast of his great wealth,
While others with stern hunger howl.

Though cares and griefs are all unknown,
And only pleasure seems to shine;
Yet he can't call one day his own,
Or say, in truth, that 'this is mine'.

Ah, no; the plague that stalks this land
Doth evidence enough this truth;
And shews the brink on which all stand,–
Whether old age, manhood, or youth.

An attitude of stoic fatalism prevailed, and few people worried that the narrow, unpaved thoroughfare from Tolbooth Wynd to the Shore was littered with mussel-shells, fish-guts and middens, while none of the houses had running water. The well in the 'Workit' or Urquhart Wynd was the favourite resort for this last commodity, although after nights of hard frost it might require to be thawed out in the morning. Epidemics of measles and anonymous fevers were prevalent, and many a young child succumbed to the 'chincough' (whooping-cough) or a 'putrid sore throat', as the parish records testify.

But not all Michael Doig's fellow-townsmen were content to sit back and wait for the Grim Reaper. On Thursday, May 27th, 1852, twelve Dykers left for the Gold Diggings of Australia, to be followed shortly afterwards by four more. They were Thomas Watson, David Rodger, David Murray, David Birrell, David Brown, John Smith, James Cunningham, Leslie Barclay, George Fowler, James Davidson, Alexander Fowler, David Wilson, William Doig, Alexander Melville, William Black and James Sharp, and the driving force behind the enterprise was Captain Alexander Rodger, of whom more later. As the nineteenth century wore on and the British Empire prospered more and more, Cellardyke men would channel that energy and inventiveness which had made them renowned among mariners into new channels, and would win their living in some of the furthest-flung corners of the globe.

Among those who stayed at home, the energy and inventiveness were channelled into finding new markets for their products. The despised 'partan' came into its own, with the arrival of the railway, and from being fished as bait for the lines developed into a prized export to Billingsgate and to the miners and spinners of industrial Lancashire.[15] The emancipation of the slaves in the West Indies cotton plantations was a bitter blow, for these poor captives had been fed largely on a diet of pickled herring; but here again a substitute was found in the shape of the red herring, which brought avid droves of English buyers flocking in by every train and steamer. Industrial Britain was crying out to be fed, and beyond her boundaries lay the traditional herring markets of Northern Europe. A boom-time was coming, a time far removed from the old hand-to-mouth existence of one's forefathers. The rise in population; the flight to the cities and consequent rise in the number of people unable to feed themselves; the growth of speedy transport facilities; the long period of peace, with the consequent disappearance of the hated press-gang: all were factors which would eventually combine to bring better times for the fishers of Cellardyke.

But this is to anticipate: for the middle decade of the century was no more exempt from its share of tragedy than its predecessors had been. On August 20th, 1855, it was the age-old cry of 'herrin' in the Haiks' which brought Cellardyke's 130-strong fleet of drave boats hastening to that familiar ground, and Adam Reid's *Venus* was only one of the many laden boats which made for home afterwards, full to the gunwales, in the face of a freshening westerly gale. One of the crew, as so often in these cases, had had a presentiment of trouble the previous night, when his dead mother had beckoned to him in a dream. The omen was fulfilled when the *Venus* foundered in the offing of Crail, with the loss of her 67-year-old skipper Adam Reid, his 8-year-old son William, and the half-dealsmen James Malcolm from Dundee, and Kenneth McLeod from Skye. Adam Reid was the son of Adam Reid and Isabella Scott and the brother of Margaret Watson (Reid), and at the age of 67 he must have been nearing the end of his active life at sea. That he perished together with the child of his old age makes this a peculiarly poignant tragedy.

We close this chapter with a look at the Cellardyke of the late 1850s, seen through the eyes of William Smith (Cowper) ('Auld Wull'), who was born in the old Bishop's Palace about a decade earlier. The Cellardyke he knew was one where the houses had as yet no numbers, and where letters addressed to a local man might bear his wife's name in brackets, so common were some of the fisher surnames. A man might be distinguished by either of two female appellations – that of his boat, or that of his wife. Two cousins named Robert Cunningham, for example, were known respectively as 'Harmony Rob' and 'Baxter Rob'. So numerous were the ubiquitous Watson 'clan' that sub-groups were distinguished as the 'Barony' Watsons, the 'Singing' Watsons, the 'Forrester' Watsons, etc. before individual 'by-names' could be applied.

Living conditions, as we have seen already, were primitive by modern standards, and the wooden floors of the houses were sprinkled with sand. Both men and women dressed plainly, the older women wearing mutch-

Adam Reid (Jack) with Margaret Davidson and his granddaughter Margaret Reid (later Mrs. Barclay), at 20 Shore Street, Cellardyke. Undated, probably 1880s or early 1890s. Adam was a survivor of the *Venus* disaster of 1855 when his father Adam Reid (Wood) and his brother William were drowned. Adam's son, Adam Reid (Brown), was skipper of the sailing Fifie *Reliance*, the steam-drifter *Guerdon*, and numerous other boats.

caps while the younger ones went bareheaded, and the men wearing blue serge seamen's jackets and trousers. Oatmeal was still a staple food in the form of porridge, bannocks and oatcakes, and neither fruit nor milk were plentiful. Except at the New Year pastry and cakes were unknown, and when a busy wife and mother had lines to bait or nets to mend her children had to make do with a syrup or treacle 'piece'. A cooked meal at teatime was almost invariably fried fish.

Of course, there were special occasions when no expense would be spared. A wedding was a great affair, with feasting and dancing, and the prospective bridegroom's boat would carry a special 'marriage flag' at the masthead during the week preceding the nuptials. It was usual to be married in the bride's house by the minister of her church. And on the way to church for a christening ceremony, the person carrying the infant would present a 'christening piece' of bread or cakes to the first person they met on the way.

Apart from James Fowler's general store at Cellardyke harbour, most of the town's shops consisted of a little room set aside in the owner's house. Some of these places sold liquor, and altogether there were nine or ten licensed premises in Cellardyke, five of which were proper public houses. Both men and women drank freely, and as the open undecked boats of the day had no cooking facilities, the fishermen would resort to the whisky bottle for a spot of warmth at sea. At the end of the herring-fishing season the 'settling-up' would often be conducted in Tammas Anderson's pub amid noisy, drunken brawls which were the delight of the small boys of the neighbourhood.

Apart from such entertainment as their elders unwittingly provided, the boys and girls of Victorian Cellardyke had many other ploys to divert them. Football, 'bools', pitch and toss, 'spy oh', 'corntag', 'Scotch and English', 'hit the boar', 'dummy tracks', 'blind man's buff' and 'jinger ring' are only some of the games remembered by an old man in the next century, and of course these fishermen's sons had their predictable seaside pursuits of fishing and playing at boats with a flat rock for a boat and a spar for a mast. Long before returning fishing-boats reached the harbour, these keen-eyed watchers on the shore could tell one from another. Every boat carried on its mast the distinctive mark of the fish-curer to whom its crew were engaged, and boats engaged to a Cellardyke curer would discharge their catch at Cellardyke while those of the Anstruther curers would land theirs at Anstruther. But a new yard or mast alone, the rake of a sail or some new cloth – these in themselves were telltale signs that identified a boat still several miles out to sea.

In the same way the Cromarty stonemason, geologist and religious controversialist Hugh Miller writes of how he learned at an early age to distinguish his father's sloop by 'the two slim stripes of white which ran along her sides, and her two square topsails', and of how not even the walls of the schoolroom could inhibit such useful learning: 'As the school-windows fronted the opening of the Firth, not a vessel could enter the harbour that we did not see; and, improving through our opportunities, there was perhaps no educational institution in the kingdom in which all sorts of barques and carvels, from the fishing yawl to the frigate, could be more correctly drawn on the slate, or where any defect in hulk or rigging, in some faulty delineation, was surer of being more justly and unsparingly criticised. .... All the herring boats during the season passed our windows on their homeward way to the harbour; and, from their depth in the water, we became skilful enough to predicate the number of crans of each with wonderful judgment and correctness'.[16]

Regrettably, the girls seem to have been relegated to the role of the patient wife preparing her husband's tea – useful training, no doubt, for the real-life roles that awaited most of them.

More daringly, there were the cheekier pursuits which have delighted children at their elders' expense since time immemorial: such as remote-control devices for tapping at windows and for knocking off hats. At the top of the 'Little Wynd', in West Forth Street, a one-storey house of two rooms was used as a schoolhouse by a Mr. Gourlay – the brother of our old friend the author of *Fisher Life* – and some of the local boys, knowing that he was shortsighted, would place obstacles in his path in the hope that he would fall over them.

When not engaged in various sorts of mischief, the fisher-children were usually to be found playing their part in the economy of the fisher-household. Nets in those pre-factory days were made by hand, and this was a task the children might be put to on returning from school. Or they might be sent as far afield as Caiplie to gather limpet bait, or 'up the country' to gather grass from the roadside to lay the hooks on when baiting the lines. These small errands were a considerable help to a mother who might have to rise at four in the morning to bait a fresh set of lines and carry them down to the boat, bringing back the used ones for the next day's baiting – a ceaseless treadmill of exhausting and monotonous toil. In the herring season the wet nets had to be laid out to dry every day – another task for the womenfolk. William Smith's father rented ground for this purpose at 'William Fowler's park', the present Burnside Terrace.

The overall picture, then, is one of unremitting toil, with many dangers and hazards run and precious little reward at the end. Yet it is not an unhappy or depressing picture this old man paints of the Cellardyke of his youth. While it is certainly a cliché to talk of the 'good old days' of the past, and foolishly naïve to suppose that poverty and discomfort in some way confer virtue on the sufferer, there is surely something to be said for a way of life which binds old and young together in a common purpose, and devises useful tasks for young, old, infirm and able-bodied alike. From the youngest children pulling roadside grass or gathering limpets, to the elderly widow 'barking' nets; from the coopers, carters and curers to the old veterans tying on hooks for tobacco money – no-one was superfluous. All had a part to play, however humble, in the life of the community. There, perhaps, lies the biggest difference between our society and that of our ancestors a hundred and thirty years ago.

7

The Nineteenth Century, Part III:
Revival, Reconstruction and Respectability

In the autumn of 1856 the East Neuk acquired a new weekly newspaper in the shape of the *East of Fife Record*, published every Saturday morning in Anstruther. The news of the area was covered on a parish-by-parish basis, and from these snippets of local gossip, together with the contributions of anonymous correspondents, we can reconstruct the burning issues of the day.

As far as Cellardyke is concerned, the picture that emerges is a grim one, and then – as now – newspapers were not slow to exploit the more sensational type of story. On November 8th, 1856, for example, we read that Penelope Barclay in Cellardyke has been apprehended and taken under escort to face trial in Cupar for an unprovoked assault on her husband Alexander Smith. The unfortunate victim had been seated at his dinner after a day at sea when his wife, under the influence of drink, hurled a plate at his head, severing an artery in his temple. Luckily a doctor had been summoned in time, and the *Record* was able to report that '... Smith is now progressing favourably'. Penelope Barclay's reward for her folly was 20 days in Cupar jail.

Other delinquents of the time included James Fleming, fisherman in Cellardyke, fined in the burgh court for an assault on James Wallace and Robert Graham; and Andrew Scott and George Watson, carters, who were convicted of indecent assault on Jane Birrell, an unmarried woman in Anstruther Easter. The prevalence of this latter type of offence gave rise to an angry editorial on February 21st, 1857:

CELLARDYKE.

DISGRACEFUL CONDUCT.– We regret to learn that for some time past, a number of young men (if they are deserving of such a designation) have been so utterly oblivious of the propriety and decency which ought to be the pride and ornament of youth, as to get themselves concealed in closes and entries about the town on the evenings, and from thence pounce upon every young female who chances to pass their places of concealment, treating them in a manner fitted to fill every right-minded individual with indignation and disgust. Even married women have not always escaped their indecency. To such heights have these malicious practices grown, that it has been found necessary to require the cognisance of the police officer, who is actively investigating the matter; and now that the case is in his hands, we trust that such an example will be made of the unmanly offenders as will secure the protection of all classes of the community for the future, and purge our spirited town from the disgraceful odium.

Just how serious these 'assaults' were is impossible to say at this distance in time, and it may well be that they were prompted more by a coarse and misplaced sense of humour than by any spirit of malice. The young carters of Cellardyke were among the most persistent offenders, and indeed the antisocial activities of this fraternity were not confined to uncouth attacks on the fair sex, as the following item makes clear:

EAST OF FIFE RECORD, Saturday, August 14th., 1858.

[Three speeding carts had collided at the nasty bend by the Tolbooth or Town Hall, where James Street, Tolbooth Wynd and John Street converge.] It is really marvellous that there are not more accidents of the same kind on our narrow streets; yet scarcely a day passes without such furious driving on the part of some of our carters as endangers the lives of old and young, and such as would be allowed in no place but this. We would rejoice to see the whip as vigorously applied to their own shoulders as they are in the habit of doing to their half-starved animals; we think this is the only punishment that would have any effect.

Hard drinking lay behind many of the town's ills. On New Year's Eve, 1857, the Cellardyke Abstinence Society presented every household in the town with a free copy of the pictorial temperance tracts 'Dissolving views' and 'Who takes the sap out of us?', which, they later claimed, worked wonders; but the correspondence columns of the *Record* told a different story. At the end of the summer herring drave the harbour area at Anstruther was awash with reeling fishermen, and to add to the degradation an 8-year-old boy was seen crawling along the gutter on hands and knees, dead drunk, mouthing oaths and obscenities. It was a situation that cried out for reform. But a change was on the way.

On December 8th, 1859 the *Heroine*, owner and skipper William Birrell, was lost close to the shore after prosecuting the small-line fishing in the vicinity of the Marr Bank. The victims, apart from the skipper, were his son David, aged 17, and his nephew Thomas Birrell, together with James Davidson, William Wood, George Keay and James Reid. Five widows and eighteen children were left to mourn their dead.

The tragedy was of a kind only too familiar to the people of Cellardyke, yet this time their mourning took a different and quite unprecedented turn. On the day following the disaster the minister of the Free Kirk in Anstruther, Mr. Gregory, was asked to hold a prayer-meeting in

The old town hall in Tolbooth Wynd (pre-1881). Note the blind corner where speeding carts sometimes collided.

Cellardyke. On arriving at the hall he was taken aback to find a crowd of some two hundred people, most of them men, and an atmosphere of strained emotionalism which was wholly new in his experience. Some of those present later compared the meeting to those held during the great cholera epidemics.[1]

In the succeeding weeks the prayer-meeting became a regular event, with no let-up either in attendances by the fishermen or in the highly-charged emotional atmosphere in which worship was conducted. At the same time, in other east-coast ports from the Moray Firth down to Eyemouth, an evangelical religious revival was under way, and this fact was not lost on the fishermen of Cellardyke. The intensity of religious feeling in the town grew ever stronger, and more and more of the inhabitants came under its spell. On the evening of Sunday, March 12th, a local youth – one of a crew the rest of whom were already converts – experienced a spiritual awakening at the evening meeting. The following day he went to sea in a state of mental anguish, and for three days, as the boat drifted helplessly on the open sea, his fellow-crewmen prayed over him and struggled to restore his peace of mind. On the third day he sprang up from the bottom of the boat, where he had lain huddled in misery, and shouted out that he had 'found Christ'. The other men were beside themselves with joy, and, as Mr. Gregory recorded at the time: 'They could attend to nothing; and how their boat drifted safely into the harbour they cannot yet tell'.[2]

The 'meetings' grew in number and intensity. On the forenoon of Friday, March 16th, the atmosphere was tense, for 'great numbers throughout the town were known to be burdened with a heavy sense of sin'. At the close of that day's meeting over a hundred worshippers of both sexes and all ages remained behind to talk to the minister, and 'at the first word that was spoken to them, they gave way to tears and sobs, presenting a most affecting sight'.[3]

After this, meetings were held daily. When word spread that another convert had 'seen the Light', crowds would gather outside the house, and ministers were called in from neighbouring parishes to help the local clergy control the surging masses of humanity in the narrow old main street. Many individuals were close to hysteria, and a kindly word of comfort might become the spark that would set a soul on fire. In the house of a sick man Mr. Gregory was addressing 'a few plain words in calm conversational style' to some women who had come in, when one of them suddenly launched herself at his feet, screaming 'Oh, save me! – save me from Hell! I'll take him; I'll take him; save me! save me!' One old fisherman knelt all night on a chair by his bedside. In the small hours of the morning, as he felt the spiritual burden lifting from his soul, he ran outside and climbed the adjoining wall to awaken his neighbour and tell him the good news. Many others, including married couples, endured this 'dark night of the soul', often spending many nights on their knees and taking little food. One woman spent night after night kneeling in agony in her cellar. On a more practical level grocer James Fowler poured his stock of liquor into Cellardyke harbour, declaring that all the profit he ever made from sales of strong drink had fallen through holes in his pockets.[4]

One by-product of this religious awakening was that even those who did not share in it were shamed into examining their consciences. In the process, many past vices and weaknesses were brought to light for the first time. Mr. Gregory noted the difference: 'There is a visible change on the town; there is less drinking'.[5] Self-righteousness and envy had abated. One fisherman declared: 'I had many a spite and grudge before . . . but now I love everything I see – I love the very stones under my feet'.[6] 'From not a few boats at sea', Mr. Gregory observed, 'the voice of holy melody, of prayer and praise, is wafted over the surface of the deep, mingling sweetly with the sighing of the wind and the murmuring of the waves.'[7]

At the end of the Lammas Drave the herring-boats were laid up in three tiers at the Town's Green. In the foreground are (L. to R.) KY 1578 *Globe*, owner and skipper David Christie; KY 1477 *Georgina Anderson*, Thomas Pratt; KY 1545 *Beautiful Star*, John Smith; KY 1386 *Petrel*, Thomas Murray (Birrell); KY 1373 *Roberts*, Robert Cunningham (Wood); KY 1901 *Florence*, Robert Brown.

'Auld Wull', in his reminiscences, gives an example of one of the more practical benefits of the religious revival. At the end of the herring-fishing season it was customary to 'lay up' all the boats not needed for the winter line-fishing: an operation which involved hauling the boats up the slipway on two pairs of iron wheels, then using horses to pull them to the Town's Green. A skipper wishing to have his boat laid up in this way had to hire men to help him, and he paid them, traditionally, with a glass of whisky. Thus in one day a man who offered his services to several skippers could end up well and truly drunk, with all the consequences resulting from that condition; and it might take six weeks to lay up all the boats. After the revival, the whisky was dispensed with. Instead the men of the town met in the Town Hall and operated a ballot system. The boats were henceforth to be hauled up in strict sequence according to the number on the skipper's ballot ticket, and they were divided up into groups of thirty or so boats known as 'clubs'. As the first club was finishing, the bellman would go through the town crying, 'The second club to meet at the capstan at (such and such a time)'. It was a more orderly and efficient way of doing things.

Of course, the 'revival' could not sustain its momentum indefinitely, and it would be foolish to pretend that all the negative aspects of fisher-life were wiped out overnight. Yet the events of that turbulent year of

1860 do seem to have left a permanent mark on the town. Perhaps it would be fair to say that after the initial fervour had died down, the townspeople settled for a steady, decent piety – that unostentatious form of Presbyterianism which is still so marked a feature of the East Neuk fishing-villages. Cellardyke had finally entered the Victorian age.

The period immediately following the Revival saw several significant innovations. Not the least of these was the sacking of the parish school-teacher, who for almost a decade had been a thorn in the flesh of heritors and kirk-session alike. As early as 1854 Admiral Drinkwater Bethune had complained that Mr. Fleming was totally unfit for office due to his addiction to drink, but it was not until 1861 that he was officially deprived of his post by the sheriff. Undeterred by this development, the Kilrenny dominie succeeded in persuading Lord Ormidale in the Court of Session to issue an interdict prohibiting the heritors from appointing another master in his place; and coolly informed them that he would happily resign if they paid him his full salary for the rest of his life! Not surprisingly, the heritors failed to respond to this offer. Finally, the following year, they succeeded in ejecting Mr. Fleming and in his place appointed Mr. George Dalrymple of Edrom, in Berwickshire: the parish – by a strange coincidence – where one of the heritors, the Rev. Sandys Lumsdaine, had his residence. To avoid future misunderstanding it was made clear to Mr. Dalrymple that his duties were to teach 'English, Grammar, reading, writing, Arithmetic, History, Geography, Mathematics, Navigation, Latin and French', and his salary was fixed at £35 sterling. Previously, by the old-fashioned method of computation, the salary had been 2 chalders of oatmeal at £13/6/3¾d. per chalder, payable at Whitsunday and Martinmas. The female teacher's duties were defined as 'to give instruction in knitting and plain sewing work, as well as in English, Grammar, reading, writing, arithmetic and Geography', and her salary was raised to £12.[8]

While the educational facilities offered by the parish were being thus regulated and improved, more practical reforms were also under way. James Peebles was persuaded to sell his house opposite the Town Hall so that it could be demolished and '... the site thrown into the Public road'.[9] Forth Street – first mentioned under that name in 1868 – was put on the list of statute labour roads in order to defray the cost of repairing damage caused by 'carting traffic ... on the way to the Union Harbour'. The decision was taken to lay a proper road to the east of the Tolbooth, and to repair the outside stair at Wilson Birrell's house. George Sharp the fish-curer agreed to put a boiler in the wash-house at the east end of the town, 'repair the roof thereof, and employ a suitable person to take charge of it, and to charge one penny for the use of the Green and threepence for the use of the Boiler, including Green'.

The Town's Green today, with Croma House and, beyond, Kilrenny Mill farm and caravan site. The area adjacent to Croma was used for fish-curing and packing, and salt cod were hung out to dry where now there are swings and chutes for children.

Croma House, the imposing edifice at the east end of Cellardyke opposite the Town's Green, was built by Thomas Cormack, a native of Coldingham in Berwickshire. By the time of the 1861 Census Mr. Cormack's fish-curing premises and cod-liver-oil manufactory were giving employment to a total of 10 men and 11 women: a useful and appropriate addition to the town's manufacturing base. Another fledgling businessman of the period was Robert Watson, who in 1859 founded Watson's factory in George Street for the manufacture of fishermen's oilskins, herring nets and buoys. Like many another Dyker, Robert Watson was the product of a marriage between cousins. His father, Alexander Watson, was one of the band of Cellardyke fishers who succumbed to the typhus epidemic at Wick in 1829. His mother was the daughter of David Watson and Grizel Tarvit, and a sister of David Watson (Salter). The business seems to have prospered from the outset, to the extent that Robert Watson's descendants were able to open branch factories in Newburgh and Buckhaven, and a London office in High Holborn.

Another successful, if small-scale, business 'ist the toon' was the general merchant's store run by George Sharp and David Murray, who in 1861 were aged 31 and 28 respectively, and employed 4 assistants. Later their fishing-gear would win gold medals at exhibitions in Edinburgh and London, and in 1878 they would commission the *Onward*, one of the first two steam drifters to operate successfully on the east coast of Scotland.

A great fillip to local pride and self-confidence was the return in 1868 of full local democracy, after almost four decades during which the burgh's affairs had been run by managers appointed by the Court of Session. The way in which the burgh's ancient privileges had come to be suspended makes interesting reading, and demonstrates the acrimonious nature of local politics at the time.

We have already seen that the coastal burghs, and in particular Kilrenny, were a byword for political corruption in the eighteenth century. The following century saw little improvement. In Kilrenny things came to a head in the spring of 1819, when the following petition was drawn up on behalf of the townspeople and presented to the House of Commons:

SHEWETH – That this is one of the few burghs in Scotland, by the set of which so much of the original constitution of all the burghs is retained, as that the annual election of the MAGISTRATES and TREASURER is appointed to be made by poll of the whole burgesses.

That this poor remnant of their ancient privileges has, however, become quite useless to your petitioners, from the countervailing operation of a right claimed and exercised by the Councils under the authority of the Act 29. Parliament 5. James III., of naming *all* the *Councillors*, who compose eleven of the fifteen Members of which the Council consists; and the choice of Magistrates and Treasurer is limited to lists of persons put in nomination by those very Councils, who of course take care to include in their lists only their own friends and partisans; so that this is, in fact, as much a close burgh as if the burgesses had no voice at all in the elections.

That, accordingly, the office-bearers in this burgh have continued themselves from year to year with little variation, beyond the inevitable effect of death and occasional jealousies, past the memory of man; and under the management of these self-elected rulers, the patrimony of the burgh has entirely vanished, there not being as much of their lands left as is sufficient for drying your petitioners' fishing-nets.

That your petitioners have further to state, as a most serious evil arising out of this system of self-election and its concomitant irresponsibility, that they, in common with all the other burgesses of Scotland, are deprived of the franchise vested in them by the principles of the British Constitution, of voting indirectly in the choice of their representative in Parliament; from which it has occurred, that the Learned Lord who now represents the district of burghs of which ours is one, has been placed in that situation by the *narrowest* majorities of the Councils, contrary to the will and wishes of every individual burgess, save those Members of the Councils who were gained over to support the Ministerial Candidate by influence which, it now appears, was not *gratuitously* exercised.

That your Petitioners shall not trespass on your Honourable House, by a repetition here of the several grievances arising from the close system, which are so fully stated in numerous petitions already on your table. They shall only declare their full conviction that nothing but the total repeal of the Scots Act of Parliament, 5th James III. c.29, will remedy these grievances, or satisfy the expectations which a firm reliance on the wisdom and justice of Parliament has excited in the minds of the burgesses of this part of the United Kingdom.

May it therefore please your Honourable House, to take the premises into your early and serious consideration; to cause a bill to be brought into your Honourable House for the repeal of the foresaid Act of the Scots Parliament, and for regulating the elections of Magistrates and Councils in the Royal Burghs of Scotland according to their original charters, and to cause the same to be passed into a law; or to do otherwise as to your Honourable House shall seem just and expedient.[10]

Nothing much seems to have come of this petition, but four years later the whole issue boiled up again when James Gardner, on behalf of a group of disgruntled burgesses, raised an action in the Court of Session to have the result of the last council election set aside due to irregularities in the voting. The case of 'James Gardner against the Town Clerk of Kilrenny' can be reconstructed from a mass of documentation in West Register House in Edinburgh, of which the following is a bare summary.[11]

James Gardner's grievance was that Matthew Conolly, town clerk of Kilrenny, had refused his request for a copy of the minutes of the town council's 'sederunt' or meeting of September 18th, 1823, when – in accordance with the burgh's constitution – first a new council, then new magistrates, had been elected. Mr. Conolly had offered to let him *inspect* the Poll-book, with its list of burgesses entitled to vote for the magistrates, but James Gardner wated much more than that. As far as he was concerned, he '. . . was entitled not merely to a full extract, instead of a few garbled and selected passages from any *one* minute, which it might thus suit Mr. Conolly's caprice, or convenience to furnish, – but to a full extract of *each* and *every* minute connected with any part of the whole business of the election'.

The reason for James Gardner's stubbornness was simple. As his counsel reminded the court, any petition of this nature *must* be accurate down to the last detail. Any slip or inaccuracy, however innocent and unintentional, would result in the petition's being automatically rejected. By refusing Mr. Gardner a detailed copy of the relevant minutes Conolly was forcing him to guess, on the evidence of hearsay, what had actually happened in the closed council meeting. *Some* minor errors of fact were almost bound to be included in the allegations. Only when the petition was presented in court would Conolly finally produce his trump card, and, with minute-book in hand, proceed to demolish his opponent's case by quoting chapter and verse at him.

In the town clerk of Kilrenny James Gardner had picked on a formidable opponent. Born in 1789 in Crail, where his Irish immigrant father was landlord of the Golf Inn, Matthew Forster Conolly had graduated from Dominie Macmin's 6 a.m. Latin classes to weaver Black's rickety barn of a schoolhouse in Kilrenny, where Mr. Orphat taught the crabbed 'secretary hand' of mediaeval charters and legal documents. A legal apprenticeship served partly in Pittenweem, where his father had once been overseer at the salt-pans, and partly in Edinburgh, had culminated in his election to the post of town clerk of Anstruther Easter at the tender age of 22: strings having been pulled along the way by such influential backers as Methven Erskine, later 10th Earl of Kellie.[12] Shortly afterwards he was also appointed town clerk of Crail, Kilrenny and Anstruther Wester, so that almost overnight the young notary became privy to the deliberations of no fewer than four of the rival East Neuk burghs – a unique position of influence.

Matthew Conolly was a Tory in politics, an Episcopalian in religion and a shrewd lawyer by profession – a combination hardly likely to endear him to the Cellardyke fishermen. Nor was he any more popular in his role as Procurator Fiscal, especially after the débâcle of 1838 when his attempt to prosecute Skipper John Sutherland for his part in the May Island pleasure-trip disaster was thrown out by the High Court in Edinburgh.[13]

In the autumn of 1823, however, Mr. Conolly was in ebullient mood as he penned his counter-petition for the Lords of Session. He was confident, he wrote, that Mr. Gardner's *legitimate* demands had been met, according to the letter of the law. He had been allowed access to documents relating to the election of magistrates, as was his right; as for the election of the new council by the old, that was no business of Mr. Gardner's or of anyone else unconnected with the council: 'He had got an extract copy of the minute in so far as it related to those matters with which he was connected; he then asked for the roll of the Poll, and he was offered inspection of it. Finding all his demands complied with, he asked something else; he demanded not only inspection, but a copy of the Poll-book. Your Lordships must perceive that this was endless. If every Burgess who voted, or was entitled to vote at the election of Magistrates, and all the Burgesses of the burgh might have done so, was to insist on the clerk making out for him a copy of the Poll-book, it would be an occupation of itself, there would be no end to it'.

Their Lordships seem to have been unimpressed by Conolly's eloquence. On December 11th, 1823, his counter-petition was rejected, having first been signed: 'The Lords having Considered this Petition They Refuse the Desire thereof'.

The case was to drag on for a further six years until finally, on April 24th, 1829, the Lords found in favour of James Gardner. The burgh was disfranchised, the sitting councillors were deposed from office, and ship-owner Archibald Williamson, weaver John Lothian and fisherman John Martin were appointed managers of the burgh for the foreseeable future. Even then the matter was not resolved once and for all, for who was to be chief manager among the three? Touchy Dyker pride was at stake. Archibald Williamson claimed the privilege, as being mentioned first in the list of managers drawn up by the court. John Lothian counter-claimed it, having been a baillie in 1818, before the controversial elec-tion which had caused all the trouble. Eventually the victory went to Lothian, and the dust began to settle. A similar situation had arisen in Pittenweem in 1823, when the council was disbanded: but that burgh's disfranchisement had lasted only two years. Kilrenny's would last for almost forty.

In December 1868 elections were held for a new council, and the first elected councillors under the new dispensation were John Martin, George Sharp, Robert Watson (Doig), David Ritchie, Brodie Nicolson, James Smith (Hamilton), James Smith (Robertson), Alexander Watson (Murray) and Martin Gardner. John Martin was subsequently elected provost, George Sharp and Robert Watson became baillies, and Alexander Watson treasurer.

One of Provost Martin's first acts on behalf of his townsmen was to apply to Admiral Bethune's legal agent for permission to lease a patch of land between Toll Road and the Windmill Road – the site of the present Holiday Camp and former R.A.F. officers' married quarters – as a net-drying ground. 'I need not say,' he wrote in his submission, 'how much difficulty and inconvenience our Fishing population has long been put to for the want of a place on which to dry their nets, the Rocks and beach along the Sea Shore, as well as the side of the Roads, are covered with nets, during nearly the whole of the summer, ground you are aware is let by Mr. Gray (the tenant of Cornceres) and others for this purpose, but that only applies to the time of the Lammas Fishing, all the rest of the year when the nets are in process of Barking, no ground can be got for this purpose'. The need was all the greater, Mr. Martin continued, because boats which had previously got by with a fleet of 20 nets were now employing 40, and in addition the boats' sails had to be 'barked' and dried. The female part of the population, he added winningly, would be spared a great amount of labour if his request were granted.[14]

The Admiral's heart however was not melted on behalf of his fellow-seafarers. He had had many offers to buy his land from individuals who wished to build there, and although he did not yet contemplate yielding to their blandishments it was possible that one day he would change his mind. Thus the Cellardyke fishermen were forced, as we have seen in the case of 'Auld Wull's' father, to cast around for a site on which to carry out this task which was so essential for their livelihood.

There were also far-reaching changes at sea during this period. Although undecked boats were still preferred by the majority, the decked variety were gaining acceptance, and meanwhile there were those who, like James Murray of the *Choice*, experimented with the innovation of a small cabin or 'bunk' forward. As early as May 9th, 1857, we find the *East of Fife Record* proclaiming the achievements of Cellardyke – '. . . now by far the most important white fishing station in the Empire, with its 30 boats and 100,000 fish at a haul' – where 'Our success . . . is owing to a new system recently adopted of doubling and trebling the quantity of line, and making more distant voyages, while, to ensure comfort, during their long stays, a deck has been put into the forepart of their boats, which is used as a bed-room; and, wishing to keep pace with the onward march of improvement, some have even got the patent American cooking-stove above, and coffee and tea now supply a want for which, not long since, spirits was thought the only remedy; in short, we are going a-head, and what is better, we mean to go a-head'.

The Dykers were less go-ahead, though, when it came to numbering their boats in compliance with the Herring Fisheries Act of 1860, which laid down that boats' sides, sails, buoys, etc. should be clearly numbered and that the intials of the port of registration should be painted on the bows. Anstruther was now placed under the Kirkcaldy district for registration purposes, and when fishery officer George Reiach reported that local men were still using the A.R. (Anstruther) registration – despite the closing of the customs-house at Anstruther – he received a stinging rejoinder from the Fisheries Board in Edinburgh:[15]

30th December, 1861.

Sir,
   In reply to your letter of the 25th. Instant, No. 48. Boats will not be allowed to pass with the letters A.R. there being no such Customs District or Collectorship. They must all be properly lettered K.Y. the crews have been already well warned of this, and additional warning should be immediately given them, – travel to the Fishing Stations for the purpose if necessary, and apprize emphatically that Boats if belonging to the District and found lettered A.R. will be seized at once as the Act directs.

Thus the now-familiar K.Y. registration came into being, although as late as 1869 East Neuk boats were still being arrested by the fishery

The Cellardyke fishing fleet at Anstruther harbour in 1873. 21 KY in the foreground is the *Morning Star*, owner and skipper James Watson (Salter), one of three boats of that name then operating out of Anstruther. (The smaller '2nd-class' boats were distinguished from the larger '1st-class' ones by the device of putting the number *before* the initials KY).

vessels for being incorrectly numbered. 'Some Fishermen think that putting the Letters & Numbers upon the Sails injures the canvas,' recorded George Reiach on May 4th, 1869, adding pedantically: 'This can only happen when not properly done. If Turpentine be used it will burn the canvas; but if White Lead and Oil alone be used, the painting, instead of injuring the canvas, will strengthen and preserve it.'

The number and size of the Cellardyke boats registered at the Anstruther fishery office at this time is an indicator of the town's prosperity. In the nine-year period from 1869 to 1878, those registered by members of the Watson 'clan' alone included the *Fiery Cross, Morning Star, Christian, Laurel, Susan, Garland, Morning Light, Goldie, Integrity, May Flower, Ruby, Janet and Mary, Brothers, Watsons, Medway, Alpha, Arab, Aldabarn, Economy, Ariel, Roberts, Agnes, Wave, Annabella, Tirzah, Trio, Advice, Medium, James, Globe, Agenoria, Agile, Waverley, Favourite, Sea Flower, Johns, Mary Wilson, Worthy, Abeona, Scotia, Blossom, Goldfinch, Advance, Britannia, Invincible, Hope, Amana, Polar Star, Margaret, Brothers' Pride* and *Cyprus*.[16]

By the mid-1860s the new fully-decked boats were venturing much further afield in search of the herring shoals, and in fact it was this period which saw the beginnings of the great autumn 'south fishing' at

Peter Murray (Reekie), known as 'Venus Peter', one of the outstanding Cellar-dyke skippers of the late 19th century.

Yarmouth and Lowestoft: an annual pilgrimage which only petered out finally in the 1950s. Here the pioneer among the Fife fishermen was the above-mentioned James Murray (Anderson) of Cellardyke, whose father Peter Murray (Cunningham) had died of typhus at Wick in 1829; and before long James's example was followed by his son Peter Murray (Reekie) – known after his boats the *Venus* and *Venus Star* as 'Venus Peter'. By the end of the 1860s more than 100 Fife boats were joining James and Peter Murray in the seasonal migration to East Anglian waters. In the age of the steam drifter the departure of the fleet for Yarmouth would become a ritual occasion, with crews handing out handfuls of hard 'bakes' (ship's biscuits) to crowds of onlookers at Anstruther harbour as a good luck gesture before setting off, sirens whooping, for the coast of East Anglia.

When disaster next struck, though, it was as usual nearer home. On a stormy December morning in 1864 young David Gellatly was on duty at the halyards out in the North Sea when the tackle slipped, and he was pitched over the gunwales. He was the only surviving son of Peter Gellatly and Grace Reid, and the grandson of David Gellatly and Catherine Tarvit; and his death at the age of 24 helped ensure that his distinctive surname would ere long disappear from the annals of Cellardyke.

Such blows seldom come singly, and it was only five months before a greater tragedy stunned the town. The date was May 10th, 1865, it was a fine spring day with a promise of summer in the air, and Henry Bett's *Helen* was only one of several great-line boats which had been tempted far out into the North Sea to the cod and ling banks. When a gale started blowing up from the east-nor'-east the small fleet turned and fled before it; but it was the following morning before the swiftest of them reached the safety of Anstruther harbour. One by one the battered vessels limped in, and with each arrival another painful vigil ended in several fisher homes. Only the *Helen* never came back to port. This time the dead were Henry Bett, Thomas Brown, Thomas Reid, Andrew Robertson, Thomas Wood, David Fleming, Francis Montidor and Thomas Muir; and five widows were left to care for eighteen fatherless children.[17]

With the death of her son Thomas, one elderly widow – Mrs. Agnes Reid (Birrell) – reached a terrible total of more than twenty near relatives lost at sea; for by the time of her death in 1873 at the age of 68, she had lost two husbands, two sons, two sons-in-law, two brothers and three brothers-in-law, to say nothing of numerous nephews and other relations. There could hardly be more eloquent testimony to the truth of the Newhaven fishwives' observation: 'Fish are no fish the day, they're jist men's lives!'

Such disasters helped to bind together the already close-knit fishing-communities, but to an outsider – in the days before the East Neuk became 'quaint' and 'picturesque' – the fisher-towns might simply present a spectacle of unrelieved bleakness. In the late '60s and early '70s the Stevenson firm of engineers were busy constructing the new harbour at Anstruther, and the youngest member of the family was dispatched there for a few weeks to learn the business. Robert Louis Stevenson's brief occupation of Cunzie House, near the Waid Academy, has been marked by a plaque, and is often cited by Anstruther patriots as proof of that town's claim to fame. Less often quoted is the budding author's opinion of his temporary home, in that unidyllic summer of 1868. One Tuesday in July, for instance, we find him writing to his mother: 'I am utterly sick of this gray, grim, sea-beaten hole'. Nor have Dykers cause to mock at the insult to their neighbours, for Cellardyke, so Stevenson tells us in his *Random Memories*, was 'that undistinguished suburb' of which he knew little, his main business lying in the two Anstruthers. It was hardly likely that the tubercular young writer, who could dismiss the stately New Town streets and houses of his native Edinburgh as 'draughty parallelograms', would appreciate the even draughtier East Neuk. Anstruther was no Samoa, and a sterner sea beat against its bulwarks than that which rolled ashore near Vailima.

In the succeeding decades the pace of development in Cellardyke accelerated, and it is to such peaceful pursuits, interrupted inevitably by the odd disaster at sea, that most space is devoted in the records of the burgh. The year 1872 saw the death of old James Fowler, one of the chief 'architects' of the modern town; and in a rare mark of respect the town's shops closed on the day of his funeral. Meanwhile, at the east end of the town, 'Pigeon Park Lane' behind the Bishop's Palace was being transformed into the modern Dove Street; while on Admiral Bethune's lands between Forth Street and Crail Road other commodious fisher-dwellings were being raised. This enterprise had started modestly enough with an application by the School Board to build the present Cellardyke Primary School, but had mushroomed when Admiral Bethune, the Superior of Kilrenny, not only gave his consent to this plan but also pointed out the suitability of the site for house-building. And so, in the area bounded on the west by the old Bow Butts, on the north by the high road from Anstruther to Crail, on the east by the 'Powcausie' – later known as 'Williamson Street', then, finally, 'Toll Road' – and on the south by West Forth Street, 'the mason's mallet and the steam crane awakened the echoes', in George Gourlay's phrase, and the modern Rodger Street and Fowler Street came into being, honouring respectively the names of Captain Alexander Rodger (of whom more later) and the late James Fowler. According to the *East of Fife Record* of May 9th, 1857, the Toll Road had already by that date been earmarked for housing, although only on a modest scale:

HOUSE ACCOMMODATION.– We are glad to hear that there is a prospect of a few additional houses being built this summer at the back of the town, two sites having been already secured for this purpose, the one on the east and the other on the north of the new house lately built by Mr. George Henderson, flesher; and a third in the same locality is, we understand, being bargained for. We would be delighted to see a row of neat cottages, each having ample accommodation and convenience for a family, up both sides of the road, leading from Tolbooth Wynd to the Toll. If such a proposal was heartily entered into, we have no doubt feus could be easily got; and with the assistance of the Experience Investment Society, of which Mr. Mackintosh, Anstruther, is an agent, this desirable object could soon be accomplished. We are glad to hear that Mr. Mackintosh purposes to give a lecture in Cellardyke on the advantages of building societies soon. We hope he will have a large audience.

Ellice Street, named after Edward Ellice, Liberal M.P. for the St. Andrews burghs, is little more than a lane connecting West Forth Street and School Road; but at the time of its building it represented the height of luxury. The land was purchased in 1862 from a farmer called Blair, the buyers being the Cellardyke Joint Stock Building Co., consisting of the Anstruther lawyer H. B. Mackintosh and Cellardyke's Robert Brown (fisherman), John Ritchie (fish-curer) and John Martin (oilskin manufacturer). Less than a year later the first houses were ready for occupation, as the *East of Fife Record* reported on March 28th, 1863. There was only one drawback. The famous red Fife pantiles, so highly esteemed by later generations, were a mite too workaday for the fastidious taste of the *Record's* editor:

CELLARDYKE
HOUSE ACCOMMODATION.– Two of the houses projected by the Cellardyke Building Company, in the newly designed Ellice Street, are now almost finished and will be ready for occupants by Whitsunday. The plans for these houses were prepared by Mr Rae of St Andrews, and were designed to give comfortable and roomy accommodation to fishermen's families, and now that two of them are erected, parties can be able to judge of their suitableness to supply the want so long felt in Cellardyke – sufficient house accommodation.

The company certainly deserve credit for taking the initiative in this matter in erecting houses of a much better class for fishermen than have hitherto been in existence. Instead of a family, male and female, all crowding promiscuously in one apartment, these houses are so designed as to supply several apartments to the same family, and may thus be the means of promoting better habits of decency and order than, we are sorry to learn, have hitherto been in practice.

The ground on which Ellice Street stands is high, and the situation is healthy, and the buildings will have a substantial and pleasant appearance when wholly finished. They have however an unfortunate drawback in the roofs, being covered with red tiles instead of blue ones or slates. These tiles greatly mar the appearance of the houses at a distance owing to their height and prominence from all directions; and tile covered roofs are so associated with coopers' sheds and kindred trades, that no one ever thinks now of covering dwelling houses with them.

For appearance sake we would advise the company yet to remove them and substitute blue ones or slates, remembering that if they wish to pay tribute to the very worthy gentleman whose name the street bears, they should exercise some taste in erecting buildings in accordance with their appreciation of him. We are glad to learn that these buildings are likely soon to be taken up by parties in want of houses; and we understand that several fishermen from Buckhaven are at present in treaty for some of them, with the view to taking up their abode here.

William Watson, skipper of the *Fiery Cross*, and his wife Lucy Moncrieff, in the 1890s. William was a grandson of 'Water Willie' Watson and Mary Galloway, and a cousin of the author's great-grandmother Margaret Watson.

Mr. Russell's advice was not taken, and the pantiled roofs survive to this day. These tiles were not popular in Cellardyke, as they did not retain heat in the same way as thatch had done. Picturesque they may have been; practical they were not.

In 1873 the Police Commissioners of Kilrenny appointed Provost John Martin to name the constituent parts of Main Street, Cellardyke. The area from Caddies Burn to the Tolbooth was christened 'James Street' after the late James Fowler. The section from the Tolbooth east to the Urquhart Wynd was named 'John Street' after the provost himself, while the remaining part was dubbed 'George Street' after Baillie George Sharp, who owned the Islet cooperage at the Craig, the rocky area at the foot of Sharp's Close in the street which now bears his name.

Of course, not everything was sweetness and light in those years. In Kilrenny the occupant of Innergellie House complained about the byres and piggeries whose effluent drained onto the main road, and the burn near the church, which was choked with rubbish. The smell was so nauseating that the windows at Innergellie had to be kept firmly closed in the summertime. Back at Cellardyke harbour Chapman Lowrie, Robert Cunningham (Baxter) and William Watson (Moncrieff) were only a few of the skippers who persisted in blocking the roadway with their boats, to the irritation of the town council. Fish-curer Thomas Cormack at Caddies Burn was severely rebuked for the insanitary condition of his yard. And so on. But all the parochial trivia of the time are dwarfed by the disasters of 1875, to which George Gourlay devotes over thirty pages of his *Fisher Life*.

This time the drama unfolded in the waters off East Anglia, where around fifty East Neuk boats had gone that autumn to try their luck. The first mishap occurred during a gale on the night of October 21st, when James Gardner, a 47-year-old bachelor, was caught by a flapping sail and hurled to his death in the offing of Lowestoft. He was the second son of Alexander Gardner and Ann Sutherland, and the family headstone in Kilrenny churchyard bears a fitting epitaph:

> A wat'ry grave we do not dread
> The sea shall render back it[s] dead
> And restore each scattered bone
> And land you safe on canaan's shore
> Where sin and death divides no more
> The glorious land at home.

During the next few weeks the gales continued to blow off and on, reaching a new pitch of fury on November 14th, when the sea-wall at Cellardyke was battered down and the few boats in the harbour had to be hauled to safety. As the hurricane-force winds lashed the whole eastern seaboard, the East Neuk fleet began the long and hazardous run home, and during the following days crowds gathered at the Braehead and other outlook points kept an anxious watch out to sea for a familiar sail breaking the horizon.

The details can be pieced together from contemporary newsletters, and from the accounts of those who returned. Skipper Alexander Watson ran into trouble rounding St. Abb's, and five other boats were forced to run for Holy Island. Others took refuge at Shields, while others again had to return to the coast of Norfolk. David Wood's *Excelsior* was tacking for Grimsby when a 17-year-old lad, Alexander McRuvie, went over the side. Skipper George Anderson's brother-in-law John Watson, 'a free-hearted and gallant mariner',[18] was washed overboard in similar circumstances, and Robert Brown, the brother-in-law of Skipper Robert Davidson, was struck on the forehead by a yardarm and suffered a fractured skull. James Murray's *Janet Anderson* disappeared off the Farne Islands, and not until her helm was washed ashore a week later at Cullercoats in Northumberland was her fate certain. Along with the 24-year-old skipper, who was to have been married on his return home, there perished Andrew Stewart, William Bridges, James Walker, Alexander Lothian and Hugh and William McKay. About the same time the *Vigilant* foundered on the Inner Dowsing, some thirteen miles to the leeward of her true course, and the dead were Robert and William Stewart; 45-year-old James McRuvie and his son James, aged 16; Alexander Doig and Leslie Brown. Luckier than these were Alexander Stevenson of the *Brothers*, William Watson (Rodger) of the *Waverley* and William Moncrieff (Scott) of the *Dolphin* who finally managed to beat a path home to Anstruther harbour.

In this, the most terrible disaster ever to hit the Fife fishing-communities, Cellardyke lost fifteen men and St. Monans twenty-one, and seventy-one children in the two towns were rendered fatherless. In St. Monans one woman lost at a stroke her husband, her son, two brothers, three nephews, a brother-in-law and a cousin. However much the material conditions of life might be improved, and the design and seaworthiness of the fishing-fleet perfected, there was still no anticipating the appalling capriciousness of wind and tide.

In the succeeding decade there were to be other martyrs to the sea. Only a year after the disasters of 1875 it was the turn of Skipper William Watson (Jack), who in the early hours of October 16th, 1876, missed his footing by the edge of the wharf at Yarmouth and plunged into oblivion. William Watson was the son of James Forrester Watson and Margaret Sime; and his fate is all the more poignant because he had only been persuaded at the last minute to take a berth in John and George Doig's *Victoria Cross*. Another member of the same crew, David Doig (Wood), was lost off the May Island, and in March 1877 yet another relative, Robert Doig, was drowned near the Marr Bank. The following year John Montidor, skipper and owner of the *Jacobina*, was drowned at Lowestoft. Just over a week later the skipper of the *Polar Star*, Alexander Watson (Bett), was swept from the helm by a heavy sea in the offing of

Lowestoft pier. 'Star Elick' was the son of James 'Star Jeems' Watson and Margaret Reid, and the brother of that 'Star Davie' who would be one of the leading skippers of his generation.

On January 28th, 1880, skipper James Bett perished in the offing of Stonehaven, and on February 29th Andrew Brown (Brunton) and Andrew Fleming were washed overboard during a gale. Andrew Muir was another casualty of the same storm. On April 21st skipper Adam Watson's *Garland* was engaged in line-fishing over a hundred miles beyond the May Island when one of the most violent southerly gales of the season blew up out of nowhere. While Thomas Watson held fast to the foresheet and his namesake David Watson busied himself on the lee gunwale with the guard ropes, the *Garland* abandoned her lines and turned for home. Suddenly, a tremendous wave burst over the boat, and both men were hurled into the sea. Thomas Watson let go the sheet, thereby probably saving the boat, and was not seen again. David Watson, after an incredible forty-five minutes in the sea, was rescued at the fifth desperate attempt. Another crewman, John Stewart, was hurled along the deck with such force that his leg was broken against a projecting plank.

Thomas Watson, who left a widow and one child, was the son of Thomas Watson (Martin), and a grandson of 'Water Willie' Watson and Mary Galloway. His brother James Watson ('Hansey') was to become a well-known trawler skipper in Aberdeen. The year after this disaster the *Garland* was involved in another near-tragedy when her lines became entangled with those of the *Good Design* out in the North Sea. David Watson was dragged overboard, but once again escaped by the skin of his teeth.

In comparison with these tragedies events ashore pale into insignificance, although as usual there was no shortage of controversial issues to excite the townspeople. Principal among these, as the '70s gave way to the '80s, was the new church at Toll Road.

It is difficult now to recapture the mood which led to the split in the Kilrenny congregation, but the dissatisfaction of the Cellardyke fisherfolk with the new Kilrenny minister was at least partly to blame. The Rev. George Anderson, a Glaswegian by birth, was admitted to the ministry of Kilrenny in November 1878; and before very long he had, it seems, alienated a large section of his flock. One of his leading opponents was the Anstruther banker and lawyer Philip Oliphant, and matters finally came to a head one Sunday morning when Mr. Oliphant rose from his pew and stalked out of the church, the minister calling after him from the pulpit, 'The wicked flee when no man pursueth' (Prov.28:1)![19]

Stung by this public humiliation, Philip Oliphant approached some of the more well-to-do local skippers, and before long a sum of money had been collected towards building a new church for Cellardyke alone. There were already many Dykers who preferred to worship in the Free Kirk in Anstruther or to attend the gospel meetings in the Forth Street hall: but on March 6th, 1881, they were presented with their very own church at Williamson Street opposite the new primary school.

The first minister, a young licentiate named Charles Ross, served only from April 1881 to March 1882 before being succeeded by the Rev. James Hiram Watson of Eccles in Berwickshire. So tenuous was this pastor's attachment to his seafaring parish that after some eight months he threw up the ministry altogether to devote himself to the profession of literature, and the production of such masterpieces as *Black Agnes, a Romance of the Siege of Dunbar*, and *Trick, Trial and Triumph: a Clerical Detective Story*. One wonders what the Rev. Anderson in his Kilrenny manse made of it all.

On March 28th, 1883, Cellardyke was disjoined from the parish of Kilrenny – breaking an ecclesiastical link of three centuries – and only weeks later the Rev. James Ray was ordained first minister of the new parish. It was a case of third time lucky, for the busy, energetic little pastor was to rule his flock for some thirty-three years: the seal of acceptance being his marriage in 1888 to Agnes Bonthrone Oliphant, the daughter of Philip Oliphant.[20]

Somewhat less controversial than these events was the building of the new town hall, the brainchild of the London merchant David Fowler – son of the late James Fowler – and his old schoolfriend Stephen Williamson M.P. The foundation-stone was laid in April 1882, and a sealed jar containing copies of town-council minutes, together with George Gourlay's *Fisher Life*, various editions of the *Scotsman*, the *Daily Review*, the *Fife News* and the *East of Fife Record*, a list of the current magistrates and councillors and a photograph of the old Tolbooth, was inserted in a wall cavity.

A year and a half later, on September 19th, 1883, the new Town Hall was officially opened by Stephen Williamson; and for an account of the proceedings we can turn to a little book entitled *The Lights and Shadows of a Fisher's Life*, by local fisherman William Smith (Melville).[21] The day started in lively fashion with Mr. Williamson being carried shoulder high to the accompaniment of a band playing 'See the Conquering Hero Comes'. On arrival at the hall, the M.P. was joined by Provost Watson, ex-provost Martin, the new minister of Cellardyke Mr. Ray, and James Fowler, son of the late David Fowler. Then, mounting a bench, he

James Street, Cellardyke, looking east towards the Town Hall. Taken on April 23rd, 1906.

launched into an encomium on the town of Cellardyke and the unprecedented extent and value of the local fisheries in that year of 1883. The
number of boats had now risen to 203, employing 650 men and boys, and
the total value of boats now stood at £63,940 – almost double the figure
for so recent a date as 1868. In fact, Cellardyke stood second only to
Buckie among Scottish fishing-ports; and, in conclusion, '. . . he was
sure that so far as concerned industry, energy, bravery and good conduct the Cellardyke fishermen were second to none in the United
Kingdom'.[22] The applause of the listening crowd may be imagined.

In the days following the grand opening of the hall café facilities were
added, and a committee consisting of William Moncrieff, David Reid,

John Wood, Adam Reid, James Walker, Peter Murray and Thomas Brown obtained permission for two hours of light entertainment to be offered on Saturday evenings, with the stipulation that only light refreshments would be available. Here was a refined alternative to the town's many taverns and beer shops. A few years later an act regulating licensed premises laid down that public houses should not open before 8 a.m. and should shut at 10 p.m., except for travellers or guests. Here was Temperance indeed!

To complete the picture of Victorian gentility we read in the *East of Fife Record* of the formation of Cellardyke cricket club. This band of enthusiasts met at Rennyhill in Kilrenny until 1884, when it was decided to move to a park beside the railway line at St. Andrews Road, Anstruther. In May 1884 the committee of the club consisted of G. Black, Captain; D. Clark, Vice-Captain; J. Dick, Secretary; A. Doig, Treasurer; and W. Morton, D. Doig, D. Christie and D. Ritchie, members. A moderate sum was charged to gentlemen spectators, but ladies were admitted free of charge.

After the tragedies of the 1870s there was a happier period when no lives were lost at sea, although the above-mentioned year of 1884 saw the deaths of two well-loved young men. One morning in June 20-year-old Thomas Fleming was found dead in his bunk in John Barclay's boat at Shetland, and only four months later his exact contemporary Alexander Doig died on the eve of departing for a new life in New Zealand. Alexander had been treasurer of the cricket club, and a full-sized portrait of the team intended as a parting gift was presented instead to the grieving mother. The boy's father, Michael Doig, was a prominent local skipper, and the family lived at 58 James Street.

There are two other issues which are pertinent to this year of 1884: both of them illustrating the way in which old ways were yielding to new, as the pressures of the modern world encroached on old Cellardyke.

The first issue was an educational one. In 1883 a new Education Act had for the first time made provision for parents to be prosecuted if their children regularly absented themselves from school, and the following year saw the first prosecutions under the Act in the East Neuk. Hardbitten fishermen who had traditionally relegated such concerns to their womenfolk found themselves, to their surprise, in court – and the experience was a chastening one. On March 14th, 1884, it was Robert Anderson of 30 West Forth Street who was forced to account for his 12-year-old son George having been found 'selling herrings near Kilrenny'. In his defence the unfortunate father pointed out that he had been away for five months at Shetland, then at the Peterhead fishing, then at

Scarborough. Only at intervals of several months did he have any contact with his son.

James Moncrieff of 4 George Street had even greater problems with his son Alexander, aged 10. The boy was completely beyond his parents' control. 'I have tried speaking to him, and I have tried licking him until I was sorry', reported the despairing parent. A few hours in the lock-up at Anstruther, he told the court, might provide a useful lesson. Similar cases were related by George Brown, David Muir, David Watson (53 George Street), Robert Wallace and George Corstorphine. A new spirit of respectability might be in the air, but the youth of Cellardyke seemed to be blissfully impervious to it.

For those who *were* alive to the benefits of education, the opening of the Waid Academy at Anstruther in September 1886 ushered in a new era of opportunity. Children aged 10 and over were offered a range of subjects from Classics to Vocal and Instrumental Music, and the more fortunate sex could expect to be prepared for 'Commercial or Professional life, the Civil Service, the Royal Navy, the Universities, &c.'; while their sisters made do with 'the Branches usually taught in similar Seminaries'.[23] However, the quarterly fees and the requirement of a pass in the entrance examination must have deterred many a potential young seeker after knowledge.

The other major issue in 1884 was much more prosaic, if no less important. Cellardyke's drinking water – still fetched in the time-honoured way from wells in the Urquhart Wynd and elsewhere, and still a source of pride to many of the older inhabitants – had been found to be contaminated with organic matter. The question now arose of whether or not to close the wells and bring in a piped supply from outside the town. Veritable battles had formerly been fought in the council chamber for less than this, and the combative spirit of local statesmen was still far from dead. On June 5th, 1884, a meeting of the town council provided an opportunity for opposing views to be aired, and the presence at the meeting of Dr. Henry Littlejohn of Edinburgh – the emissary of the Board of Supervision – did little to cool tempers. The whole proceedings were reported in the following day's *East of Fife Record*.

The first outburst of indignation was provoked by Provost Skinner's incautious admission that he was not satisfied with the Edinburgh professor Macadam's analysis of the local water, and that he had accordingly ordered another, independent, analysis:

BAILIE SMITH – That analysis was ordered by the Water Committee.

TREASURER THOMSON – I call that in question. I am a member of the Water Committee, and they never agreed to get such an analysis.

BAILIE SMITH – But I say that they did.

TREASURER THOMSON – It is a private analysis, and no authority was given either by the Council or Committee to get it.

BAILIE SMITH – You are a member of the Committee, and you knew all about it.

TREASURER THOMSON – I was never consulted in the matter at all.

BAILIE SMITH – You were consulted.

TREASURER THOMSON – No such thing.

MR. MARTIN – I may inform Dr. Littlejohn that . . .

BAILIE SMITH (interrupting) – You were consulted about the opening of the wells.

MR. MARTIN – Order, Mr. Smith. (Hear, hear).

BAILIE SMITH – You are Chairman, are you? . . . (No.) . . . Well, hold your tongue.

With difficulty, Dr. Littlejohn endeavoured to prise out of the council some objective information about the various wells then in use in the town. Then, with prophetic foresight, he touched on a subject which was to exercise future generations:

DR. LITTLEJOHN – Suppose you got a good supply of water into the town, would that not induce summer visitors to come here?

THE PROVOST – Who would come here?

DR. LITTLEJOHN – I don't know, but I will tell you my experience of your East of Fife Coast Burghs. Some years ago I took my children to Lower Largo. They were not long there when I had to take them away – they were all laid down by typhoid fever on account of the bad water supply. Therefore, I don't look with a kindly favour upon the eastern villages at all.

This affront to local pride was too much for the volatile baillie, but indignation was no match for urbanity: and before long he was reduced to a fuming silence:

BAILIE SMITH – But it is different with us here. I have known people who have lived to past 90 years of age with the present water.

DR. LITTLEJOHN – But these are only the people that survive. (Laughter)

BAILIE SMITH – It shows that the water is not bad.

DR. LITTLEJOHN – I beg your pardon, Some people can never be poisoned – (great laughter) – they are so tough. I could put you into as unsanitary a house as you will find, and it would do you no harm, but if I were to put a stranger in he would be struck down at once.

BAILIE SMITH – I can believe that.

DR. LITTLEJOHN – For instance yourself, you are about as tough a man as I have seen for a long time – (loud laughter) – and I say disease would have very little effect upon you (Renewed laughter).

BAILIE SMITH – I don't agree with your medical opinion. We don't want the water.

For centuries Dykers had endured all manner of perils by land and sea, and emerged triumphant. But against the new-fangled menace of bureaucracy there was no defence. In the second week of July the council received the Board of Supervision's conclusion that a water supply or supplies by gravitation must be introduced into the burgh of Kilrenny at the earliest opportunity.

We cannot leave this interesting year of 1884 without commemorating a cause which, for once, united rather than divided the townspeople. At this date the burghs of less than royal origins, such as St. Monans and Kingsbarns (Kilrenny still clung on to the spurious status of royal burgh), were still deprived of the right to vote for a Member of Parliament, and a Franchise Bill which would have put right this anomaly had been thrown out by the House of Lords. Furious at this high-handed treatment of their just demands, the Liberal voters of the East Neuk declared a half-holiday on Friday, September 18th, and set about organising a demonstration to show the strength of their feelings. In the event, the turn-out was even better than expected, not least in Cellardyke. Let the local news media take up the story:

EAST OF FIFE RECORD, Saturday, September 26th., 1884.

In Cellardyke there were a great many manifestations of approval on the part of the inhabitants with the object of the demonstration. Messrs. Duncan & Black at their net factory had the words painted in large bold letters, 'The Lords caught in their own', at which was hung a net. A little further along on their premises was an effigy of Lord Salisbury, with his right hand uplifted grasping a scroll of paper and supposed to be giving vent to his 'flaunts, jibes, and jeers'. The likeness, which did not bear a very striking resemblance to the leader of the Opposition in the Lords, was placed outside the door of the loft, with the words above his head, 'Salisbury out in the cold'. The representation afforded much amusement, and was received with roars of laughter by the processionists. Above their shop in James Street Messrs. Thomson & Son had a large flag, on which an old worn-out shoe was meant to represent the House of Lords, with the words underneath, 'The Upper House can't be mended. 'Tis thoroughly worn out.' In the same street, and immediately in front of the Town Hall, Mr. P. Thomson had a very beautiful display. A row of flags was stretched across the street, and on the centre one the following appeared:– 'Gladstone – Williamson – the East of Fife fishermen will hook the House of Lords', underneath which there was a representation of herrings being hung on a hook. Ex-Provost Watson displayed a number of flags, on one of which he asked the crowds to give 'three cheers for the Franchise Bill'. This was complied with in a hearty manner again and again.

Prosperity and progress were the order of the day, for the herring-fishery had been enjoying boom conditions since the early '50s. Now that steam drifters were coming into circulation – and Fife fishermen were among the first to make the transition from sail to steam – greater quantities of herring than ever could be caught, and as the drifter could also be adapted for great-line fishing in deeper waters, the same was true of white-fish catches. Yet it was a fragile prosperity, at best. The expansion of the industry had been promoted first and foremost by the curers, who in order to retain the services of fishermen contracted to them were forced to promise them higher and higher rates per cran – rates which depended on the price of cured herring being kept artificially high. If a glut occurred, or a foreign competitor – such as one of the Scandinavian countries – entered the market, then prices were depressed and the curers found themselves in trouble. As most of them financed their commercial ventures by borrowing heavily from banks or money-lenders, they had no margin for error, and a bad season with low profits could lead them into bankruptcy. In 1884 just such a situation arose, triggered off in early summer by a more than adequate catch from the Lewis fishery of low-grade herring which proved difficult to sell in the finicky German market. Prices dropped, commitments to the fishermen on the one hand and the banks on the other could not be honoured, and the greater part of the season's catch had to be sold to the curers at a loss, in many cases, of £1 a barrel. It was a good ten years before trade picked up again. One effect of the slump, meanwhile, was that the curers lost their dominant position as backers of the fishing industry to the salesmen, who eventually succeeded in imposing their unpopular auction system on the fishermen of Scotland.[24]

What effect, if any, did the advances of the '70s and '80s have on the daily life and circumstances of the fishermen themselves? The net financial effect is difficult to calculate, for men might have shares, and different amounts or types of gear, invested in more than one boat; and the wealth accruing from bigger catches must be balanced against the

F

Some advertisements for Cellardyke firms from the endpapers of George Gourlay's *Anstruther*, published in 1888.

higher costs of the new technology. But for at least one commentator, writing in the year 1884 in a spirit of true Victorian optimism, there was no doubting the new-found prosperity of the fisher-class: 'Well-to-do fishermen are sure to possess, first, a house and furniture; second boat and gear, or perhaps shares of a large and a small boat; third nets, lines and other fishing materials. The heads of families are generally tolerably comfortable as regards means. A small proportion may, through unfortunate circumstances, be poor for a time, but perseverance soon overcomes the poverty. The various banks receive a goodly amount of money on deposit from them; and when we consider that mostly all the houses in the fishing villages which they inhabit belong to themselves, for the greater part, we must allow that as a class they are both powerful and rich. Young fishermen as they earn and save money, invest it in their friends' or relatives' boats, thereby securing an interest in the boat, and therefore in the industry'.[25]

Yet there was more to the Cellardyke fishermen of the late nineteenth century than this classic depiction of Victorian capitalism would suggest, for the break with the past was not total, and the skippers and crews of the new drifters carried with them into the new age a large share of the attitudes and preconceptions of past generations. It is notoriously hard to pin down fishermen's superstitions to definite beliefs and practices, but from the reminiscences of William Smith (Melville) and his namesake 'Auld Wull', aided by modern oral tradition, we can piece together something of the mental world of the nineteenth-century Cellardyke fisherman.

One belief which has survived into modern times, and which is well attested in Gourlay's *Fisher Life*, is that of precognition – usually taking the form of a dead ancestor beckoning in a dream to a member of a doomed crew, on the eve of disaster. Another concerns the use at sea of taboo words for persons or animals regarded as 'uncanny', or the undesirability of such taboo items being brought on board – as the following anecdote illustrates:

'The most superstitious of the fishermen in the Cellardyke community at that time (the 1890s) was a skipper named Tam Bett. A fisherman going aboard for a week or so's trip usually carried his food in a small barrel, but if he had any left over, maybe a loaf or so, he would often carry this tied up in a 'cloot'. If Tam got you with a cloot fastened with a safety-pin instead of a knot he would throw the cloot and all into the sea.

'Pigs (Taboo-name: cauldies) were of course extremely unlucky. On one occasion some of the lads played a trick on Tam Bett. They got the carcass of a pig and hoisted it to the top of his mizzen-mast before a trip. When the fleet had set sail and were about a mile out of harbour one of Tam Bett's hands spotted this. Tam himself was at the tiller and looking ahead. 'There's something at the top o your mizzen-mast, skipper,' shouted the sailor. 'What is't?' said Tam. 'I'm fear't to tell ye.' 'Well, let's hae it down and see what it is.'

'If Tam had got the laddie that did that, said Mr Carstairs, he would have knifed him for certain. Anyway Tam's boat turned about and spent the period of that trip in harbour. . . . The antidote for the infringement of a taboo is of course to touch cauld iron. . . . When Tam Bett had the pig's carcass on board he had all his crew touching one of the anchors that was lying on the deck.'[26]

Another set of beliefs sought to explain why the elusive herring so often disappeared completely from east-coast waters, and fisheries inspector George Reiach was moved to set down a total of seventeen reasons advanced to him by the fisherfolk. These were: 1. burning kelp;

2. running steamboats; 3. ringing church bells; 4. firing large guns; 5. fishing on Sundays; 6. fishing with seine trawl; 7. catching immature herrings; 8. using herrings for manure; 9. herrings being caught, and allowed to lie rotting in the sea; 10. fishing during daylight; 11. garvie fishing; 12. using small-meshed nets; 13. rainy season; 14. dog-fish; 15. thunder; 16. stormy weather; 17. wickedness of the people.[27]

Through all this varied list a common thread of logic – a determination to explain a natural phenomenon by natural means – is combined with an atavistic linking of the availability of fish stocks *with acceptable human behaviour*: an attitude which recalls the Dark Age legend of St. Thenaw. The last-named reason – the wickedness of the people – was especially dear to the hearts of the fisherfolk, and scoffers were referred by the pious to the Book of Hosea, chapter 4, verses 2 and 3: 'By swearing, and lying, and killing, and stealing, and committing adultery, they break out, and blood toucheth blood. Therefore shall the land mourn, and every one that dwelleth therein shall languish, with the beasts of the field, and with the fowls of heaven; *yea, the fishes of the sea also shall be taken away*'.

Yet another belief concerned the 'unluckiness' of certain surnames, which could not be uttered at sea. In Cellardyke the name in question was 'Marr'. Charles Marr senior and his wife Isabella Watson (a grand-daughter of 'Water Willie') were the parents of a large brood of sons, all of whom were fishermen like their father,[28] and while at sea both father and sons were addressed or referred to by the appellation 'the laud (i.e. lad)': as, 'Auld Chairlie the laud', 'Young Chairlie the laud', 'Tam the laud', etc. They were not permitted to help shoot the nets, but *were* allowed to help haul them in, by which time the size of the catch had presumably been decided by Fate. This strange superstition may be connected with the fact that Marr ends in a double consonant, for similar names, such as 'Watt', 'Ross' and 'Coull', have traditionally been re-garded as unlucky in various parts of the north-east.[29]

These, then, were the Cellardyke fishermen of the late nineteenth century: conservative in belief but radical in practice. But what of their many fellow-townsmen and -women whose 'industry and energy' drove them to the even more radical expedient of forsaking their native shores? We have already noticed the emigration of Cellardyke men to the Australian goldfields, and the headstones in Kilrenny churchyard bear testimony to many who died there, as well as to the few who came back. There we learn of shipmaster David Watson, who died on his way to St. George's Sound in 1870, and of his son Robert, buried at Adelaide; of Margaret Cunningham, the niece of 'Baxter Rob', who died at Melbourne,

Captain Alexander Rodger, master of the China tea-clippers *Kate Carnie* and *Ellen Rodger*, and owner of the *Min*, *Lahloo* and *Taeping*. Captain Rodger's shipping firm was based in Glasgow. Among other generous acts, he bought the Town's Green at Cellardyke and presented it to his fellow-townspeople.

and Thomas Birrell in Geelong; or of William Doig who lies buried at Williamstown, George Fowler at Mitcham, and John Crawford at Melbourne. Both John Meldrum (Gellatly) and William Jack returned from the gold-diggings at Matakanui, Otago, New Zealand, to lie in their native soil. Others died at Halifax, Nova Scotia, or Vancouver, or Evansville, Indiana; while Alexander Smith died at Hangkow, China, and Alexander Fowler on board the *Northern Bride* on the river Hooghly. Wherever men 'go down to the sea in ships', the mariners of old Cellardyke were there.

Three men in particular deserve a special mention here. Only six years before the ceremonial opening of the new town hall there died in Glasgow one of the foremost sailors of Cellardyke. Captain Alexander

Rodger (1802–77) was the son of Elizabeth Watson and of that David
Rodger who perished at the Burntisland drave of 1814. As a young man
Alexander was 'one of the most active young fishermen of his time',[30]
and most of his leisure moments were spent in the study of navigation.
At the age of nineteen he moved over to the merchant service as a sailor
on board a collier, and by the age of 22 he was in command of a brig
trading to the Mediterranean. Later he became captain of the first large
ship to sail from Glasgow to Australia. Once, when a sunken reef in the
Indian Ocean almost brought him to grief, he took careful soundings and
reported its position to the Admiralty, whose charts were thenceforth
amended to include 'Rodger's Rock'.

In later life, when ill-health forced him to retire from the sea, Captain
Rodger devised a series of business ventures: one of which was the
expedition by Cellardyke fishermen to the Australian goldfields. Then
his interest turned to the China tea-trade, and before long he was the
owner of a fleet of tea-clippers including the *Kate Carnie, Taeping,
Lahloo* and *Min*: vessels which have been numbered among 'the most
beautiful and yacht-like merchantmen that ever sailed the seas'.[31] If
Alexander Rodger has any claim to lasting fame, it is perhaps as the
owner of the ship which in 1866 was to break all previous records for
the trip from the Pagoda Anchorage of Foochow to London's grimy
dockland.

As a historian of the China tea clippers once put it: 'It is probable that
no race ever sailed on blue water created so much excitement as the great
tea race of 1866. For some years past the public interest had been
growing, until it had now come to pass that even those who dwelt in
sleepy inland villages looked eagerly down the shipping column of the
morning papers for news of the racing clippers. And if this interest was
shown by landsmen who had no connection with either the ships or the
trade, it is not surprising that the great shipping community of Great
Britain looked upon the tea races much as the British public look upon
the Derby or the Boat Race'.[32]

Even the City of London, financial hub of the empire and home to
some of the most cynical gamblers of the time, was stirred to a fever
pitch of speculation: all the more so when, after ninety-odd days out, the
dash up the English Channel became a two-horse race between the
Taeping and her great rival the *Ariel*. Yet nowhere was the suspense more
keenly felt than in far-off Cellardyke and its neighbouring burgh – for if
Captain Alexander Rodger was Cellardyke's own, Captain John Melville
Keay of the *Ariel* was a son of Anstruther Wester. (The crew of the
Taeping included, at various times, George Fowler, David Watson

(Murray) and John Watson (son of James Watson (Salter)) of Cellardyke, and there may well have been Anstruther men aboard the *Ariel*.)

The end of the race had all the drama of a first-rate thriller, even to the final twist in the tail. The *Ariel* arrived outside the East India Dock well before the *Taeping*, which made for the more distant London Dock, arriving there a full thirteen hours later. However, the *Taeping*, drawing less water than the *Ariel*, was able to enter her dock a nail-biting twenty minutes before her rival. Leaving the Min River of South China on the same tide, the *Ariel* and *Taeping* had docked in the River Thames on the same tide. It was a spectacular achievement. No less spectacular was the generosity of the *Taeping*'s master, Captain McKinnon, who promptly offered to share his winner's bonus of £100 with his defeated adversary. The two owners also split the bonus of 10 shillings per ton of tea which was traditionally added to the price of the winning ship's cargo. Captains Rodger and Keay occupy an honoured place in the folklore of this most romantic of all maritime pursuits, and today plaques mark the houses, in Cellardyke and Anstruther respectively, where once they lived; while their portraits hang side by side in the Scottish Fisheries Museum in Anstruther.

Our next hero was not only born in the same year as Alexander Rodger, but was also his classmate in Dominie Moncrieff's school at the Braehead.[33] Although born in Pittenweem, Sir Walter Watson Hughes was brought up in Cellardyke, where his first taste of work on leaving school was at George Sharp's cooperage. Later he spent a winter at the lines in skipper Robert Cunningham's boat the *Friends*,[34] before trying his luck as a curer. There followed a brief spell on Captain Smith's Leith whaler the *William and Anne*, and a trip to the Gulf of Finland on the *Ocean* of Dundee, before the young sailor's restless spirit led him on board a ship bound for the East Indies.

'I sling my hammock in the forecastle, but I am resolved to spread my cot in the cabin',[35] he wrote to his father, and indeed before long he was owner and master of the brig *Hero* – and dodging imperial war-junks on the opium run through the China Seas to Bangkok. Having won the friendship of the Siamese royal family and lulled their suspicions of the foreigner with rich gifts, Hughes felt secure to pursue his nefarious trade, but his activities were discovered, and a trap was laid. Only the timely intervention of a friendly courtier prevented him from attending a banquet in the royal palace which would have climaxed with his arrest. Without pausing for the niceties of leavetaking he regained his ship and ran for home. It was the end of Walter Hughes's career in the Orient.

Never one to wallow in defeat, our 'hero' was soon deeply involved in another commercial venture: this time in the infant colony of South Australia, where sheep provided a more wholesome speculation than the deadly poppy. But the colony's treasures were not all on the hoof, for already large mineral deposits had been uncovered here as in the rest of the continent. When Walter Hughes brought his flocks to graze at Wallaroo and Moonta, in the arid Yorke Peninsula – a sheep-run the size of Fife – it was not the pasture that attracted him, but his seaman's keen-eyed observation that the tree-roots here burnt with a green flame.

To cut a long story short, the copper deposits discovered at Wallaroo and Moonta made Walter Hughes the richest man in Australia, while the miners imported from Britain would eventually form the largest Cornish community beyond Land's End. In the grim shanty town that sprang up by the seashore, Welsh smeltermen kept their language alive for forty years in sermons and hymns. 'Visitors who came by ship on a stormy evening could see across the water the glare of furnaces reflected in the clouds and white smoke trailing across a black sky. Morning did not soften the landscape.'[36] Victorian capitalism had come to this barren landscape with a vengeance.

Like most of Hughes's ventures it had been a close-run thing. The dubious manner in which his mineral leases had been acquired led to a select committee finding against him, but neither Supreme Court nor Privy Council could dislodge him. Yesterday's opium-runner was today's respectable industrialist, and generous donations to carefully-chosen 'good causes' only served to enhance his standing. In 1872 a gift of £20,000 to the Presbyterian Union College of Adelaide allowed that institution to dream of higher status, and today Sir Walter Watson Hughes is honoured as the founding father of the University of Adelaide.

There were other ventures too. Hughes owned large properties north-east and north-west of Watervale, and planted the first Riesling vines at Springvale, where in the early 1860s he established Hughes Park Station. The 896 square miles of his Gum Creek pasturage fed 60,500 of his sheep, and in 1872 he bought the Lake Albert and Peninsula estate, which eventually grew to over 33,000 acres. More spectacularly, Hughes and his fellow tycoon Thomas Elder provided the financial backing for Colonel Egerton Warburton's epic trek from Alice Springs to the north-west of the continent in 1872. Elder, a native of Kirkcaldy, was an enthusiastic advocate of the Asiatic camel as the solution to Australia's long-distance transportation problems; and it was with 17 of these excellent beasts to carry his provisions that the intrepid colonel set out on his epoch-making expedition. Two years and 2,000 miles later, having conquered the Great Sandy Desert and eaten the last of their camels, the remnants of the little party staggered into the coastal settlement which was journey's end. Invaluable knowledge had been gained about 'some of the driest and most difficult areas of the continent',[37] and part of the credit must go to Walter Hughes.

In 1873 Hughes retired to England, and in 1880 he was knighted for his services to South Australia: the first native of the East Neuk to be so honoured for other than political services. Finally, on New Year's Eve, 1887, Sir Walter Watson Hughes died peacefully in his villa at Chertsey, in the heart of suburban Surrey. 'Shrewd, gentle and kind' is a biographer's somewhat curious verdict on the old buccaneer whose career so nearly ended on a Siamese gallows.[38]

Our last eminent Dyker was made of soberer stuff. Stephen Williamson was born in 1827 to Archibald Williamson, a future manager of the burgh in the years of disfranchisement, and his heiress wife Isabella Lawson, and at the early age of 24 he became the co-founder of the Liverpool shipping firm of Balfour, Williamson & Co. Soon the firm's activities had spread to the Americas, with branch offices in Valparaiso and San Francisco, but Stephen's ambition went beyond mere commercial success. In April 1880 he entered Parliament as Liberal M.P. for the St. Andrews district of burghs (i.e. the East Neuk), and although he was later to transfer his allegiance to Kilmarnock, he remained from first to last a champion of British shipping interests and in particular of the Scottish fisherman. Stephen Williamson died in 1903 at his home in Cheshire, and was survived by his eight children and by his wife, a daughter of Dr. Thomas Guthrie of 'Ragged School' fame.

The name Williamson is an honoured one in our burgh, for an earlier Stephen Williamson was a councillor of Kilrenny from 1693 until 1719, and at least seven generations of the family worshipped in Kilrenny church.[39] Stephen's father and grandfather were both in their day baron baillies to the lairds of Kilrenny, and like any other son of Cellardyke the M.P. had strong links with the fisherfolk. His father was a cousin of fisherman David Watson's wife Elspeth Salter, so that Stephen and David Watson junior (Murray) were second cousins. Stephen's son Archibald Williamson junior was raised to the peerage as the 1st Baron Forres of Glenogil. David Watson's son James Murray Watson (Watson) followed his father to the fishing. Archibald junior's great-grandson Alastair Williamson, 4th Baron Forres, is a successful businessman in Australia. James Murray Watson's great-grandson is the author of this book.

Ever the realist where the fishing industry was concerned, Stephen Williamson had been an early advocate of the trawler. Not until 1890, however, did he receive backing from the East Fife men, and then the support was a trickle rather than a flood. In a letter to the *East of Fife Record*, published on May 23rd, he set out his position on the issue with the dry logic which was his hallmark: 'Now I have been asked to take an interest in one or two steam trawlers with the view of endeavouring to restore some life to the white-fishing industry at Anstruther. I am quite willing to do so, but only on condition that the experiment does not meet with strong opposition from the great body of the fishermen. When I had to do with the representation of the burghs their opposition to trawling was often very strongly expressed to me, but I am informed that their views are now greatly modified. When I hear (as I recently did), of a crew toiling a whole week at sea and only making, during all that time, four shillings per man, it appears to me that matters cannot be worse than they are now'.

The local skippers were not slow to respond, and for weeks to come the correspondence columns of the newspaper were awash with passion, polemic and – occasionally – good sense. Skipper Michael Doig took the M.P.'s part:

'... In the year 1883 five fishermen joined together to get a trawling vessel, as we believed that trawling was sure to increase, and the sooner we went into it the better. But the opposition amongst fishermen was so strong that in the spring of 1884 we gave it up. I was of opinion at the time we did wrong to do so. Had we done so and succeeded it would have been better for the most of the fishermen, as plenty of them would have started trawling, who are not in a position to do so now.'

'Wives and mithers, maist despairin',
Ca' them lives o' men.' (Lady Nairne, *Caller Herrin'*)

Boats and gear might change, but not the cruel sea. On the morning of April 7th, 1890, the *Garland*, *Carmi II*, *Alaska* and *Lavinia* left for the North Sea fishing-grounds under a threatening sky full of scudding clouds. By ten o'clock the gale had risen to such a fury that the *Alaska*'s head-rope, all twenty-two plies of it, snapped like a cotton thread. This was followed by a mighty wave of such magnitude that skipper David Davidson, his mate Peter Muir, John Watson and Alexander Falconer were swept helplessly along the deck. The rail saved the first three, but the 19-year-old Falconer was lost to sight among the breakers. A native of Fisherrow, he had been much loved in his adoptive home for his quiet and unassuming ways.

Yet worse was to come. The *Carmi II*, making her maiden voyage, let

The *Carmi II*, skipper Tam Anderson ('Carmi Tam'), at Yarmouth. Built in 1890, she made her maiden voyage in the storm which wrecked the *Garland*, and her crew were the last people to see the doomed boat.

go her nets around noon and trimmed her sail for home. Before long she was shooting like an arrow past the stricken *Garland*, still plunging wildly at her nets. It was the last time the doomed vessel was seen above the water. Not until a week later were fragments picked up far out at sea – her bowsprit, and some other sad relics.

The loss of the *Garland* was a peculiarly emotive tragedy, for several reasons. Her usual skipper, William Watson (Smith), had been prevented by illness from making this trip, and his elderly father Adam Watson had only taken his place at the last minute. David Watson (Murray) had had two earlier brushes with death, as we have seen, and on another occasion had fallen from the mizzen of the tea-clipper *Taeping* into the China seas. Robert Brown (22) was the breadwinner of his family, his father having been disabled aboard Robert Davidson's boat in the dreadful gale of 1875. Robert Watson, at 16 the 'baby' of the crew, had repeatedly asked his father to let him go to the deep sea in the *Garland*, and each time had been refused – until now (Robert's father was William Watson (Moncrieff) of the *Fiery Cross*). The other victims, John Brown (30) and Alexander Smith (Gardner), left two widows and a child. They were as fine a crew of seamen as any upon the coast, with a boat to match. Ironically, the *Garland*'s ballast had been set in concrete, making her more stable than the average vessel of the period. Now that concrete in her bowels kept her firmly anchored to the seabed.

In the following weeks many affecting addresses on the fate of the *Garland* were made in the local churches, and these, together with an account of the disaster itself, were collected by the old bookseller George Gourlay into a pamphlet entitled *The Sorrow of the Sea: being a Narrative of the Loss of the 'Garland' and other disasters to the fishing fleet by the late gale, with the Pulpit References on the occasion.*

Adam Watson had been one of those Cellardyke fishermen 'saved' in the religious revival of 1859–60, and as the Rev. George Anderson reminded his Kilrenny congregation the Sunday after the disaster, 'They all worshipped together in this church on their last Sabbath evening upon earth'. Several of the men had been active in the Y.M.C.A., and they were all practising Christians. Of David Watson, Mr. McAlpine of the Free Church in Anstruther said, 'His life was a burning and shining light. . . . Latterly in the Y.M.C.A., in the Mission School, and at open-air meetings, he seems to have possessed some premonition that his grave was to be a watery one. Three times before this sad gale has he been overboard . . . and do not some of you think that that assurance of his, expressed a few weeks ago, and so much commented upon at the time, that "should he die in the next storm he was perfectly ready", was an utterance from the very lip of his watery grave? . . . Surely from his watery bed, sixty miles from the harbour, he yet speaketh'.

Mr. McAlpine next spoke of 'that bright and happy Christian James Salter', and concluded, 'Methinks you hear them saying "Good night" in the midst of the shrieking storm, but follow onwards, and do you not hear them saying "Good morning" on the threshold of glory?'

John Dick, a young fisherman on his uncle's boat the *Zephyr*, wrote the following lines on the loss of the *Garland*:

Slowly the morning dawned upon
  Our gallant little fleet.
As o'er the bounding sea they sped,
  Each little craft complete.

The heavy sky showed silent signs,
  Which some alone can know;
But brave are they who face the storm
  As they would meet a foe.

We watched them as they sailed away
    Across the watery main;
But little thought that one of them
    Would ne'er come back again.

But it was so, for all next day
    The wind a tempest blew,
And from that day no tidings came
    Of her, or of her crew.

Her name the *Garland* was, and she
    Had often fought her way
Through raging storms, through trackless paths,
    Amidst the foaming spray.

But she is gone, we know not how;
    She, and the seven brave men
Who formed her crew, shall never plough
    The raging sea again.

And now we mourn the loss of those
    Whose lives we have admired;
But oh! to see them as they sing
    In beauteous robes attired.

Sad grew our hearts, as, day by day,
    Each ray of hope grew dim;
But God is good, he knoweth best,
    We leave it all with Him.

He holds the waters in his hand,
    He sees the widows' tears;
'I will not leave you comfortless'
    He whispers in their ears.

'Although mysterious it has been,
    Though dark thy path may be,
I through the cloud will lead thee on,
    If thou but trust in Me.'

And though their home has darkened been,
    We know it was in love,
And we shall meet our friends again
    In that bright home above.

The *Garland* disaster was talked about in Cellardyke as long as there were any alive who could remember it.

In May 1895 the boat *Providence*, whose skipper David Watson (Cunningham) – known as 'Pip' – was a relative of Adam Watson, lost a crewman overboard while fishing seventy miles from the May Island.

The headstone of Adam Watson (Ainslie) of the *Garland* and his son William Watson (Smith) of the *Brothers*, in Kilrenny churchyard.

William Motion was forty years of age, and left a widow and seven children. Just over a year later, on August 25th, 1896, the mate of the same boat, Alexander Tawse, was knocked overboard by the sail and drowned twenty-five miles offshore. On June 9th, 1897, Adam Reid's *Reliance* arrived at Crail and reported that the skipper James Anstruther Moncrieff had been drowned during a heavy gale two nights before. So it went on, the inexorable toll of sacrifices to the sea.

By this time there is little trace in the records of the 'wickedness of the people' so evident to earlier generations of ministers and elders. By 1896, for example, the kirk-session of Kilrenny could fix on November 8th as a suitable time for resuming the morning service in winter, 'as by that time many of the Congregation and especially the young Men of whom the Bible Class is largely composed, will have returned from the English fishing'. And at a congregational soirée to mark the Reverend Anderson's semi-jubilee the fortunate minister was presented with an illuminated address and a purse of sovereigns, while his wife received a gold ring set with opals. The generosity of the gifts is a sign of the increased prosperity of the Kilrenny congregation. It also looks suspiciously like a snub to the little band of dissidents at the new church in Cellardyke.

Even the goldfields of Australia and New Zealand, with all their promise of material rewards, could not shake the new-found piety of the fishermen-diggers, and many a prayer went up from rude tents in the wastes of Bendigo and Ballarat. Unlike the compulsive gambler who must always have one more spin of the wheel, the average Cellardyke emigrant would return after accumulating sufficient wealth to build himself a new house on the braes above the old town, and fit out a boat in which to resume his natural trade. When a man *did* remain behind it was usually to pursue a career or vocation to which he had long aspired.

Typical of the new breed of Dyker were various members of the Cunningham family who by the last decade of the century were to be found in the new fisher communities of West Forth Street, Ellice Street and Rodger Street. An oral tradition in Cellardyke credits some of these Cunninghams with having designed and built the first 'Fifie': the distinctive sailing-boat favoured by the East-coast fishermen for much of the later nineteenth-century, at least until the advent of the Zulu in 1879:

> She told me that the first boat known as a 'Fifie' was built in that field (east of Cellardyke harbour) by a family called Cunningham, and one of them had told her that they first modified the Scaffie to have a near-vertical sternpost. And when they then tried a model with a vertical stem as well as a vertical sternpost, they thought it should have a new name. Somebody suggested the 'Fifie', and there it was. About the family of Cunningham, the boatbuilders, she said the last one emigrated to Australia.' (Peter Smith recalling his great-aunt Barbara Doig, born in 1854 at the East End of Cellardyke).

At 34 Rodger Street lived Alexander Cunningham, son of Robert Cunningham and Janet Fowler, with his second wife Agnes Pratt. The house belonged to their son-in-law David Watson ('Pip'), skipper of the *Providence*. Alexander's son by his first marriage to Janet Horsburgh, Robert Cunningham, lived with his wife Annie Meldrum at No. 20 (later they would move back to the old family home at 50 George Street, for after losing three fingers of one hand while at sea, Robert would leave the fishing to keep a grocer's shop). On the other side of School Road, at 2 Ellice Street, lived Alexander Cunningham (Nicol), whose father Thomas Cunningham (Smith) – a cousin of Alexander Cunningham (Pratt) – died in 1884 at 3 Ellice Street. (With the Cunninghams, as with the Watsons, one needs the wife's maiden name for correct identification!) Alexander Cunningham (Nicol) was the brother of the Reverend Thomas Cunningham jun., minister of Furner in South Australia, where in 1890, according to the *East of Fife Record*, his congregation presented him with a new buggy. Another brother was James Cunningham (Doig) whose only son Thomas Cunningham lived at 'Craignoon House', Bircham, Victoria, Australia. Alexander's brother-in-law John Martin (Nicol) was first manager then provost of Kilrenny for a total of twenty-four years, while Alexander's son Thomas Cunningham (Moncrieff), a ship-chandler in Anstruther, was a future provost of Anstruther Easter.

In May, 1899, Alexander Cunningham (Nicol) wrote a letter which was published simultaneously in the *East of Fife Record* and the *Southern Cross* of Melbourne. Peculiarly Victorian in its coupling of religious fervour with the pursuit of Mammon, Alexander Cunningham's letter is also an impressive testimony to the intelligence and expressive powers of the more thoughtful type of nineteenth-century fisherman, and to the generations of ministers and dominies whose example and teaching, aided by the Authorised Version of the Bible, had moulded his character and mind:

EAST OF FIFE RECORD, May 19th., 1899.

EARLY CHURCH LIFE IN BENDIGO.

Mr. Alexander Cunningham, 2 Ellice Street, Cellardyke, writes to the Southern Cross, Melbourne, as follows:–

Dear Sir,–

I have been a constant reader of your valuable paper for a long time past, and have perused it with much pleasure and profit. But your descriptions of the Churches of Bendigo have rather surprised and refreshed me, more especially when you speak of the placing of Dr. Nish, for I was present at that service when a Dr. Mackay, I was told, placed him over the church there. It was only a framed tent we were met in, but truly God was in that place, although we had by no means a large gathering. I relished very much the late Dr. Nish's preaching; it was indeed water in a thirsty land, and at this day I bless God from old Scotland's shores for the means of grace enjoyed on Bendigo diggings. I may say that I was about fourteen months on the diggings at Dead Dog Gully, Back Creek, then on Eaglehawk Flat, so that we were three or four miles from the township, however, we managed to get to church, although the surroundings were not of the best. Later on there was a stone building put up, which was more comfortable to worship in. When one compares Bendigo as it was then to what it is like now, there must be a vast difference indeed. I am glad that Dr. Nish is succeeded by such men as Mr. James, Mr. Mackay, and others who believe in the Gospel of Scripture, which is the power of God unto salvation to every one that believes. We have seen something of its power here in the years of '59 and '60, when many were taken from the ranks of Satan and translated into the Kingdom of God, and who remain to this day as standard bearers for Christ in our community. This we call the proof of the Gospel, when it not only causes a man to profess Christ, but live soberly, and righteously, and godly in this present world. We pity those who seek the real cure for man's fallen state apart from this only cure for all the diseases of the unrenewed heart. But with the grace of the Holy Spirit men can alone be taught of him who came to bind up the broken hearted, and to give sight to the blind, and to set at liberty those who were bound. I have still a very warm heart to Australia, and I hope and pray that Christ may be glorified in that sunny land.

The form of worship in the local churches had changed little over the years, and the organ or 'kist o' whistles' was still unheard of. When Alexander Reid, tinsmith in Cellardyke, was appointed precentor of Kilrenny church, his salary was fixed at £12 per annum, '... and the proceeds of two collections from the Congregation on the second Sabbath of January, and the second sabbath of June, after the ordinary Collection is deducted'. His duties were 'to conduct the Psalmody in the Church when required, also teach and train a Choir at least once a week in the Infant School, where it has always been done'.[40]

But in late Victorian Cellardyke it was still inadvisable to walk by land or sea with both eyes on the heavens. In October 1896 John Mitchell offered £9 'for the customs and Shore Dung', while carters Robert Christie junior and D. & G. Pattie outbid each other for the privilege of 'lifting and carting of the Dung from the Streets and Wynds of the Town'. Thomas Christie, on September 28th, 1897, was appointed 'Scavenger and Lamplighter' at £1 per week, and he must have been cheered by the council's ruling that from 1st. January following, 'no person will be allowed to put out nuisances on the streets except in buckets or other vessels, and that public notice thereof be given by handbills, which the Clerk was authorised to prepare'.[41] Godliness might rule in Cellardyke, but cleanliness would not be far behind. Perhaps it was this period in the town's history which gave birth to that stock character of East Neuk folklore – the Cellardyke housewife who polishes her doorstep with merciless zeal, and washes the coal before putting it on the fire!

The following year, Bailie Williamson agreed to sub-let his field on the west side of Toll Road (formerly Williamson Street) for a public recreation park, and stringent regulations were drawn up for the use of Kilrenny Common. These included a ban on 'horses, ponies, mules, asses, carridges or vehicles of any kind, or tents, portable or otherwise'; nor would 'obscene language or improper behaviour be permitted at the upper and lower Common, and no intoxicated person shall be allowed therein'. At the same time steps were 'built up' at the Tolbooth Wynd, and the Shore, Tolbooth and Little Wynds were all 'improved'. Progress and improvement were the order of the day. Then came the ruinous gales of mid-October, and the worst storm damage in Cellardyke for over sixty years.

This time, thankfully, no local men were lost, but after the phenomenal seas of Monday and Tuesday, October 18th and 19th, the piers of Cellardyke harbour were completely wrecked. To be sure, the larger boats had long since flitted to Anstruther's Union Harbour, but

Cellardyke harbour in the 1920s. The white house in the centre (5 Shore Street) has since been demolished.

Cellardyke was still home to a dozen or so yawls which prosecuted the crab and lobster fishery, providing a living for those too old or infirm for the deep-sea fishing. Not only piers but houses and boundary walls were wrecked, and an appeal was soon got up for money to make good the damage.

Before the storm ceased its fury, both land and sea had given up their dead. On Thursday morning a body floated on to a skelly to the west of Caddies Burn, and was tentatively identified as a Norwegian sailor. He was buried in Kilrenny churchyard, the local fishermen walking four abreast behind the hearse. Even the prehistoric dead were not safe in their tombs. Sailmaker James Smith, of Crichton Street in West Anstruther, took a stroll along by the Billowness (between Anstruther and Pittenweem), and stumbled across a stone coffin containing bones protruding from the ground near the pinnacle rock known as 'Johnny Doo's pulpit', where the young Thomas Chalmers had taken his first nervous steps in the art of preaching.[42] Under the massive impact of the sea the very earth had opened up. It might have been the Last Day. The ancients of Anstruther were not surprised. Only half a century ago there had been burial mounds here, wrote one to the *Record*. 'Tread softly!' says George Gourlay of the Billowness, 'every step is on a grave'.[43]

From the ancients of Anstruther to the children of Cellardyke now, for as the year turned it was time once again to rehearse the school play. We know from Gourlay that the fisher children were no mean actors, for long before Waterloo, in the adventure school for whalers' children, they had struggled manfully with the Rev. John Home's melodrama *Douglas* – their old dominie's favourite text. Feelingly the old bookseller writes of 'blubbering Nelly', 'little Isa Boyter squeaking in reply', of Willie Morris, 'sublime as a hero', and 'tousy Tam Murray', of Jock Salter 'with his black eye and bloody nose' and Ned Bauldie, 'the blinking herd'.[44] One would give much to have seen that performance.

This time public taste was more refined, though never perhaps in the history of the theatre was there a more confusing gallimaufry than J. G. Grieve's *Flowers o' the Forest*. Not only did 'Wandering Willie', impersonated by Master W. Donaldson, share the stage with 'Tom Thumb' (Master John Murray), 'John Gilpin' (Master George Davison), 'Tam o' Shanter' (Master Robert McLeod) and 'Robin Hood' (Master Robert Watson), but feminine interest was supplied by 'Jeannie Deans' (Miss Maggie Reid), 'Black Eyed Susan' (Miss Williamina Murray), 'The Lass of Richmond Hill' (Miss Cecilia Deas) and – a curious stray from across the Irish Sea – 'The Colleen Bawn' (Miss Betsy Keay).

'Very many pretty voices were heard among the girls', wrote a critic in the local paper, 'but the boys with the proverbial deep voices of those brought up on the East Coast were a little too strong ... and no doubt Mr. Davidson ... will be able to rectify this'. So much for the deep, drawling drone which marks the true Dyker.[45] The harmonium was 'most sympathetically manipulated' by Miss Mitchell.

The century ended with renewed feuding between the fishertown and its sister burgh. Hostilities were triggered off by an 'indignation meeting' in Cellardyke to protest against the Union Harbour Commissioners' decision to remove the collector's office and steelyard from Shore Street, Anstruther, to another situation near the west pier. As usual, the local newspaper offered a forum for jibes and sarcasm from either side. The Commissioners' pompous talk of Anstruther's 'increased traffic' (i.e. trade), for instance, caused great hilarity beyond the Burn, where no traffic except that in fish was held in much esteem:

> There was not a bawbee earned from potatoes last year, there was £8 the year before that. Some years it had been more than that, but the harbour did not exist for potatoes. It was the fishing that kept it up. (Applause).
>
> *Mr. George Ritchie* – If they had not the laid-up rates (i.e. for fishing-boats) they would be bankrupt. Let us get the wheels again and pull up our boats in Cellardyke, and keep our money for Cellardyke. (Laughter and applause).

The Chairman – It is my opinion that this is on a line with what they have done all along, throwing away money foolishly. In anything they have ever done for the benefit of the harbour nothing has ever been done proper, and everything they have tried has just been thrown to the winds.

Mr. Ritchie – They were told that pretty plainly by our worthy Provost, but it does not matter, as long as they have the majority, they will always have the power to crush the poor Cellardyke fisherman. (Laughter and applause).

Nevertheless the proposed change of site went ahead as planned, to the evident approval of the *Record*'s editor. The only opposition, he concluded in a self-righteous editorial on May 12th, had come from '. . . a few who can be counted on to oppose anything concerning Anstruther'.

One of his correspondents was less restrained in his comments. Signing himself – in the manner of a local Kirkcaldy-registered fishing-boat – 'K.Y. Red Herring', he launched into a virulent denunciation of the Dykers and their well-known habit of picking over their neighbours' vices and shortcomings while ignoring their own. After commenting briefly on the steelyard controversy, he opted for an indirect method of attack. There was currently talk in Cellardyke of landscaping Kilrenny Common for the benefit of local people. He could hardly contain his contempt for this notion. Why desecrate the Common when the Dykers' idea of recreation was to pollute the Shore at Anstruther with the grossness of their fisher manners?

To interfere with it (i.e. the Common) with the view of making a pleasure park is simply ridiculous. The people of Cellardyke have no more need of the fresh air in a public park than a pig has for a jewel in its nose. Provost Thomson would do well if he wishes to make a name for himself, and serve the ratepayers he represents, by having two portable shelters of an artistic design placed in the Folly (i.e. the paved area between Shore Street and Anstruther harbour) for the accommodation of his public park resorters. Then the quiet people of Anstruther in Shore Street would at least have some chance of peace and quietness in their houses on the Saturday and Sunday nights. The noise and language used by what are called 'the young Dykers' crowding round the windows and corners of and on the pavements in that Street are past describing. All this goes on on Sunday nights while Provost Thomson and their parents may be worshipping in Church or Chapel . . .'

This was grossly insulting, and not to be borne; but Cellardyke had a champion waiting in the wings. In the very next issue (May 26th), after pointing out that not only Cellardyke 'lads and lassies' but also those of Anstruther, Pittenweem and St. Monans resorted to the Folly at weekends, 'A LOYAL DYKER' continued:

I am a Dyker, and proud of the fact, for I claim for Cellardyke that she has sent out into the world many brave and noble sons and daughters. Think of the Rodgers, Fowlers and Williamsons, benefactors of their race, men known throughout the world, and many more noble men and women, who if they have lived and died 'among their ain folk', have been none the less worthy, and today, where will you find in a place of like size, a greater number of more devoted men than are numbered as Sunday School teachers than in Cellardyke?

The latter-day Dyker can only nod his head in agreement, reflecting with satisfaction that, as the old century gave way to the new, local patriotism was still alive and kicking between Caddies Burn and the 'Golden Strand'.[46]

These 'Old Worthies' at Cellardyke have been tentatively identified as: *Back Row* (L. to R.) John Muir ('Codlin' Jockie'); Alex. Murray; David Davidson; Leslie Brown ('Buller'); Thomas Brown; Isaac Harrell (born in Harwich); Peter Fleming ('Pimple'); Thomas Mathers (the burgh scavenger); Charles Carstairs (grandfather of Provost Carstairs). *Front Row* (L. to R.) A. Thomson ('Lummie'); David Hodge ('Hodgie Bow'); James Keay; Thomas Cunningham ('Black Tam'); Thomas Fleming; Alex. Myles ('Laird'); William Watson; James Cunningham.

8

The Twentieth Century

The New Year's Eve of 1900 fell on a Sunday, so fewer revellers than usual were out on the streets of Cellardyke at midnight to welcome in the new century. Those who did brave the chilly night air to gather at the Cross or in Rodger Street soon dispersed, after the usual exchanges of greetings and the occasional snatch of song, '. . . with flutina accompaniment'. Coloured lights in a few windows indicated households where first-footers were welcome.[1]

The nineteenth century had dawned on a Cellardyke embroiled in war and depleted of its young men by the press-gangs. A hundred years later not everything had changed for the better; but now the Boers of South Africa had supplanted the French as the bogeymen of a new generation. In only its second issue of the new year, the *East of Fife Record* printed a letter from a Lance-Corporal Moir of the 1st Gordon Highlanders, stationed at Camp Enslin near Kimberley, to his mother in Cellardyke. A chapter on the twentieth century could hardly begin more aptly than with this young soldier's heartfelt protest at the horrors of war:

> We lost our Commanding Officer, two or three officers killed and one wounded, and four men killed and sixty wounded. It was an awful sight. I never saw the like of it. We buried over 150, they were all brought into camp after the battle, and we had 1200 wounded altogether. The bullets were like a shower of hail, and shells bursting all over and around. God knows how I got off, for I was in the thick of it. I found the heat of a shell and the wind of it in my face. I never was so near in all my life. There were bullets hitting all round me and bristling over head. I have been in a few battles but nothing like this. . . . I wish it was all over. There is not so much fighting spirit left in me now for I am always thinking about my wife and little one. . . . Go and tell Mrs McLeod I saw William here. He was in the fight, but I saw him the day after the battle, and he was all right.

The anxious mother in Cellardyke can have found little to comfort her in this dispatch from a 'foreign field'.

Each new century seemed to commence with a baptism of tragedy. On February 24th, 1800, a boat's crew had perished at the entrance to Cellardyke harbour. On February 12th, 1900, the Shields-registered

The *Morning Star* at Yarmouth in 1900. (L. to R.) Charles Anderson; Thomas Smith; Thomas Fleming; William Anderson; Thomas Murray (Geddes); David Boyter; George Anderson; James Watson ('Star Jeems'). Over 80 feet in length, she was thought to be the biggest Fifie ever built.

steam-liner *Bernicia* left Anstruther harbour with her Cellardyke crew, and was not seen again. Skipper Thomas Watson left a wife and three children. He was the son of Alexander Watson and Jean Horsburgh, and a first cousin of Robert Cunningham (Meldrum) and Margaret 'Granny Mags' Watson. The other crewmen were Daniel Henderson, who left a wife and a grown-up family of five; Alexander Boyter, a wife and six young children; Alexander Gardner, a wife and five young children; Thomas Gardner, a wife but no children; Alexander Murray, a wife and eight children; James Stevenson (20) and Thomas Ritchie (18), young unmarried men, and an engineer and fireman from Shields.

For the incoming town council there were the usual mundane problems to solve: in particular, the question of harbour repairs, and how to pay for them. The dignitaries who confronted this problem, with effect from November 1900, were Provost Peter Thomson, draper; Baillies Robert Williamson and John Butters; Treasurer James Fortune and

Councillors John Clark, George Birrell, Alexander Black (soon to succeed Mr. Thomson as provost), Robert Melville and Martin Gardner. It was resolved to build the south pier further seaward, so as to give the harbour an additional breadth of ten feet, and to build it on the ledge of rock known as the Skelly Point, then to carry an arm to within 26 feet of the west pier, on which booms would be placed.[2] Meanwhile, an official document prescribing the dues to be paid on goods landed at Cellardyke, even before the rebuilding was complete, presents an optimistic picture of the battered little harbour's future potential:

CELLARDYKE HARBOUR DRAFT PROVISIONAL ORDER, 1901[3]
Rates on Goods
Shipped or Unshipped, Removed or Delivered at the Harbour, or within the limits thereof, or at any Pier or other Work connected with the Harbour.

	s.	d.
Ale and Beer, per 36 gallons	0	1½
Apples, per ton	1	0
Berries, viz.:– Bay, juniper, yellow and cran, per cwt	0	2
Biscuits, per ton	1	0
Boots and Shoes, per ton	2	0
Carrots, per ton	0	4
Cattle, viz.– Bulls, each	0	4
Cows and oxen, each	0	3
Calves, each	0	1
Horses, each	0	6
Pigs, each	0	1
Sheep, each	0	½
Lambs, each	0	¼
Asses and mules, each	0	6
Wild animals, each	1	0
etc.		

One wonders how many 'wild animals', or for that matter even asses and mules, ever stepped groggily ashore at the ancient creek of Skinfasthaven.

'They have heard evil tidings. There is sorrow on the sea.' (Jeremiah 49:23).

But we must return yet again to the sorrows of the sea. On Wednesday, September 3rd, 1902, a severe gale raged the length and breadth of the eastern seaboard, and the S.S. *Tinto* of Bo'ness ran into difficulties near the May Island. By good fortune the Anstruther fleet was homeward bound from the northern fishing grounds at the time, and skipper Robert Stewart's *Rothesay Bay* went to the aid of the stricken vessel. In

Anstruther harbour at the turn of the century. KY 159 is the *Mayflower*, skipper Robert Ritchie, built in 1884 for Kilrenny town councillor Alexander Watson (Murray). In the centre of the picture can be seen the funnels of some steam-liners.

the subsequent rescue operation the engineer of the *Tinto* was drowned, but the rest of her crew were pulled to safety. Skipper Stewart would later be presented with a pair of binoculars by a grateful Board of Trade representative at a public meeting in Anstruther. A life had been lost, but a greater tragedy had been averted.

Not until the weekend did the appalling consequences of the gale become apparent. As the rest of the fishing fleet steamed back into harbour, the *Celerity* and the *Brothers* were found to be missing. Then, as fears began to grow for their safety, the *Celerity* came limping home with the news that the *Brothers* had last been sighted in difficulties some forty miles off the Aberdeenshire coast. Immediately the crew of the *Anster Fair* offered to return to Aberdeen and look for the missing boat. Four other crews, exhausted though they were after a hard week at sea, voted to go with them as soon as they had unloaded their catch. In this they were overruled by their friends ashore, who persuaded them to take a well-earned rest, and volunteer crews were quickly formed to take their place. At four o'clock on Saturday afternoon the *Anster Fair*, *Innergellie*, *Rothesay Bay*, *Glenogil* and *Rob the Ranter* put out to sea, their crews promising to wire from Aberdeen if there was any news. Beyond the harbour bar the boats parted company, some sailing to seaward and some

177

to landward of the May Island, sweeping the North Sea for any sign of their missing comrades.

The promised wire brought no balm for the strained nerves of relatives and friends. Neither by sea nor on land was there any trace of the *Brothers* or her crew. It was a sombre crowd which gathered at Anstruther harbour the following night to greet the returning liners.

The skipper of the *Brothers* was that William Watson whose life had been so providentially spared back in 1890 when, at the last minute, his father had taken his place aboard the ill-fated *Garland*. With him perished his sons Adam (24) and Alexander (22), one of them a cabinet-maker to trade who had only accompanied his father on that one trip to sea in hopes of restoring his indifferent health. Another victim, William Peat, was about to be married, and indeed his banns were to have been proclaimed in church that very Sunday. The other members of the crew were James Watson Muir, an unmarried man of 22, and the half-dealsmen Charles Norrie and his brother-in-law David Ferrier from Broughty Ferry.

'No fisherman was better known over the whole north-east coast of Scotland', commented the local paper, 'than Skipper William Watson, nor can one be found who was held in more universal respect and esteem by all classes. He was a leading man in the community, being an elder in Kilrenny Church, a member of the Cellardyke Christian Association and took part in many other movements for the welfare of the community.'[4] It was always the brightest and the best who were taken.

Other disasters followed, almost too numerous to mention: John and Alexander Deas, lost off their father's boat in July 1904 in the very act of leaving Anstruther harbour; Robert Smith, drowned in February 1905 when Thomas Bett's *Cornucopia* (K.Y. 174) was rammed and sunk by the naval gunboat *Speedwell*; Robert Stewart, aged 21, drowned near Yarmouth off his father John Stewart's drifter *Rambler*; and Andrew and William Henderson, drowned three weeks later when the trawler *Star of Hope* ran aground on the coast of Aberdeenshire. John Watson, fireman on Adam Reid's drifter *Guerdon*, was lost at Yarmouth, and John Sutherland at Hartlepool. William Smith of the *Amethyst* was drowned in February, 1908.

If little could be done to improve safety at sea, more vigorous measures could be taken on land. In September 1907 the council received a letter from four residents at Caddies Burn – Mrs. Gardner, Mrs. A. Thomson, Mrs. J. Thomson and William Boyter – regarding the advisability of placing two lamps there, 'as they considered that on a dark night, the road was at present dangerous both to life and limb'. The suggestion was

The *Midlothian* in 1900. (L. to R.) John Watson (skipper's brother); Thomas Lowrie; James Deas and young son; skipper William Watson (Smith); David Dick; James Dick; James Dewar. Skipper Watson was the son of Adam Watson (Brown), and should not be confused with his uncle William Watson (Smith) of John Street, nor with William Watson (Smith) of the *Brothers*, son of Adam Watson (Ainslie) of the *Garland*.

accepted, and it was resolved that the houses at the Burn be known henceforth as Burnside Terrace.[5]

Another cause for concern was that latest menace to life and limb, the motor car. Anstruther Wester town council had already petitioned the neighbouring burghs about joint action to have the existing speed limit for cars reduced, when, on 5th September, 1911, the Kilrenny councillors debated a letter from the Automobile Association & Motor Union stating that the road between Anstruther and Kilrenny was 'covered with metal over its full width, making it almost unfit for motor traffic'. Would the council in future, when laying down metal, arrange for a track to be left at the side of the road free from loose metal, so that motor cars might pass through without any damage to their tyres? The council would not. With that special degree of scornfulness reserved for all that was new-fangled and without precedent, they agreed 'to take no steps in connection with the matter'.

As the nations of Europe moved inexorably towards war, things took
their accustomed course in the parish of Kilrenny. A dispute with the
presbytery of St. Andrews over the lack of a morning service at Kilrenny
church was resolved to Kilrenny's satisfaction, and recorded in an exul-
tant minute in the kirk-session register. Mr. David Williamson was
asked by the council to have the private streets at the back of West Forth
Street and Burnside Terrace put in order, and it was decided to put
down foot pavements at East and West Forth Streets and School Road.

More momentously, the town councils of Kilrenny and the two
Anstruthers agreed reluctantly to apply for a Provisional Order for the
amalgamation of their historic burghs. They were motivated by the need
for a new deepwater harbour at Anstruther, which was unlikely to attract
a harbour grant unless substantial sums could be guaranteed from the
local rates. It was imperative that the three burghs should present a
united front. However, it was not likely that a quick agreement would be
reached between such 'auld enemies' on issues like equal rating and a
shared water supply, and indeed before long Anstruther Wester with-
drew from the negotiations in disgust. Further progress was hindered by
events beyond anyone's control.

'Great excitement was created in the town on Monday morning', reported the *East of Fife Record* on August 7th, 1914, 'when it became known
that fully 40 half-dealsmen, who were members of the Naval Reserve, had
been ordered to report themselves at Methil. The Shore Street and piers
were crowded with knots of fishermen, eagerly discussing the situation.'
It took a lot to stir the fisherfolk up to such a pitch of anticipation.
'Never since 1860 – when the news of the Government grant to the new
harbour was received – has there been such excitement in the town.' The
half-dealsmen, most of them from the West Highlands and Islands, were
seen off on the 11.18 train by a great crowd of local fishermen, and were
reported to be 'quite cheery at the prospect of active service'.

The summer herring fishing thus came to an abrupt end, and pros-
pects for the winter fishing at Yarmouth looked bleak. Those Anstruther
drifters caught out in northern ports by the outbreak of war were
escorted home on Tuesday evening by a torpedo destroyer. But when the
insurance companies – who at first had refused to accept responsibility if
the boats continued to fish – relaxed their hard line, it was not long
before a semblance of normality returned. On August 19th the *Plough*
and the *Kilmany* ventured gingerly out to the fishing grounds again,
followed the next day by nineteen other drifters. The German High Seas
Fleet was at worst a distant menace, and when, after all, had the sea *not*
been perilous?

The driftermen's bravado lasted barely three weeks. On Saturday, September 5th, afternoon strollers at Crail and Balcomie gazing idly at warships out in the Forth saw the cruiser *Pathfinder* suddenly enveloped in spray and smoke. In less than five minutes she had gone to the bottom with her crew of 250 men. There had been rumours of suspicious-looking trawlers in the area, and Royal Navy minesweepers had not yet had time to clear the whole estuary. It was the end of the fishing for the foreseeable future. (The *Pathfinder*, it later emerged, had been sunk by the German submarine U21 – the first submarine strike of World War I.)

Later that month twenty young fishermen left for Portsmouth to join the Royal Naval Reserve. By October 8th the number had swelled to forty. A week later there were sixty Dykers in the R.N.R., and forty in the Territorial Army, and already at least one local man had bled for King and Country. On 12th October Mrs. David Brown of George Street heard that her husband Private David Brown, known in Cellardyke as 'The Silent Postie', had been wounded at the River Aisne. Luckier than many of his comrades, the wounded hero would eventually return from the Western Front to his quiet cottage by the shore of Cellardyke.

To convey the sense of loss which must have pervaded every home in the parish, we can hardly do better than to quote from the rolls of honour which appeared in the local churches, listing the names of all those currently serving in the armed forces at home and abroad by the end of this first year of the Great War:[6]

TERRITORIALS, 7th BLACK WATCH

David Barclay, 7 John Street.
James Birrell, 13 John Street.
John H. Birrell, 66 James Street.
Harry A Bowman.
Alexander Boyter, 1 Rodger Street.
Thomas Christie, 4 George Street.
John Doig, 5 Rodger Street.
William Gardner, 5 Urquhart Wynd.
Adam Lowrie, 18 Shore Street.
Angus Mackay, Kilrenny.
Peter Murray, 33 Rodger Street.
George Nicol, 67 George Street.
John Parker, 32 Rodger Street.
Robert Shireff, 59 George Street.
Alexander Stevenson, 64 James Street.
John Swinton, 53 George Street.
James Tarvit, 42 James Street.
Peter Tarvit, 49 James Street.

Alexander Watson, 30 John Street.
Andrew Watson, 30 John Street.
Robert Watson, 17 James Street.
Thomas Watson, 16 East Forth Street.
John Wilson, 12 James Street.
Joseph Wilson, 12 James Street.
Wilson Wilson, 12 James Street.
Robert Wood, 21 Rodger Street.
John Young, 1 George Street.

OTHER ARMY UNITS

Allan Clement, Pitkierie farm	Fife & Forfar Yeomanry.
James Clement, do.	Queen's Own Royal Yeomanry.
H. Edie, Cornceres farm	Fife & Forfar Yeomanry.
George McKay, George Street	1st Battalion, Cameronian Highlanders.
George Moncrieff, 10 George St.	Lowland Mounted Brigade.
David Pratt, Ellice St.	H.L.I.
Philip Oliphant Ray, The Manse, Cellardyke	Cameronian Highlanders.
Alexander Smith, Harbourhead, Cellardyke	Canadian Army Service Corps.
T. Swinton, George St.	Canadian Army 6th Battalion (Regimental Staff).

ROYAL NAVAL RESERVE

David Anderson, John Street.
Henry Bett, 3 Fowler Street.
Thomas Boyter, 31 Rodger Street.
Peter Carstairs, 30 Rodger Street.
John Christie, 4 George Street.
G. Corstorphine, 41 John Street.
A. Davidson.
John Deas, 67 George Street.
George Doig.
John Doig, 3 George Street.
Martin Gardner, 44 James Street.
Robert Gardner, 20 James Street.
Robert Gardner, 2 Rodger Street.
Robert M. Gardner, Williamson Street.
John Gowans, 27 George Street.
David Hodge, 28 George Street.
George Hodge.
Robert Keay, 28 Shore Street. (H.M.S. *Cochrane*).
David McRuvie, 42 George Street.
James McRuvie, 42 George Street.
James Mitchell, Harbourhead.

James Moncrieff, West Forth Street.
Alexander Muir, 77 James Street.
John Muir, 20 John Street.
Robert Muir, 20 John Street.
Alexander Murray, 28 Rodger Street.
William Reekie, 18 Rodger Street.
Thomas Ritchie, 28 James Street. (H.M.S. *Riviera*).
James Smith, 21 James Street.
Martin Sutherland.
G. Tarvit, Urquhart Wynd.
T. Tarvit, 37 George Street.
David Thomson, 24 George Street.
Robert Thomson, 42 West Forth Street.
William Thomson, 4 Burnside Terrace.
Alexander Watson, 9 Burnside Terrace.
James Watson, 12 East Forth Street.
William Watson, 29 East Forth Street.
George Wood, 6 John Street.

By early 1915 the fishing had picked up again, although the crews were operating under severe restrictions. The Firth of Forth was now closed by an imaginary line drawn from Crail to Dunbar via the May Island, and although line-fishing was permitted between Kirkcaldy and Crail, fishing with nets (i.e. for herring) was absolutely forbidden within the limit. However, as admirals-depute and the like had discovered to their cost through the ages, it was one thing to draw up regulations for the fishing, and quite another to ensure that they were obeyed. Among the first skippers to be fined at Cupar for net-fishing west of Crail were Martin Gardner of the *Vanguard III*, John Muir (Keay) of the *Camperdown*, Thomas Bett of the *Scot*, Henry Bett of the *Breadwinner* and Robert Anderson of the *Sunbeam*: to mention only five of the forty-three boats seen using their nets inside the Firth one night in late February.

Before long the Admiralty had found more pressing employment for the drifter crews. Already by the end of January the *Dreel Castle* (W. Sutherland), *Golden Strand* (J. Stevenson), *Craignoon* (A. Rodger), *Kilmany* (M. Gardner), *Coreopsis* (P. Gardner), *Guerdon* (Adam Reid) and *Cromorna* (A. Henderson) had been enlisted for patrol duty, and they were followed in the week ending 22nd May by the *St. Ayles*, *Eva*, *Venus*, *White Cross* and *Scot*; then, a few days later, by the *Vanguard III*. Forty local drifters were now engaged in this work, and two hundred and fifty men had joined the ranks of the R.N.R. (Patrol Boat Section).[7] A week later the *Camperdown*, *Lily*, *Maggie* and *Andrewina* left for an unspecified destination 'somewhere west of Suez'. It was the height of the Gallipoli campaign. One unnamed Anstruther drifter was instrumental in saving three hundred passengers from the emigrant ship *Ancona*, torpedoed by an Austrian submarine in the Mediterranean.[8]

Meanwhile those Cellardyke and Kilrenny men who had opted for the soldier's life were in training with their units: the majority being with the 1st. Battalion the 7th Black Watch at Kinghorn, where the rigours of training camp alone were to prove too much for one young recruit:

A TERRITORIAL'S DEATH. – Much sympathy has been expressed this week for the parents of Private Robert Watson, of the 1/7th Black Watch, in his untimely death. Private Watson was one of the many young men who heard and responded to the call for men for service. Although not of a robust constitution, he threw himself eagerly into the work of training, and was a most promising young soldier. Unfortunately, he contracted a bad chill when out on manoeuvres, and was invalided home fully two months ago. Unremitting attention proved of no avail, and he died on Sunday evening. The funeral yesterday was largely attended. Provosts Black and Readdie were among those present, while Major Sibley, the Recruiting Officer for the Kirkcaldy District, who was passing through on duty at the time and stopped his car instead of passing the cortege, on learning what was happening, immediately joined the mourners. A squad of the 2/7th Black Watch, under Sergeant Watt, were sent along from Kinghorn to represent the regiment. The service was conducted by the Rev. Mr. Anderson, E. Anstruther.[9] (Robert Watson was the author's uncle.)

Three days before Private Watson's death his battalion had left for the Front, and only a few weeks later they were in action for the first time. 'The first of our Territorials to fall for his Country', in the words of the Rev. Urquhart of Chalmers Church in Anstruther, was Lance-Corporal W. B. Watson of 'Craigholm', the son of Mr. and Mrs. Alexander Watson of Watson's oilskin factory in George Street. Privates Alexander Boyter and Adam Lowrie were wounded in the same attack, and from now on the tally of dead and wounded in the local papers is greater than we can do justice to in these pages.

The *East of Fife Record* during this period resounds with stories of long-separated Dykers reunited with one another in the unlikeliest of places: in a trench on the Western Front, in a field hospital at the Dardanelles, in a Canadian troopship in mid-Atlantic. A veteran in his thirties would recognise a beardless youngster because of his family resemblance to the Boyters, the Martins or the Watsons. There was something oddly comforting in the thought that one's son or husband had a familiar companion at his side with whom he could reminisce about the safer, saner world they had both known.

Any serviceman returning briefly on furlough was assured of an attentive hearing if he felt any inclination to relate his experiences: but how could such horrors be described for an uncomprehending audience of non-combatants? One can sympathize with the reticence of Captain G. M. Black, son of the old baker David Black and commandant of a military hospital in Brighton, who would only admit that his work was 'most interesting'.[10] A more colourful account, however, was provided by Captain C. H. Maxwell of the 1/7th Black Watch, who on September 24th granted the *East of Fife Record* a calculatedly morale-boosting interview:

> No words can fully describe the readiness and gallantry of the boys from the East of Fife in tackling the business in hand ... Our boys are a cheery lot, and great on music. Both in the trenches and on the march, the voices of the Anstruther and Cellardyke boys can be depended on to strike up a tune, which is lustily taken up by the whole Company. It is a cheery sound, and keeps up our spirits wonderfully.

Two East Neuk men were singled out for special mention:

> A word of praise must also be given to our two local stretcher-bearers, Drummer Harry Bowman, Cellardyke, and Drummer Robert Hughes, Pittenweem. The doctors could not compliment them enough on their work, not only for the prompt attention they gave to the wounded, but in carrying them to safety over open ground under heavy fire, and returning at once to carry more wounded, sometimes through miles of trenches packed with soldiers. They would work until they were fit to drop, and were always ready when called upon.

It was a nice tribute for the men's families to read.

What was happening meanwhile on the home front? For one thing, the controversy over what the *Record* scathingly referred to as 'The Lighting Farce'. The problem was that no-one knew who had ultimate responsibility for enforcing blackout regulations:

> MR. MITCHELL – In whose hands is this lighting business? Who has the authority to order restrictions?
> BAILIE MARR – That is the mystery.
> MR. MITCHELL – It is a perfect farce.
> MR. SWINTON – There seems to be one authority for Anstruther and one for Cellardyke.
> Mr. Mitchell said that the lights in George Street, south side, which showed northwards, were complained of by the police on the grounds that they were frightened for Zeppelins. In Anstruther the street lamps formed perfect torchlights, offering more guidance to Zeppelins than the lights in private houses, which only shone to the other side of the street. It was utter rubbish to allow the brilliant lights and compel others to darken.
> ... Mr. Laverock said the glare from the street lamps of Anstruther could be seen for miles. He did not see why Cellardyke should be restricted.[11]

It was only to be expected that, even in wartime, Anstruther would contrive to get the better of its unfortunate neighbour!

Considering that it was an official organ of local government, the town council of our ancient royal burgh had a refreshingly sceptical attitude towards bureaucracy and all higher authority. The Chief Constable's advice to have the waterworks watched, and the Scottish Office's initial memorandum on extinguishing lights in the event of aerial attack, were both in turn quietly shelved; while later missives from the Live Stock Section of the Ministry of Food on the utilisation of household waste for pig feeding, and from the Scottish Office on the urgency of collecting all fruit stones for the war effort(!), were openly derided.[12]

The women and children of the town were making their own more practical contribution. By the end of January 1915, the list of garments made by female members of Cellardyke Church for local soldiers and sailors comprised 336 pairs of mittens, 110 pairs of socks, 42 pairs of hose-tops, 36 belts, 30 jerseys, 15 day shirts, 11 mufflers, 9 knitted jackets, 6 night shirts, 2 bed-jackets and 2 dozen handkerchiefs. The children of Cellardyke school had raised enough money to send specially-inscribed pocket-knives to fathers and brothers, and had even gathered dandelion roots which an Edinburgh chemical works was able to convert into dressings for wounded servicemen. Others picked sphagnum moss for the same purpose.

But even in the darkest years of the war, life was not unrelieved gloom. Since November 25th, 1912, weekly picture shows had been held in Anstruther Easter Town Hall under the auspices of the East of Fife Electric Cinematograph Company Ltd., and the silent posturings of Fatty Arbuckle and Buster Keaton must have provided a few hours' diversion for appreciative audiences. Nor were they short-changed for their 3d. entrance fee (children 2d.). On Saturday, February 26th, 1916, for instance, they could thrill to 'The Prisoner of Zenda' and 'Jane's Declaration of Independence (A Sensational Drama)', and rock with laughter at 'The Clubman (An Amusing Comedy)' and 'Mabel, Fatty and the Law (A Keystone Comedy)'. Lovers of Ruritania would be back the following Saturday night for 'Rupert of Hentzau', followed by 'Innocence at Monte Carlo', 'Jimmy on the Job', and – intriguingly – 'A Dismantled Beauty'! It was therapeutic stuff, although there must always have been some wives and mothers who, like Mrs. James Watson of 3 Dove Street, had little stomach for Hollywood's synthetic tears and laughter. By early 1916 Mrs. Watson headed the league table of sacrifice with no fewer than seven sons in the armed forces: Thomas, David and Wilson in patrol-boats; John in minesweepers; James in the H.L.I.,

Alexander in the Scots Guards and Robert in a unit of the Canadian Army.

Let us not leave this section on the early years of the Great War without commemorating the appointment of Miss E. Gardner, in March 1915, to an assistant teacher's post at Cellardyke Primary School. Euphemia Watson Gardner – 'Phame' to generations of school-children – was the daughter and granddaughter of enterprising Cellardyke skippers, and a relative of those Watsons who had perished with the loss of the *Garland* and the *Brothers*. For more than four decades her stern but kindly personality would compel the respect of even the most unruly elements among the bairns of Cellardyke, until, in the late 1950s, she taught her last class (one of whom was the present writer) – by which time some of her earliest pupils had become grandparents.

As the war continued the casualties mounted: James Moncrieff, killed at the Battle of Jutland when the battle-cruiser *Invincible* blew up, killing all but six of her crew; George Moncrieff Cunningham, son of the ship-chandler and future provost Thomas Cunningham, killed at the Somme; Robert Louden of Rennyhill Farm, riddled with bullets on a barbed-wire fence at Loos. Philip Oliphant Ray, son of the old minister, was killed in action with the Royal Flying Corps. A fleet of drifters, including the *Craignoon*, was sunk by the Austrian navy in the Adriatic, and a terrible gloom descended on the villages of the East Neuk when word came from the Admiralty that the crews were missing, believed lost. This story, however, has a happy ending. Alex. Watson of Watson's factory, a major shareholder in the *Craignoon*, joined with the Anstruther fishery officer and a local G.P., Dr. Wilson, in contacting the International Red Cross, who made secret overtures to the Austrian government. It emerged that the crews of the missing drifters had been rescued and interned in P.O.W. camps in Austria and Bohemia. Even before the Admiralty itself had official notification of the men's whereabouts, their grieving families were reassured as to their safety. But not until the end of the war would the unfortunate sailors be allowed home, and the tale of their return journey, through Austria to Venice and then by cattle trucks through France, is a minor epic in itself.

Another stirring story concerns the St. Monans motor-boat *Watchful*, which was sunk by a U-boat when twenty-two miles off Shields. The crew were forced to row some nine miles in their yawl before being picked up by a Lowestoft drifter and landed at Shields. Dyker Alexander Watson, reported the *East of Fife Record*, '. . . thinks he has had enough of fishing during the war, and is now inclined to go into Naval service and in that way do something to the enemy as compensation for wrecking such a valuable motor boat' (Alexander Watson was the author's uncle).

There are also many tales of bravery rewarded. Harry Bowman of the Black Watch received his Military Medal from Provost Readdie of Anstruther Easter during an interval in the panto 'Puss in Boots' at Anstruther Town Hall. Captain J. Montador's D.S.C., for 'zeal and devotion to duty in the Eastern Mediterranean', was presented to him by King George V at Buckingham Palace. Leading Seaman Alexander Watson – fresh from his ordeal in the *Watchful* – was in the news again when the Royal Humane Society awarded him their Bronze Medal for lifesaving in recognition of his rescuing the sole survivor of the trawler/minesweeper *Recepto*:

> *COAST BURGHS OBSERVER*, May 17th., 1917.
> *BRAVERY REWARDED.*– A Cellardyke man, we are pleased to notice, has been awarded the Royal Humane Society's Bronze Medal and Certificate for saving the life of a sea-comrade under circumstances which made the rescue fraught with considerable peril to himself. The hero of this plucky and daring adventure is Leading Seaman Alexander Watson, fourth son of Mr William Watson (Cunningham), 17 James Street. Like most of our gallant lads who follow the sea in these perilous days, Leading Seaman Watson is of an unassuming disposition and has been characteristically reticent regarding the occurrence. But the main facts are that Leading Seaman Watson, who is an excellent swimmer – a perfect water-rat – to use a colloquial expression – dived into the sea and at great risk to his own life succeeded in rescuing from a watery grave a seaman named Donald McIver, R.N.R. McIver was one of the crew of a minesweeper which had been mined, and he was the only man on board the ill-fated vessel who was saved. Mr Watson sen., it may be mentioned, has four sons in the Navy. The eldest is mate of a patrol boat, another who was in the Black Watch died for his king and country two years ago, a third son is stoker on a pilot cutter, the fourth has already been mentioned, and a fifth son is almost ready to go – a patriotic record that will be very hard to beat.

But it would be hard to beat the record of another (unrelated) Watson – Chief Skipper David Watson, son of James Watson of the *Morning Star* ('Star Jeems'), who by 1918 had collected the Italian Medal for Valour, the French Croix de Guerre and the Serbian Gold Medal. (By this time, incidentally, the Russell family's *East of Fife Record* had been transformed, via the short-lived *Coast Burghs Observer*, into *The East Fife Observer, The only advertising medium for the East of Fife, extensively circulated in Anstruther, Cellardyke, Crail, Kingsbarns, Pittenweem, St. Monance, Elie, Earlsferry, Kilconquhar, Colinsburgh, Arncroach, Carnbee, and surrounding districts*; and it is to this grandly-entitled organ of the Press that we owe most of the following facts and figures.

As the above-mentioned exotic decorations imply, these were strange and stirring times for the veterans of the North European fishing-grounds, many of whom could claim – like the skipper of the *Carmi III* in the winter of 1917 – that they had been 'much about Egypt, Greece and Bulgaria', had assisted in the evacuation of Gallipoli, escorted the supporters of the Greek statesman Venizelos to their island sanctuary, and visited Salonika and the terrible charnel-house of Suvla Bay (*East Fife Observer*, November 1st, 1917).

Then, one day, it was all over. Crail heard the news first, and not till after midday on that eleventh of November did the glad tidings reach Cellardyke and Anstruther. In the 'bracing weather and sunshine' which had succeeded the recent gales, the flags and bunting went up, and all the bells of the little sea-towns rang out in unison.

For a time, it must have seemed that Peace was all, and nothing else mattered. Even the unexpected influenza epidemic caused little stir at first, and in any case a local chemist had proposed oil of eucalyptus sprinkled on the handkerchief as a simple preventative(!). More impressive by far was the sweep of the German High Seas Fleet as it cruised slowly down the Firth with its Royal Navy escort a few days later, drawing crowds of thousands to the braes of the East Neuk for a day-long vigil.

The local paper's change of name was not the only innovation in those years. In 1917 the Rev. Mr. Ray, having built up the congregation at Cellardyke from 40 to over 700, was translated to St. James's Church, Portobello; his successor being the Rev. James R. Lee, late of Glengarry. On the political front, the St. Andrews Burghs were merged with the rural East Fife constituency, and in the election campaign of December 1918 ex-Prime Minister Asquith, M.P. for East Fife since 1886, duly presented himself for the first time to the sceptical voters of the East Neuk. On December 12th a whistle-stop tour from Lundin Links to St. Andrews meant eight speeches in as many different venues: only the Anstruther electorate being deprived of the great man's presence as he motored straight from Pittenweem to Cellardyke without stopping. There had been a misunderstanding about the booking of Anstruther town hall. The Cellardyke fisherfolk, doubtless unperturbed by Anstruther's loud indignation, gave the Liberal statesman a polite hearing before joining with their neighbours in voting in his Unionist opponent, Colonel Sir Alexander Sprot of Stravithie. Asquith's friends and supporters could hardly contain their fury. 'I feel humiliated as an Englishman at such a result', wrote the Bishop of Chelmsford. 'I am left today wondering whether this is really England', wrote his fellow bishop of Southwark. But it was not England that had ditched Asquith, it was the East Neuk of Fife, whose natives are not renowned for doing the expected thing. Augustine Birrell, himself a former member for a Fife constituency, summed up the Establishment's wrath:

> Now that it is over I don't mind telling you that *I never did like East Fife*, although I imagine the blunder is attributable to the absorption in the County of those plaguey boroughs with that fishing population which has broken the hearts of so many good (and bad) Liberals ere now.[13]

Almost before the dust had settled on the battlefields, the burghs were at loggerheads again. Whoever first suggested a joint war-memorial at the Billowness, the most distant part of Anstruther from Cellardyke, was a foolhardy optimist, and his plan was given short shrift at the next meeting of Kilrenny town council:

> 'Provost Black said so far as he could learn the inhabitants of Cellardyke were against it.
> *Bailie Marr* – That is so. They are in favour of it being in Cellardyke.'

Cellardyke's war-memorial now stands, gaunt and weather-beaten, in a commanding position on the Braehead opposite the Cardinal's Steps, looking out over the Firth to the May Island. The Anstruther memorial went ahead as planned at the Billowness.

Once the euphoria attending the Armistice had evaporated, hard reality returned with a vengeance. These were poor years for the fishing, and the increasing dependence on expensive steam drifters created social divisions among the fisherfolk as skippers and owners became more sharply differentiated from crewmen than ever before. While admirably suited for minesweeping, where the Admiralty footed the bill, the drifters were ruinously expensive for the average three- or four-man partnership of fishermen to maintain, and control of the industry gradually passed to wealthy landsmen who functioned both as owners and as extensive creditors. Even in 1900 the cost of a drifter was £1,500, compared to £700 for a sailing-boat of the largest type; while by 1912 the new standard steel drifters might cost £3,200.[14] Heavy coal bills, and the regular weekly wage paid to the non-shareholding 'black squad' of fire-man and engineer, were costs which had to be met irrespective of how many fish were caught. To be cost-effective the drifters had to be almost constantly at sea – great-lining for white fish when herring were not to be had – but the collapse of the great Russian export market after 1917 was a body-blow to the industry (in 1913, some 80% of cured herring exports had gone to Russia).

In 1919 a strike of machinists at Watson's oilskin factory in George Street was followed by a fishermen's strike: the men demanding that the drifter-owners adopt the 18-share principle employed at Peterhead (6 shares to the boat, 6 shares to the nets and 6 shares to the crew). A local branch of the National Sailors' and Fishermen's Union was set up. The once-despised trawlers were attracting more and more recruits from the East Neuk, for although the life was hard and the rewards, for ordinary crewmen, less than princely, each man was at least guaranteed a fixed weekly wage. This was enough to lure a number of Cellardyke fishermen up to Aberdeen during the inter-war period (including three of the author's uncles).

There is little good news from this period, but plenty of the other sort. William Gardner, engineer of the *Venus*, was lost at Yarmouth. Martin's factory in East Forth Street was gutted by fire. The old minister of Kilrenny, Mr. Anderson, was no longer able to carry out his duties, but no amount of pressure could budge him from his manse. (Almost alone among the churches of Scotland, Kilrenny still lacked an organ.) Concern was expressed at a meeting of the Anstruther District School Management Committee, on October 28th, 1920, that about 700 children from the area were missing schooling by going south to the Yarmouth fishing with their parents. They were allowed to sit in the schools there, replied Mr. Steele of St. Monans, 'but they received no lessons as the teachers in England could not understand what the children said'. It was agreed that local teachers be dispatched to East Anglia to cater for these unfortunate little seasonal migrants.

More pleasant to relate, a presentation made to Mr. Peter Thomson, to mark his fifty-two years as superintendent of the Anstruther Baptist Church Sunday School, gave the old ex-provost the chance to reminisce about fellow-Dykers who had been founding fathers of the little church at the East Green (only yards from the west end of Cellardyke). Grocer James Fowler had been the original pastor and preacher when the church was opened in 1859, and even before then the Sunday School had been started by the fish-curer James Horsburgh in his house at 17–21 James Street (later the home of the author's grandparents). Seeing the local children playing down at the seaside on the Sabbath day without benefit of religious instruction, Mr. Horsburgh had fetched them up to his house, where his spacious cellar had been converted into a subterranean schoolroom. It would be interesting to know how the children viewed this adult interference with their liberty.

Meanwhile history was repeating itself as Cellardyke fishermen once more set out for a new life in the colonies. This time it was Canada, not Australia or New Zealand, which beckoned. As early as 1912–13 the brothers Robert and William Davidson and their brothers-in-law Alexander Brown and Thomas Murray, along with another Dyker named John Wood, had set out for Hamilton, Ontario, where work had not been hard to find. Another man, Stephen Doig, opted for Port Dover on Lake Erie, where he found employment with the W. F. Kolbe Fish Company. On being told that many more experienced Scottish fishermen were currently living in Hamilton and practising other occupations, Mr. Kolbe set out in person to recruit the men; and the story goes that he found them sitting in Hamilton city park.[15] Thus began the little ex-patriate community of Dykers on the shores of Lake Erie.

Between 1920 and 1931 the Dyker colony received reinforcements, with the arrival of Jimmy Reekie, Jimmy Woodward, John Salter Watson, John and Tom Tarvit, Sandy Parker, Alex. Wood and Alex. Gardner; and before long the herring fishing in the Great Lakes was being prosecuted by tugs with names like the *Lashero* (cf. the Brunton family's steam drifter *Lasher* in Anstruther) and the *Dyker Lass* (skipper John Salter Watson, son of John Watson (Salter) of the *Pride o' Fife*). It was home from home for the Dykers, for whom the pursuit of herring was second nature.

Second nature too was another kind of trade which grew up in the '20s. When innate American puritanism led to the great drought known as Prohibition, many Port Dover crews took to running what was jocularly referred to as 'the midnight herring' down the Great Lakes to the U.S.A.:

> Whisky and beer were legally produced in Ontario and were listed on the ship's manifest as being destined for Cuba or some other legal point. Customs officials were usually inclined to look the other way when tugs returned from such exotic places within 24 hours of their departure, ready to pick up another shipment. During the daylight hours they tended their pound nets. There were reports of small swift vessels sneaking into the boat yards of Charlie Gamble in Port Dover for repairs to bullet holes in their hulls.[16]

Whether working for Kolbe or Capone, it was more profitable than remaining in Cellardyke; and the relationship was sealed when George Ingram, son of an Anstruther fish-merchant, married W. F. Kolbe's younger daughter Mildred Mary at a ceremony in Buffalo, N.Y.

An attempt to introduce Prohibition into the East Neuk itself in 1920 had failed miserably when most of the burghs voted resoundingly for

'No Change'. In Kilrenny and Cellardyke the figures were: No Change, 470; No Licence, 216; Limitation, 2. Similar results were recorded in Crail, the two Anstruthers and Pittenweem, where over-exuberant cele- brations ended with 'dry' voters' houses being bespattered with mud and several windows being broken. Only St. Monans, known irreverently to some in the East Neuk as 'the Holy City', went calmly against the tide with a decisive 459 votes for 'No Licence'. This result was attributed to the village's unique religious tradition, St. Monans being a well-known stronghold of the Open and Close Brethren and various other funda- mentalist religious sects.

We may mention in the passing two old Cellardyke veterans of the days of sail who died at this time. Peter Macaulay, who died at Port Chalmers in New Zealand in 1925, aged 89, had been orphaned young and brought up by his maternal grandmother Lizzie Small in Cellardyke. After trying the fishing he shipped before the mast in 1858 aboard the Anstruther clipper *Marco Polo*, then went on to become a gold-miner and then a merchant seaman again, before settling as a fisherman at Port Chalmers. His contemporary, John Sutherland, had also served aboard full-rigged merchant vessels before fate found him a berth on the famous steamship *Great Eastern*, when in 1865 she successfully laid the trans- atlantic cable from Ireland to Newfoundland. During that epic voyage John Sutherland was in the main cable tank. On another occasion he was serving aboard the sailing-ship *Lord of the Isles* when she was wrecked on an atoll in the Philippines, and for several weeks, until a passing trader dropped anchor in the vicinity, he was forced to lead a Robinson Crusoe style of existence in idyllic surroundings.

Men like Sutherland and Macaulay have a familiar air to them, for we have met their like in the stories of Joseph Conrad and John Masefield, and other romances from the days of 'sturdy ships that were a glory of white canvas'.

Many old things were passing away now, and yet greater changes loomed on the horizon. On November 19th, 1925, the *East Fife Observer* published an imaginary conversation 'overheard' at Anstruther harbour, which treated in a lighthearted fashion one of the longest-standing pre- occupations of the Dykers in this or any other age:

HARBOUR HEAD GOSSIP
Stranger (re drifters) – Do all these men belong to Anstruther?
Speaker – Oh, no no. I see you are a stranger here. The fishermen a' belong to Cellardyke, a different place or burgh a' thegither. (Pointing to Cellardyke) It's east that way the fishermen bide.
Stranger – A different burgh, dear me.
Speaker – Aye, there's long been a crack aboot 'gaun thegither' wi Anster, but tae tell ye the trith auld prejudice has keepit it back. Oor fethers used aye to say, 'Dinna gaun in wi' onything Anster wants ye tae dae or else you'll be dune. They aye did hes and they'll dae the same tae you. Awthing for thersels.'

But there was no holding back the tide of 'progress': 1929 saw the passing of the Local Government (Scotland) Act, and on November 12th the town council of Anstruther Easter met for the last time, followed on the 25th by Anstruther Wester – whose provost, Mr. Brodie, thus ended forty-six years' service on the council. Kilrenny council, meeting on the 26th, was therefore the last of the three municipal bodies to surrender its independence.

The evening commenced with routine business. There were walls to be repaired, and houses and fences to be painted. Then Provost Mitchell rose to present the parchment of the Royal Humane Society to James McLeod, who on August 22nd had saved a young boy from drowning in Cellardyke harbour. It was a pleasant duty with which to conclude the affairs of Kilrenny town council. The provost then invited the councillors and officials to the Reading Room to enjoy what the *Observer* termed 'a sumptuous repast'. It was a time for reminiscence, and for looking forward – partly in trepidation, partly in anticipation – to the future of the United Burghs. Baillie W. W. Carstairs, of Martin's factory in East Forth Street, had no regrets for 'time past': 'I, myself, can look back to the days when it was hardly possible for an Anstruther boy to show his nose in Cellardyke, and vice versa. It was then an occasion for divots and stones in such a way that it was often a pitched battle, the spirit of animosity being then so prevalent even amongst the young boys.' Anstruther had probably missed its chance, he thought, the title of 'premier fishing port of the east coast' having been yielded to Aberdeen; but there was still cause for optimism if the three burghs worked together.

One amusing example of past disharmony was given by town clerk J. Gordon Dow: 'Bailie Carstairs has referred to the anomaly that has existed with three burghs and one town clerk. I recollect when I was town clerk when Anstruther Easter had occasion to complain against Kilrenny dumping rubbish inside Anstruther's boundary. I wrote to myself as clerk of Kilrenny stating that the practice must cease at once.'

Bailie Bett, who had been associated with the council for 18 years, remarked that he was not an amalgamationist, and he regretted that the pleasant nights they had had in the council chambers had come to an end. Councillors Hunter and Thomson spoke next, then the provost was toasted to the strains of 'For He's a Jolly Good Fellow'. Thus ended the last meeting of Kilrenny town council, a body whose earliest records date back to 1592, and whose first council chamber had been erected in 1624. As the councillors wrapped themselves up against the chill November night and took their separate ways home, it was left to the caretaker of Cellardyke town hall to lock the door on over 300 years of history.

On December 10th, 1929, 25 candidates offered themselves for the 12 seats on the first town council of the United Burghs of Kilrenny, Anstruther Easter and Anstruther Wester. (Yet again an opportunity was missed to give the name 'Cellardyke' official status, 'Kilrenny' being by now a decayed and depopulated little rural hamlet.) W. G. Readdie of Anstruther Easter was elected first provost, to be succeeded only three years later by Baillie Carstairs of Cellardyke: a controversial figure to whom we shall be returning.

Scarcely had the councillors taken their seats when the recriminations began. For some reason, Kilrenny's rates had dropped by 9d., while Anstruther Easter's had risen by 6d. and Anstruther Wester's by 2/7d. 'Anstruther Easter and Wester are paying for the privilege of uniting with Kilrenny' was a common opinion given vent to in the local paper. 'Not so!' cried the Dykers:

> The people of Cellardyke do not think that their portion of the united burgh is receiving a full measure of treatment, and whether this be right or wrong the fact cannot be ignored that where there is smoke there is fire.
> This leads us to the old, old question of amalgamation, and while many may say that the old days of rivalry are gone, others know that that rivalry exists to-day and that Cellardyke will never be Anstruther. (*East Fife Observer*, October 23rd, 1930)

Perhaps not so much had changed after all! Controversy over a new coat-of-arms was however avoided by adopting the anchor of Anstruther Easter, the three interlaced salmon of Anstruther Wester and the open boat crewed by five mariners of Kilrenny.

It would have taken more than 'amalgamation' to change the age-old ways of the Cellardyke housewife. Here is an eyewitness report from an incredulous Glasgow 'visitor', published in the local paper on June 19th, 1930:

A street sign at the east end of Kilrenny village, showing the combined coat-of-arms of the United Burghs.

'Doing the door' is, apparently, a morning task over which Cellardyke housewives spend much time. Passing through the narrow streets the other day, I was quite amused to observe not only the brass and doorsteps being cleaned but also the pavement and half across the street being washed down. I am informed that this regularly takes place, no matter the weather. It seems a foolish task, and one does not know whether to commend or censure Cellardyke's wives, as pedestrians soon obliterate work expended on the pavement. This is the first place I have been in where women wash the street. Does this practice prevail elsewhere?

The need for such obsessive cleanliness had passed, but the women of Cellardyke could not help themselves, for they were heirs to those indomitable creatures described so vividly in verse by 'Poetry Peter' Smith, the fisherman-poet of Cellardyke, in his collection *Fisher Folk* (Peter Smith was born in 1874 at 34 George Street, the descendant of generations of Cellardyke Smiths, Doigs, Murrays and Cunninghams):

> Yon days oor women gaithered whiles,
> Tae pairt the mussels doon the Giles,
> Or when the snaw lay on the tiles,
> Doon tae the Skaup:
> Or gaithered limpits, traivelled miles
> Tae fill a caup.

Nae hats or gloves were worn they say,
But only on the Sabbath day,
Then tartan neepyins held the sway
Ower heid or shoother.
Be their hair black, or broon, or gray,
Lass, wife or mither.

Nae kilts wore they, but guid long claes.
It was the fashion – if you please.
Then a' ye saw was jist their taes,
As they gaed by;
Nae lang bare legs on wintry days
As blue's the sky.

What were the men up to while the women scoured the streets? Football, for one thing – and there was no need to travel to the nearest city when Anstruther had its own 'Bluejackets'. Here is 'Poetry Peter' again, in 'Tae Jeems':

I, and you tae, can mind it fine,
Tam Dug ran doon along the line,
And no a man hooever swift,
But Tam could left far oot o' sicht.

And when the Crailers cam' tae play,
The hale Toll Road was fu' that day.
Hoo Little Duggie taen the lead,
Coupit lang Morris ower his heid,
Hoo you and Crieff fair had the knack,
Tae mak' wha eer cam' near – stout back,
'Whiteheid' in Dyker fitba' story,
As famous as the great McGrory.

Golf, the Fife sport *par excellence*, also had its followers, and they must have enjoyed the following news item on July 10th, 1930, relating the success, in the United States, of Cellardyke-born golfer John Watson (the author's uncle):

INDIANA CHAMPION

CELLARDYKE MAN'S SUCCESS

BRILLIANT GOLF

Golfing fame has come to Cellardyke through the success of a native in America.
Mr John Watson, the popular professional golfer at Erskine Park Club, South Bend, Indiana, recently won the Indiana State Open Championship with a score of

The *Nancy Hunnam* at Yarmouth before the First World War. (L. to R.) Jimmy McRuvie ('Kye'); Wull Kermack; John Deas; – Jack; unknown; skipper Charlie Gen ('Chairlie the Frenchman'); Peter Smith ('Poetry Peter'); Adam Watson. In the hold: Jocky Watson sen. (Martin). Adam and Jocky Watson were the author's great-uncles.

281 for 72 holes. Proof of Mr Watson's golfing skill is found in the details of his rounds, which yielded 69, 71, 73, and 68, one of the lowest scores returned in a United States open championship. . . .

Mr Watson is the sixth son of Mr and Mrs Wm. Watson, 21 James Street, Cellardyke, and a nephew of Mr H. Duff, one time of St Andrews. On leaving Cellardyke School Mr Watson was employed as a joiner at Pittenweem and at the age of 18 he decided to cross the Atlantic as an assistant to his uncle as a golf professional. His success was immediate and after serving at Louisville with his uncle he decided to strike out on his own and accepted a post at Wanasee where he remained for two years. Later he became a professional at Marion, Indiana, and for the last four years he has been professional to the Erskine Club and is the first professional to bring the State Open Crown to South Bend. His uncle is at present professional at Nashville.

In the land of his adoption Mr Watson has achieved signal success as a golfer and has met many of the big guns of the American golfers including Bobby Jones and Walter Hagen, with whom he had a particularly close struggle to the last green.

Possibly Watson will one day join the ranks of competitors after the golfing honours of Great Britain.

Later in the decade ambitious plans were drawn up for a golf course to
the east of Cellardyke – the 'architect' being the great James Braid of
Earlsferry. Unfortunately the scheme fell through on the grounds of
expense. But a proposal to cut out a swimming pool at the east end of the
town was more successful, largely because much of the labour was
undertaken by unpaid volunteers. The 'Pond' was opened on June 17th,
1933, and at the suggestion of Provost Carstairs was officially named
'The Cardinal's Steps'. Nearby a hut was erected for the East Neuk
Model Yacht Club. A putting green had been laid out there some ten
years previously. Thus the Town's Green, where the 'Fifies' of yesteryear had been pulled up by traction engine, became the recreation area of
a more leisured age. Once again we turn to the gently ironic pen of our
local bard for a full history of the enterprise:

THE POND (From *The Herring, and other Poems*)

> Jist draw inower your chair or stule,
> And if the muses dinna fail
> I'll tell ye a' a canty tale
>   O' oor ain folk
> Which happened jist within a mile
>   O' Basket Rock.

> Ae day, no awfu' lang, lang syne,
> Some steery chiels, I kin them fine,
> Tae clean a dub made up their min'
>   And redd it oot,
> Three cables length frae 'Skimfast Hyne'
>   Or there aboot.

> A bathin' pond they thocht tae mak' it,
> So wi' some mair they cuist their jacket,
> Skellies and rocks and stanes they whacket,
>   Baith big and little;
> And mony a lempit's shell they cracket,
>   And mony a knuckle.

> 'Twas ca'ed the 'Shaulds' by aulder chaps,
> And lies fornent the 'Caunle Staps',
> But, jist for fear o' South East slaps
>   Some winter nicht,
> A dyke was built tae save mishaps,
>   And keep it richt.

The Cardinal's Steps bathing-pool and Croma House today (27th September 1985), with a haar coming in from the sea. Cellardyke's war-memorial can be seen on the right of the picture.

Some workmen cam frae Anster Pier,
Built up the dyke and wi' their gear
Cleaned oot a bit – losh I'll say here
            They did their best,
But left it tae the volunteer
            Tae dae the rest.

And fegs, they cam frae a' the airts,
Frae fishin' boats and ploomen's cairts,
Left joiners shops and makin' tairts
            Tae brak up skellies:
Clerks, grocers, slaters did their pairts,
            The hearty fellas.

The very laddies frae the skule
Gobbled their parridge and their kail,
Syne yerkit at it teeth and nail,
            Wi' heirt and haund.
The lassies fain wad ta'en a spale
            I understand.

It didna' need nae magic stroller,
Or weel read, educated scholar
Tae tell them that it needed sillar,
      Fine did they ken
'Twad need the great and Mighty Dollar
      Ere it was dune.

Yet even then they didna' stick,
A' plans were tried – clear o' 'Auld Nick',
The best o' talent they did pick
      Frae near and far:
Then crooned a' wi' this magic trick
      A Grand Bazaar.

Gifts cam tae it frae Jock, Tam, Jeannie,
A new tarred net, a set o' cheeny,
A guernsey and a lassie's pinny,
      Sweeties and caundy,
A soo, some hens, a concertina,
      Wad a' come haundy.

At first the pond was meant for soomin'
For lads and lassies, men and women,
For sweeps or clerks, fishers or ploomen,
      For laird or cottar;
As long's ye proved that ye were human
      And payed yer copper.

Noo hoo it cam, I'll no say richt
If 'twas a dream or second sicht
Made them see yachts some munelicht nicht
      Sail ower the Dub;
The slogan rang – and rang wi' micht,
      A Yachtin' Club.

Yachts, oot they cam, baith auld and new,
O' various shapes and varied hue,
Some no been seen since Waterloo,
      Don't think I'm vulgar;
Some carved wi' some o' Nelson's crew
      Before Trafalgar.

Frae closets, cellars, kists and garrets,
Some pretty models, some nae merits,
Like Joseph's coat, wi' nebs like parrots,
      Sic a display.
They minded me o' scoots and marrits
      Aboot the 'May'.

> But losh, the thing taen on new life,
> Models were made, baith braw and rife,
> Some built, some carved wi' jist a knife
>   Wi' cunnin' haund,
> Wad shamed the buildin' yairs o' Fife,
>   They were sae graund.
>
> They sailed, jist like some living thing,
> White sails like sea birds on the wing,
> While frae their boos the spume did fling
>   Past their lee side;
> I'm sure if seen their praise'll ring
>   Frae Cowes tae Clyde.
>
> The Racin' Cups, no ane, but three,
> Gifted by men wi' sportsman's ee,
> Draw croods the races for tae see,
>   Frae far and near;
> Sic men, I think you'll a' agree,
>   Deserve a cheer.
>
> Nae mare I'll say aboot the race,
> For gosh, I've neither time nor space,
> But shud ye think it's no the case,
>   Flee, bus or hike
> Tae yon auld farrant, auld world place
>   Named – Cellardyke.

For those who preferred more passive pursuits, there was always the new phenomenon of the 'talkies', which arrived at the Empire Picture House in Anstruther on December 10th, 1931. Although the Town Hall Picture House was to close on January 9th, the Empire, next to the *East Fife Observer* office in High Street, Anstruther Easter, and the Regal Cinema, in Crichton Street, Anstruther Wester, were to survive into modern times: a powerful lure on Saturday nights to Dykers who had no such glamorous entertainments on their side of Caddies Burn.

To more sober topics now. The shortcomings of the steam drifter were the subject of much discussion at this time, and some of the more far-sighted owners were casting around for more efficient and economical types of boat. In 1928 Provost (then Baillie) Carstairs had had two motorboats, the *Winaway* (skipper John Gourlay) and the *Onaway* (skipper Jocky Watson), launched at Anstruther. Both boats were powered by 48 h.p. semi-diesel Gardner engines, and were 53 feet in length. The *Winaway* continued to fish out of Anstruther under the same

The crew of the *Gleanaway*, including some of the author's relatives, in the early 1930s. (L. to R.) John Cunningham (great-uncle); Eck Meldrum (from St. Monans); George Flett; skipper Jocky Watson jun. (father's cousin); Jimmy Watson (father's cousin); Leslie Henderson. In lifebelt: John Ballingall (son of local policeman).

skipper for the next twenty years or so, but the *Onaway* was purchased by the Ministry of Agriculture and Fisheries in 1930 for experimental and research work. Her successor, the *Gleanaway*, was confidently expected to run at a cost of £8 10s. per week. compared with £26 15s. for a steam drifter, and in 1931 her crew (it was claimed) netted £40 2s. 6d. a share for the Yarmouth fishing compared to the driftermen's £22. In 1936 the *Gleanaway* was sold to South Africa and her successor, the *Royal Sovereign*, was built and launched at Cellardyke harbour. Part-owners with Mr. Carstairs in all three boats were the brothers Jocky and Jimmy Watson (cousins of the author's father).

Tragedy struck in those years too. In February 1934 Tom Anderson of Cellardyke was lost overboard from the motor-boat *Just Reward*, while in August Charles Anderson of 24 Rodger Street and Robert Hodge of 33 John Street, crewmen on the *Mace*, were drowned at Fraserburgh. Only a few days later a whole ten-man crew escaped, miraculously, when their drifter was rammed and sunk in the North Sea.

On the night of Wednesday, August 22nd, 1934, the *Venus* was lying at her nets off Scarborough and most of the crew had turned in, leaving Robbie Bett alone in the wheelhouse. Suddenly – and none of the crew could later explain how it had happened – a trawler loomed up out of the darkness and hit the old wooden vessel so hard in the side that within four minutes she had crumpled up like matchwood and gone to the bottom. The crew, hastily roused from sleep, were forced to jump onto the pitching deck of the trawler – the *Staunton* of Grimsby – abandoning all their possessions in the frantic scramble. The *Staunton* later transferred them to the Berwick drifter *Janet*, which landed them at North Shields. The crew of the *Venus* (a name which has attracted more than its fair share of bad luck in the annals of Cellardyke) were Peter Murray (son of 'Venus Peter'), Tam Birrell, James Smith ('The Kitlin'), John Peat, Michael Doig, Martin Tarvit, Robert Bett, George Bett and Henry Watson (the author's father), all from Cellardyke, and Andrew Anderson from Pittenweem.

Less fortunate than these men were skipper James Tarvit of 22 Fowler Street, his brother John Tarvit of 8 Fowler Street, and David Birrell of 2 Toll Road, all lost when the Leith trawler *May Island* was washed ashore at Lamba Ness in the Shetlands two years later.

Municipal improvements continued apace. Twelve houses had been built on the east side of Toll Road in 1928, and in 1932–33 twelve more were added at Blyth's Park, between Fowler Street and Toll Road. Those east of Fowler Street were named 'Fowler Place'. Cellardyke architect Martin Gardner designed an enclosed sale-ring and offices at Anstruther harbour, on the site of the old shore-dues office. A new cemetery was consecrated at St. Andrews Road, Anstruther, and Dykers resigned themselves to sharing eternity with their Enster cousins. Then, for the second time in living memory, the world slid downhill towards war.

Mr. Chamberlain's declaration on September 3rd, 1939, found the people of Cellardyke and Kilrenny, like much of the nation, at church. When the first air-raid warning sounded, at ten to twelve, the congregations dispersed quietly, without any show of panic. The minister of Kilrenny at this period was the Rev. J. Marshall Pryde, a veteran of the trenches in the First World War, who had succeeded the late Mr. Anderson in 1925 and had lost no time in equipping his church with a much-needed organ. With their four strapping grown-up sons Mr. and Mrs. Pryde cut a very different figure in the parish from their predecessor. By the autumn of 1939 all four sons had become pilots in the

R.A.F. Three weeks after the declaration of war, Flying-Officer William Pryde was killed during a practice flight in the East of England. He was in his 23rd year.

It took only another three weeks before the reality of war impinged with brutal suddenness on the East Neuk. On Monday, October 16th, the streets of Anstruther were crowded with shoppers (including the author's mother) when a large black plane appeared flying low over the rooftops. The interested onlookers craned their necks for a better view, until bus conductress Zena Wood spotted the swastikas on the wings. Fourteen German bombers, the *East Fife Observer* later reported, had attacked naval vessels in the Firth of Forth in Britain's first air-raid of the war.

As in 1914 the local fishing industry was an early victim, with drifters and motor-boats alike being pressed into war service. However, there is no sign that the fishermen were reluctant to join up, at least as far as the Royal Navy was concerned. As in the First World War, fishermen were in great demand for the patrol service and boom defence, and some veterans of that earlier conflict were ready for the fray again: veterans like William Davidson, aged 56, who had held skipper's rank on H.M. drifters *Guerdon* and *Clara Wood* at home and in the Adriatic. A skipper who stayed with his vessel in wartime went straight into uniform and kept his command. Thus in 1939 when the steam drifter *Acorn* (K.Y. 194) was requisitioned by the Admiralty, her skipper Martin Gardner ('Acorn Mairt') of 29 James Street was signed on as skipper under Merchant Navy articles before being transferred in February 1941 to the R.N.R. The following list, preserved among the records of the Anstruther Fishery Office at West Register House, gives the names of Cellardyke men who applied to go fishing for mines in the early years of the war (N.B.: 2nd Hand = Mate; A.B. = Able Seaman; O.S. = Ordinary Seaman):

R.N. Patrol Service and Boom Defence (West Register House, AF 19/137

Henry R. D. Watson	12 East Forth St.	2nd Hand (the author's father)
Wm. John Barclay	26 Toll Road	O.S.
Robert Thomson	6 Urquhart Wynd	A.B.
Robert Thomson	8 Glenburn Road	A.B.
James Watson	21 John Street	O.S.
Robert S. Pattie	1 Dove Street	O.S.
Alex. Keay	44 John Street	Engineman
David Corstorphine	52 George Street	O.S.
Thomas Tarvit	10 Burnside Place	O.S. & cook
John W. Reekie	69 George Street	O.S.

Patrick O'Brien	12 James Street	A.B.
John Cunningham Bird	56 John Street	Engineman
Charles C. Gen	2 West Forth Street	O.S.
John Fleming	38 East Forth Street	O.S.
Alex. Thomson jun.	1 Rodger Street	A.B.
Robert Gardner	41 James Street	Engineman

Not all those who applied were accepted, and indeed some men's eagerness was in inverse proportion to their suitability. On November 19th, 1940, the Recruiting Officer, Royal Navy & Royal Marines, 300 Bath Street, Glasgow, wrote in the following terms to the Fishery Officer, Anstruther:

> Dear Sir,
> You will remember that I called upon you a few months back and found that you were away so wrote explaining my visit relative Patrolmen. The trouble is that men are attempting to enrol as such having *no sea experience* whatever, consequently if they manage to slip through my fingers, I get a rap over the knuckles from the Depot to which they are sent when this is found out. . . .
> Men for the Patrol Service MUST have sea experience in *seagoing* fishing vessels even for grade 'B'. . . .

No doubt a distaste for the Army, traditional in maritime communities, was behind many of these ill advised attempts to join the Navy.

It has been said that the first casualty of war is the truth, and certainly there is a distinct odour of censorship in the columns of the local paper from now on. Only with local knowledge and the testimony of survivors is it possible to fill in the gaps in news stories. There was no ban, however, on stories of heroism, and the paper's editor was only too pleased to print the story of Chief Coxswain Martin Gardner (Thomson) of 46 James Street, who on the afternoon of Saturday, February 10th, 1940, arrived back in Cellardyke on leave to find yet more danger lying in wait for him at home. A Swedish cargo-steamer, the *Göteborg*, had gone aground at the Carr Briggs, near Fife Ness, and because of the wartime ban on the firing of rockets a car had been sent round the town to alert the crew of the lifeboat. Not until the boat was being launched did someone mention that Martin Gardner was back in town. With midnight approaching the unfortunate coxswain was summoned from his bed and carried out dryshod to the boat on the back of Mr. Alex. Cunningham. The rescue was a brilliant success, both crew and boat being saved.

In June of that year Flying Officer David Douglas Pryde was awarded the D.F.C. for his part in a bombing-raid, and the *Observer* reported that his eldest brother, George, was now a Squadron-Leader. Five days later Squadron-Leader George Pryde was killed in action.

Rodger Street, Cellardyke, after the bombing raid of 25th October 1940.

Before the end of the year Cellardyke itself came under attack. On the evening of October 25th people were resting after their day's labours or getting their children ready for bed when the town was rocked by a massive explosion, and the air resounded with the roar of engines and the stutter of machine-guns:

> John McRuvie cam through and said, 'Come on, come on, get the bairns oot!' We were sheltering in a cupboard, and I couldnae get the door shut. John said, 'I'll jist go oot and see what it's like.' Just then there was a splatter o tracer bullets in the brick. Jean (a sister in Crail) cam along next day and said, 'It's a' roond Crail that Cellardyke's gettin bombed' (The author's mother, then living at 12 East Forth Street).

A house in Rodger Street had taken a direct hit, and the whole street had suffered structural damage. Windows were broken, and fishermen's backyard 'lofts' shattered. By an unbelievable stroke of fortune the worst injuries sustained were a few superficial scratches. The houses in West Forth Street were also affected, and in distant Aberdeen a resident of that street with a reputation for possessing the second sight dreamt that the frosted glass panel in her front door had developed a complex pattern of cracks: a dream which on her arrival home proved to be only too true.

Up in Kilrenny the news was worse, for another bomb had hit the isolated cottage of a shepherd named Alex. Scott, killing his wife and their eldest son. Local rumour afterwards claimed that the son had gone out with a hurricane-lamp, as the plane was flying over, to see to his pet rabbits: but we shall never know.

There were many more casualties in the following years. In January 1941 Alexander Doig (McLeod) was killed in a bombing raid on Cornwall, while James Gay of 81 George Street was killed at Tobruk. John Smith Rodger was lost in the sinking of H.M.S. *Cossack*, and Chief Skipper Alexander Watson (Reid) D.S.C. aboard H.M.S. *Flanders*. David McRuvie, skipper of an armed trawler, was decorated for bringing down a Dornier 17, but was lost at sea almost a year to the day later. Second Officer David Watson (Rankine) of the Merchant Navy met the same end. Craftsman David Smith of R.E.M.E., Driver Robert A. Fowler of the R.A.S.C. and Company-Sergeant-Major James Pratt (Thomson) died in North Africa and the Middle East. Squadron-Leader David Douglas Pryde was reported missing, and his parents in the Kilrenny manse had an agonizing six months to wait for confirmation that they had lost a third son. The remaining son, Jack, was injured in a plane crash and invalided out of the R.A.F. to become a captain in the Argylls. He was to survive the war, having served in all three main branches of the armed forces, and would later marry the widow of one of his brothers in fulfilment of a pact the two boys had made at the beginning of the war.[17]

Many Cellardyke and Anstruther men were serving in the Dover patrol, and one casualty was 30-year-old Boom Skipper Thomas Ritchie, known affectionately, on account of his handsome, dapper appearance, as 'Count Ritchie'. He died during an enemy bombing raid on Dover harbour (the author's father was wounded in the same raid).

While the young gave their lives, the old remained, and it is heartening to record the remarkable number of golden weddings celebrated at this time in Cellardyke. First came Robert Stewart and Agnes Watson, in December 1940, followed by William Watson and Jessie Cunningham on September 18th, 1941. William and Jessie had been married at the little inland parish of Dunino, a common custom for Dykers in the 1890s. In one week in 1892 four Cellardyke couples had been married there, including James Watson ('Star Jeems') and Catherine Fowler Smith, of 19 John Street, who celebrated fifty years of marriage on September 22nd, 1942. In November came the turn of Mr. and Mrs. Alexander McRuvie of 4 East Forth Street, Mr. McRuvie being a veteran of the sailing Fifies who had gone on to become mate on the steam drifter *White Cross*. His wife was a daughter of Charles Marr, skipper in his day of the *Ocean Foam*, *Queen of the Isles* and *Gem of the Sea*.

Robert Muir of 28 West Forth Street, who died aged 74 in January 1943, was an old seadog who had lost count of the number of times he had circumnavigated the globe. His favourite story concerned a journey from 'Frisco to Falmouth which took more than half a year, the crew subsisting on weevily biscuits and sips of water. It was a tale with which to thrill a more fortunate generation, but amidst the war news of the 1940s it has the nostalgic aura of a lost age of innocence.

Ironically, as the tale of carnage mounted weekly in the local paper (we have no space here to mention all the dead), the *Edinburgh Evening News* printed a poem about the winding-up of the Hearse Society of Kilrenny: a friendly society whose members had been united in their determination to avoid a pauper's funeral:

GRIM BLACK STALLIONS
Kilrenny Hearse! What memories of childhood you recall –
The burn that wimples softly past thy coach-house wall;
Its grated door through which as bairns full oft we keekit in,
Unfrightened by thy sombre plumes, as black as mortal sin;
The old church and its steeple and cock without a tail;
And the slow procession wending to the kirkyard dale;
Whither in quiet dignity, by clamours undistressed,
Ye bore the 'rude forefathers' to their last long rest.
Theirs was no fear of pauper coach to rattle o'er the stones,
Who, in their private carriage disposed their weary bones;
So now, as once ye drove them take ye your own last ride.
Gone members, horse, society – old hearse, go forth in pride.[18]

The war brought strange distinctions to natives of the East Neuk. Detective Inspector William Hughes of Special Branch, a Pittenweemer by birth, accompanied Mr. Churchill on visits to Italy and to the Allied Forces in Normandy. Betty Gardner, daughter of Martin Gardner (Thomson) of Cellardyke, exchanged the uniform of a bus-conductress for that of a sergeant in the Searchlight Regiment in London, and had a letter of thanks from a grateful pilot read out on the wireless. Private James Keay of Toll Road helped cook lunch for King George when the monarch visited the troops in North Africa. Skipper Alexander Doig McRuvie of Burnside Terrace took part in the Salerno and Anzio landings and was mentioned in dispatches. A member of the Free Dutch forces with the unlikely name of Jan Melvill van Carnbee paid a visit to the ancestral home of his forbear Sir John Melville of Carnbee, who had emigrated to Holland in the 1600s. Another 'exile', Flight-Sergeant Roy

Taylor of the Royal Australian Air Force, came to visit his Cunningham relatives in Cellardyke before taking up a Middle East posting, and was killed in action only three months later (Roy Taylor was a cousin of the author's father).

Disasters closer to home included a destructive fire at Martin's factory in 1943, and a similar outbreak in January 1945 when Watson's factory was gutted, and several families living nearby lost both their home and all their possessions. But by this time it was becoming clear that the war was won, and – a sure sign of returning sanity – a quite different kind of result was uppermost in Dyker minds. On Saturday, April 13th, 1945, Hitler had just over a fortnight to live, and England hammered Scotland at Hampden Park. 'Even the glories of the 51st Division can't console us', wrote Alex. Smith to the *East Fife Observer*:

> The schoolboys of the United Burghs must feel frustrated, knowing that they have no chance to learn football and play some day for their country. Football is Scotland's national game, yet at the Waid Academy the boys are not allowed to play it. I would like to know who is responsible for this?

Someone must have hearkened to his plea, for by the time the author arrived at Waid Academy, in the summer of 1958, football had taken its place alongside rugby as part of the sporting curriculum.

The General Election took place in July, and the editor of the *Observer* felt able to assure his readers that 'Propaganda whispers that the Services vote had tended very much to the Left are now discounted'. 'Sober opinion', he continued, had realized that a defeat for the National Government was unthinkable. The rest of the country, unaware of the unassailability of Churchill's government, proceeded to vote the Socialists into power; not that it made much difference in East Fife, where J. Henderson-Stewart of the Liberal National party was returned to Westminster with a cosy 13,845 majority.

Meanwhile the ex-servicemen and -women of the East Neuk were coming back to face an uncertain future. There were worries that Rosyth naval dockyard, an important employer of local labour, would revert to a 'care and maintenance' basis as had happened after the First World War. The outlook was also bleak for Crail Aerodrome, lately the base for No. 827 Squadron, who had participated in the last, decisive attack on the *Tirpitz* in 1944 (later Crail Aerodrome was to become one of a handful of Joint Services Schools for Linguists, where elderly émigrés conducted crash courses in Russian for services personnel. One graduate of the Crail school was Geoffrey Prime). The Admiralty was reluctant to part with boats which it had requisitioned for the war effort, and demobbed fishermen were returning from the Navy to find themselves unemployed. There were not enough boats to take full advantage of the winter herring in the Forth, and there was anger and frustration at the spectacle of large-scale herring imports from Norway. The fishermen themselves were not released all at once, and many boats continued to fish with elderly crewmen taking the place of absent sons or nephews.

It was not all gloom, however. The Inshore Fishing Industry Bill provided for loans and grants for fishermen to buy new boats, or to acquire redundant Admiralty motor-vessels, and in August 1946 James Bett became the first ex-serviceman to take advantage of the scheme when, with the assistance of his mate Donald Sutherland, he sailed M.F.V. 437 all the way up the coast from Bournemouth to Anstruther. Other skippers procured boats on loan, like John Gardner of Cellardyke, who in early 1946 became the first local skipper to prosecute the winter-herring fishing in the Forth with a steam-drifter: in this case, the Peterhead-registered *Tyrie*.

But although none or few foresaw it at the time, the days of drift-netting for herring were effectively over, and the next five years would see the total eclipse of the winter-herring fishing. Five years later again, in 1956, James Muir's *Coriedalis* became the last East Fife drifter to make the annual autumn trip to Yarmouth. The age of the seine-netter had arrived, despite much opposition, and it was the end of several 'auld sangs'.

In May 1946 a public meeting in Anstruther about the future of the East Neuk burghs gave local people the chance to air their fears and hopes. How was the area to attract new industry when it was not scheduled as suitable for industrial development? (The impending expansion of coal-mining in West Fife had persuaded the uninformed bureaucrats of Whitehall that 'Fife' was now taken care of.) The drift of the rural population was appalling, reported County Planning Officer Mr. M. E. Taylor, and if the audience could see the figures for population moving from East Fife into the towns it would make them wonder what was going to happen. Provost Carstairs announced that an attractive brochure had been sent 'far and wide', extolling the East Neuk's potential as a holiday resort.

Perhaps most worrying of all was the contribution of Mr. W. W. Thomson, rector of the Waid Academy in Anstruther – the sole secondary school in the East Neuk outside St Andrews – who remarked '. . . that there was nothing to him more depressing than the knowledge that the best boys and girls who left school every year had to go out of East Fife to earn a living. To his mind that was not right. There were no opportunities locally, and it looked almost as if the East of Fife had become reconciled to drifting into a sort of lethargy'.

At Cellardyke Primary School the roll had slumped from 438 in 1929 to 280 in 1946: a depressing statistic. Was this the future of the United Burghs: to become a geriatric desert, abandoned by its young people and living off its memories of the past? Probably no-one present viewed the problem in quite such melodramatic terms, but there was no mistaking their genuine concern that May evening in 1946 as they debated the future of their community in a bleak post-war world.

Postscript

That's how it was, and that's how it is. I was born just over a fortnight after that meeting in Anstruther, and throughout my lifetime the same questions have gone largely unanswered.

In the early '50s the influx of R.A.F. personnel brought back a temporary bustle and 'busyness', but without seriously affecting the economy of the area. At Cellardyke Primary School we looked askance at the strangely-accented incomers, and in school, shop and pub the culture clash was considerable. Servicemen's wives, often from south of the border, and accustomed to the perks of living in West Germany or the Far East, were slow to acclimatise to the East Neuk of Fife, and they were not universally welcomed by local people. But eventually lasting friendships were struck, and the end result was probably broadened minds on both sides.

The transformation of the R.A.F. camp at Toll Road into Anstruther Holiday Camp has been a more lasting change, but essentially it only put the already existing holiday trade onto a more organised basis. When I was a boy we welcomed a particular family into our home year after year, and before my time there were even some Dykers who handed over their home to the 'visitors' and took up temporary residence in their gear lofts. Hospitality can surely go no further! Every year during the Glasgow Fair, or the corresponding holiday period for Paisley, Coatbridge, or wherever, the same family would come to the same house in Cellardyke until the children on either side were grown-up, and reached the stage of exchanging wedding-presents. Today the holidaymaker comes with his family to a caravan or a barrack-room euphemistically termed a 'chalet', set in a camp which has many facilities of its own; and contacts with local people are less intimate than formerly.

What of the fishing – the lifeblood of the community from earliest times, and the very reason for its existence in the first place? The great days were over before I was born, and I regret this. I would like to have seen the winter-herring fleet strung out in a line between the May and the shore, their lights twinkling like a city out at sea, and the men's voices rolling back over the water, in the crisp, clear evenings after the New Year. Or the convoys of lorries thundering through the night to

Primary 1 at Cellardyke School, session 1951–52. *Back Row*: (L. to R.) Michael
Smith; George Finlay; the author; Michael O'Neill; Ronnie Thomson; George
N. Allan; Tom Brown; David Parry; Graham Safely; Hugh Barnett.
Second Row: (L. to R.) Mary Mackay; Sandra Murray; Sandra Birrell; Elizabeth
Christie; Senga Booth; Kathleen Bartlett; Isobel Meldrum; Agnes Bush;
Patricia Watson.
Third Row: (L. to R.) John Horne; Beatrice Cameron; Elsie Clarke; Helen
Deas; Angela Bruce; Evelyn 'Goldie' McInnes; Wilma Hughes; Pamela Burch;
Isobel Bolt; Mary Braid; Jimmy Syme.
Front Row: (L. to R.) Sandy Scott; Tom Horsburgh; Robert Taylor; Ian
Anderson; David McLean; Alec Imrie; David Appleby; Neil Mackie; Billy
Cowie; Ian Strowger.

Anstruther station and the waiting trains which would take the fish to
Leith docks, and onto freighters bound for Hamburg. The Dutch and
German cargo-boats which thronged Anstruther harbour after the potato
harvest were gone by my time. But I am just old enough to remember the
very end of the Yarmouth fishing, when I would be taken down to the
pier to get my 'bakes' from my uncle Adam, on Jimmy Brunton's
Noontide, before she set off with the other drifters on the annual pilgrimage. Their homecoming in the weeks before Christmas was eagerly
anticipated, for they brought back long pink sticks of rock and nets of
assorted nuts, exotic luxuries from the southern ports.

GOOD LUCK CUSTOM—Fishermen at Anstruther observing an ancient custom before they left for the Yarmouth herring fishing yesterday. They are seen handing out "bakes" (ship's biscuits) to the spectators. The old custom is said to ensure good luck.

Jock Martin and Jimmy Brunton jun. on the drifter *Lasher* (skipper Jimmy Brunton sen.) in the mid-1930s, giving out the 'bakes' at Anstruther harbour before setting out for the autumn herring fishing at Yarmouth. Those on the pier include Mrs. Brunton sen. and Bob Hughes, jeweller with Burd's of Anstruther.

Later most of the fishing fleet moved to Pittenweem, as their ancestors had once moved from Cellardyke to the safer haven of Anstruther, and now more and more boats are kept at Aberdeen docks, the crews travelling home at weekends.

The author's uncle Adam Watson, crewman on the *Noontide* (skipper Jimmy Brunton jun.), with his wife Annie Fleming at Yarmouth in the late 1940s. On the deck of the *Noontide* (L. to R.) Nicol Smith (from Crail), Peter Boyter and Jimmy Smith ('The Kitlin').

There were still many 'worthies' around in the '50s: old Maggie Dunbar, the last local woman to wear a black shawl over her head, taking pies to her husband down the pier when he was in no condition to come home for them himself; the 'Twinny Leslies', identical twin sisters dressed always in black who paraded slowly past our house on Sunday mornings on their way to Kilrenny kirk; Geordie Broon, horse-tamer extraordinary, who lived in the next council block to ours; and a host of others noted for some mark of originality or eccentricity which set them apart from the rest of us. It was a town of nicknames, where a man might be known as 'Lion', 'Tiger', or 'Kitlin', 'Lowpie', 'Tauttie Eckie' or 'Eckie C' (once an exasperated teacher, confronted with three Alex. Watsons in his class, had christened them Eckie A, Eckie B and Eckie C; one of the other Eckies was my uncle). Women kept their maiden name until death, or beyond. Stopped one day in Toll Road by a stranger who enquired where Mrs. Wood lived, I was baffled, although the woman in question lived only a few yards away. I had never heard her married name used before.

Let me end by retracing the steps of the census enumerators through the old Main Street of Cellardyke: the James, John, George and Shore Streets of my childhood.

Just to the east of my granny's house in James Street stood a potato-crisp factory, where once oilskins and canvas buoys had been manufactured. Across the road was Adamson's the baker's, where on Saturday mornings, towards twelve o'clock, the locals would gather for a 'clash' as they waited for the meat-rounds, pies and rhubarb tarts to arrive from the bakery in Pittenweem. There was universal acclaim when at last the van drew up outside and Hamish the vanman bore the trays inside on his head, as stately as any African matron. Saturday's 'denner' was secure at last.

Next to Adamson's stood a chip-shop where 'Gales' (Eck Gardner) was the genial host: so notable a character that the adjacent 'Little Wynd' was 'Gales's Wynd' to my generation. His great rival was 'Mymie' Cargill, a few yards further east near the Town Hall, and each brand of fish-supper had its own devotees. Once Mymie gave me sixpence to take her little Scottie 'Beauly' for a walk. Freed from the suffocating atmosphere of the chip-shop, the eager little brute pulled me all over Cellardyke and Kilrenny before it had done with me, and the sixpence was well earned. On the south side of the street was 'Tawsie's' ice-cream parlour, another favourite port of call in that delicious, succulent street. Ever alert to the sounds of language, even at an early age, I concluded that 'Tosi', as I pictured his name, was of Italian descent like his opposite number Jimmy Brattesani, dispenser of delicious cones and 'sliders' in Shore Street, Anstruther. But Davie Tawse, son of the Alexander Tawse drowned in 1896, was as much a Dyker as any local Watson, Doig or Muir.

On the north side, between the two chip-shops, stood Bobby Watson's dark little basement parlour. Known, like his father the town-crier before him, as 'Bobby Bell' (but not to his face!), Bobby was our local barber, and I suffered my first haircuts as a toddler sitting on a board stretched over the arms of his chair. Twenty-odd years later my somewhat shaggier locks were still receiving his attentions, while I regaled him with tales of student life in Edinburgh. It was a source of wonder to Bobby that one who had imbibed English at his mother's knee, albeit of the East Neuk variety, could wish to spend four years at a university repeating the process. I do not think I ever succeeded in explaining this to his satisfaction.

H

Conversation was more precious than coin to Bobby in his lonely basement. The sight of passing legs at his window 'gaun wast' would prompt hours of speculation as to their probable owner, and the nature of his or her business down in Anstruther. If a local fisherman or two drifted in during the course of the afternoon, the talk would grow to a debate, and scissors and clippers would momentarily be stilled, for Bobby could not cut or clip and talk at the same time. And so the long, slow afternoons dragged by, as we talked, and speculated, and wondered; the occasional spurts of hair accumulating on the floor.

I seldom set foot in Cellardyke Town Hall, except on rare occasions when our Sunday-school trip to Pitmilly or Kenly Green was rained off. Oh, those Sunday-school picnics of yesteryear, with cakes and lemonade and tugs-of-war, and old Kate McRuvie dancing with the little ones in a ring to the tune of 'Bimbo was his name-o'! To her own generation she was 'Kate the De'il', on account of her fiery temper, but to us infants she was a proper apple-cheeked old granny, like in the story-books. Most of our real grannies were decidedly less playful.

Past the Town Hall now, and into John Street, where the first shop was Bowman the butcher's. No restaurant, Chinese or otherwise, in the Cellardyke of the '50s! Many a trip I made between my granny's house and the butcher's, bearing the same half-pound of mince before me like a fiery cross, because however carefully weighed out it was always too much for my frugal granny. Then I would watch in silent awe while Eck Bowman, a frugal soul himself, nipped off a piece of the raw meat and popped it into his mouth. My granny's little foibles were well known, and raised scarcely an eyebrow. Eck's brother Fergie, as jovial and cheerful as Eck was taciturn, kept the sub-post-office next door.

McInnes's pub (now the Boat Tavern) was forbidden and forbidding territory for a small boy, and the next familiar emporium – no lesser word will do – was Butters's store. In its dark interior, where as many goods hung from the roof as were piled on the floor, nets, lines, buoys and ropes had been sold in the heyday of the local fishing industry. It could still supply most people's needs most of the time, from groceries to shoes to a little boy's simple requirements of rod and line. Further along John Street, at No. 21, stood Maggie Watson's more modest establishment. At one time scores of elderly women, widows or spinsters for the most part, had set aside a room in their house as a grocer's or sweetie shop, and Maggie – a relative on my mother's side – was one of the last to survive. You went down steps and through a door with a tinkling bell which might or might not summon Maggie from her inner sanctum.

There was often time to study the entire contents of Maggie's shelves before the slip-slop, slip-slop of her baffies in the passage announced her imminent arrival.

Further east in George Street was Watson's oilskin factory, a place I never entered, although I was a frequent visitor to the rival establishment in East Forth Street. My eldest sister was a machinist in Martin's factory, then owned by Provost Carstairs, and I was often delegated to take her her midday 'piece'.

At the far end of Shore Street stood the grocer's shop owned by my father's cousin Jimmy Smith, which served the 'ist the toon' folk and relieved them of the need to trek along to Anstruther for their shopping. Thanks to such little shops as this there were still in my boyhood old people like Mrs. Bridges at Harbourhead or Robert Muir (Robbie Mair) in Dove Street who for many years had never set foot in Anstruther. Thus the distinctive character of each community and of its inhabitants was preserved, long after the union of the burghs. After Shore Street came East Shore, and the last few houses in Cellardyke.

The Cardinal's Steps bathing pool, better known as 'The Pond', was the great recreational area of the town, and we rolled on the grass and sucked our ice-cream cones where once our ancestors had pulled up their boats at the end of the 'drave', or hung out salt cod to dry on 'haiks'. Beyond lay Kilrenny Mill farm, and further on, round the distant headland, Caiplie Coves, from where it was an easy hike to Crail. It was a route I often followed, from childhood onwards, sometimes – in the pretentious days of adolescence – with a book of poetry or essays for company.

That was my Cellardyke, or part of it. Did I really bowl a 'gird' up and down Toll Road, write on a slate at school and fetch accumulators for our old wireless from Dick Christie the engineer's, the acid burning itchy patches on my wrists? I have said nothing of the horses and carts which brought our milk, or fruit and vegetables, or of Jimmy Campbell – ever cheery and obliging despite his useless, damaged arm – who pushed his barrowload of fish round the streets in all weathers; or Peter Love, whose barrow brought our Sunday papers. The streets were safer for such traffic in those days. At the age of 39 I am far too young to conjure up some sentimental, imaginary Golden Age of childhood. Yet there were many good features in the Cellardyke of the '50s, and it all seems such light-years away now.

So much for the past. What of the future? The picture is not entirely gloomy, for new houses have sprouted on the Braehead, above the Town's Green, and more are springing up, unexpectedly, in the sleepy hollow of Kilrenny. Murray Square and Fishermen's Court are welcome additions to Cellardyke's street-plan, and will no doubt be part of 'old Cellardyke' for the rising generation as formerly the new terraces of East and West Forth Street were for my grandparents' generation. There has been controversy over the future of the old houses down by the shore, but they still stand where they always did, and the Dykers of several centuries ago would not be unduly disconcerted if, through some time-warp, they were to be dropped back in their former haunts.

The Fifies of yesteryear may have disappeared from Cellardyke harbour, but there are pleasure-craft there today, and a surprising number of fishermen still scattered throughout the town. Indeed there is still a Skipper William Watson living not a stone's throw from Skinfasthaven, even if these days he keeps his seine-netter *Gleanaway II* up at Aberdeen. The character of Cellardyke remains largely unaltered, and its history is still there to be read in its streets, houses, harbour and seashore, and in the distinctive speech-forms and thought-processes of its inhabitants. As long as there is still room for a little individuality in the world, the Dykers – proud, thrawn, arrogant or what you will – will survive. I suspect they are not ready to go under yet.

Appendix 1

Family Trees of the author's paternal grandparents, William Watson (1864–1945) and Jessie Horsburgh Cunningham (1869–1958).
  Pages 222–223

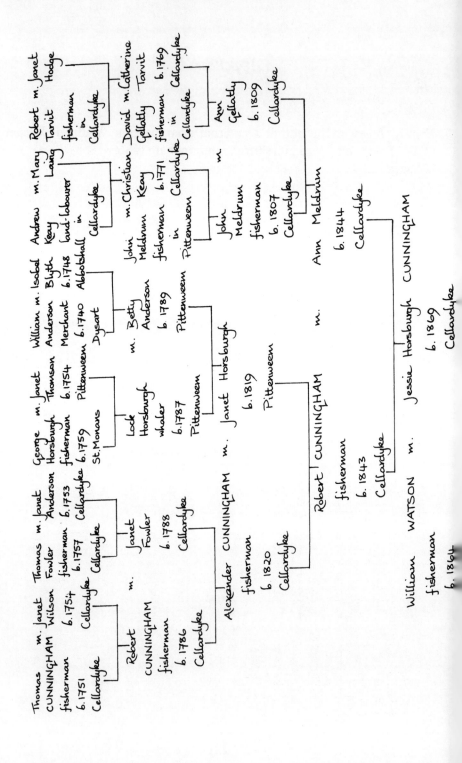

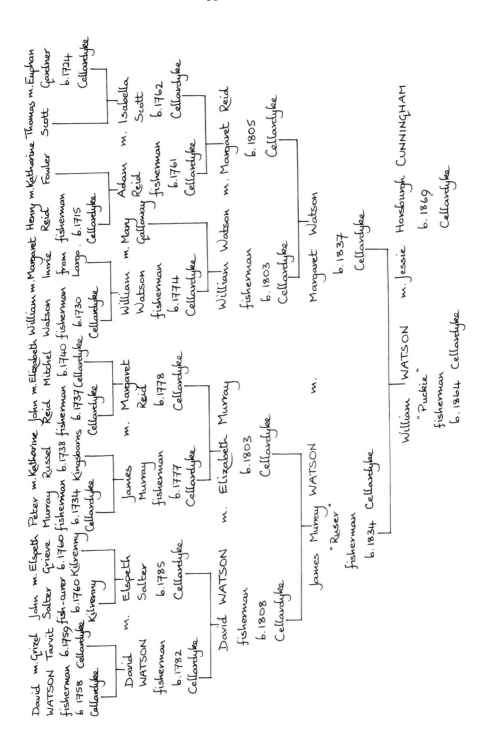

Appendix 2 The 1691 Hearth-Tax List for Kilrenny Parish

In 1691 the Scottish parliament, fearful of the threat posed by the Jacobites, gave authority to James Melville of Cassingray to impose a hearth-tax throughout Scotland. The intention was to raise money for the army. Householders were obliged to pay fourteen shillings Scots for each hearth in their house, only paupers and certain categories of official being exempt. According to Duncan Adamson, in *West Lothian Hearth Tax 1691 with county abstracts for Scotland* (Scottish Record Society), p. 4, 'the number of paying households if multiplied by seven ought to give some assessment of the population'. In the case of Kilrenny parish, this would give a population of 1,673.

Surnames have been capitalised, but punctuation and abbreviations are as in the original. The abbreviation 'yr.' = 'there', i.e. in that part of the parish.

Geo. Lumsen portioner yr.	6
Tho: Peacock	3
Jam: Peacock	1
Wil: Smith	1
James Dunkan	3
Capt: Gideon Murrys Relicks	4
Geo: Strang	1
Dav: Ramsay smith	2
Alex^r Millar	1
Geo: Louden	2
Tho: Weddel	1
Wil: Gullen	2
Wil: Browster	1
Jam: Salter	2
Wil: Pitblado	1
Jam: Davidson	1
Alex^r Myrton	1
Tho: Smith	1
Elspeth Gilchrist	2
John Red	2
Dav: Craigy	1
Tho: Dumbar	1
Dav: Fouler in Barnsmoor	1
Dav: Broun yr.	1

Dav: Broun younger yr.	1
John Broun yr.	1
John Broun elder yr.	1
Peter Bet yr.	1
Rob: Kininmont yr.	1
John Kinninmont in Silverdyke	1
Alex^r Lyng	1
John Young	1
Jam: Kay	1
Wil: Moore	1
Steven Williamson	2
Robert Lessels	1
And: Smith	1
Margret Davidson	1
David Moor	1
Jam: Lessels	1
Tho: Greive	1
Geo: Wilson	1
And: Louden	1
Dav: Red	1
Sir Philip Anstruther	25
The Laird of Scotstarvet	17
Robert Michel yr.	2
Jam: Broun yr.	1
John Smart yr.	1
Alex^r. Tailor yr.	1
Dav: Kininmont yr.	1
Wil: Smith yr.	1
Tho: Broun yr.	1
Tho: Kay yr.	1
Wil: Fairful in Pitkeery	1
And: Walker	1
Dav: Tody	1
John Forbes	1
Rob: Broun	1
Jam: Louden	1
Tho: Salter	2
Jo: Young	1
Rob: Couper	1
Tho: Cambel	1
Joh: Dunkan	1
Jo: Lawson	1
Rob: Lyel	1
Wil: Fyel	1
The Laird of Bafour for his house in Kilrenny	8
John Carmichal	1
And: Hodge	1
Wil: Salter	1

John Dunkan	1
John Gourly	1
Alex^r Lesles	1
And: Tailor	1
Jam: Robertson	2
Jean Lawson	2
Katrin Watson	2
John Rid	1
Tho: Paterson	1
Jam: Michel	1
Robert M^{c}dougle	1
Barbara Anderson	1
And: Strang	1
Jam: Young	1
Geo: Smith	1
John Lesles	1
Henry Watson	1
Dav: Watson	1
Jam: Anderson	1
Rob: Couper	1
Wil: Dog	1
John Alexander	1
Wil: Byter	1
Rob: Morton	1
John Murry	1
Tho: Young	1
Alex^r Garner	1
Tho: Smith	1
John Millar	1
Jam: Anstruther	1
John Powry	1
Janet Edy	1
Rob: Din	1
Jonet Waterson	1
Wil: Anderson	2
Wil: Watson	1
Jam: Ady	1
And: Wide	1
Dav: Moor	1
Wil: Spindie	1
Wil: Black	2
Wil: Young	1
Dav: Craigy	1
Dav: Kay	1
John Dewar	1
Catrin Carse	1
James Couper smith	2
Alex^r Iron	1

Jam: Banes	2
Dav: Red	1
And: Louden	2
Alex^r Lyng	1
Stevin Williamson	1
Thom: Wishart	1
Pat: Broun	1
Jam: Paterson	1
Jam: Salter	1
Agnes Dunkan	1
John Pitblado	1
John Robertson	1
Wil: Young	1
Tho: Fouler	1
Jam: Morice	1
John Craig	1
Jam: Tarvit	1
The Ministers manse	5
Tho: Scote	1
Capt. Murrys Relict	6
Mr Mungo Grahm	2
John Wilson	1
The Mannorplace of Innergelly	12
	TOTAL
	239

Appendix 3 Early Cellardyke Fishing Boats

Reliable information about the boats used by our fisher ancestors is hard to come by. The ancient burgh seal of Kilrenny, dating perhaps from the early 1600s, portrays a small open boat without masts, with steeply raked stern and stem, and a crew of five mariners engaged in line fishing. We have already noted that East Neuk boats were fishing at Orkney and Shetland and round the west coast at Lewis by the sixteenth century, and clearly they must have been sturdy, seagoing vessels.

In 1710 Sir Robert Sibbald writes of the Cellardyke line boats having a crew of six, while the herring boats carry seven men each. At the end of the century, in the First Statistical Account, the minister of St. Monans describes the herring boats of his parish as having from six to nine men in their crews.

George Gourlay's *Fisher Life* is another useful source of information, although Gourlay tends to be annoyingly imprecise about dates. In the period after the Battle of Trafalgar, he tells us, Thomas Cunningham of Cellardyke had a drave (i.e. herring) boat called the *Jennet* – 'a staunch and serviceable craft, though scarcely eight-and-twenty feet of keel' (*Fisher Life*, 46). At the same time the latest addition to the local fleet is described as 'the leviathan of the coast at a length of twenty-nine feet'. In the opinion of David Birrell, a recognised authority: 'She's too big, I say, either to row or sail' (*Fisher Life*, 47).

This brings us to the earliest surviving Registry Books for the Anstruther Fishery Office, which are preserved at the Customs & Excise Office, 270 High Street, Kirkcaldy, and which describe the Cellardyke fishing-boats of the 1820s and 1830s. These are rather different craft from the later Fifies, so familiar from old photographs with their vertical stem- and stern-posts. The earlier vessels were round-sterned, undecked, lugger-rigged and clinker or 'clench' built, and their two masts appear to have been of the same length. Their depth was between four and five feet. The length of keel is not given. In weight they vary between roughly sixteen and roughly twenty tons, the fractions being expressed in 94ths. This is in accordance with an Act of Parliament of 1824 which laid down that henceforth, in registering boats, the length of the keel was to be multiplied by the breadth, the product by half the breadth and the whole by 94, the quotient being deemed 'the true

Contents of the Tonnage'. The passing of this Act may have been the reason for the opening of this register in 1824.

Ownership of boats was by a share system, the total number of shares being 64. Most of the undermentioned boats were built at Leith by the firms of William Lindsay or Alexander Leckie, although some were built by the Anstruther wright James Henderson. Extracts are from Volume One only, and relate exclusively to Cellardyke boats.

Name	Master	Owner(s)	Date of Registration
Morning Star	Alexr. Watson	Alexr. Watson	30th June 1824
Johns	John Sutherland	John Sutherland	30th June 1824
Mayflower	John Parker	John Parker (22 shares)	30th June 1824
		Adam Reid (21 shares)	
		William Watson (21 shares)	
Lindsay	James Anderson	James Anderson (32 shares)	17th July 1824
		Thomas Anderson (32 shares)	
Two Brothers	David Keay	Alexr. Keay (32 shares)	22nd Oct. 1824
Unitatos		David Keay (32 shares)	
Alexander	Alexr. Pratt jun.	Alexr. Pratt	22nd Oct. 1824
Betty & Euphan	Henry Stevenson jun.	Henry Stevenson sen. (32 shares)	22nd Oct. 1824
		Henry Stevenson jun. (32 shares)	
Five Brothers	David Rodger	David Rodger (32 shares)	27th Oct. 1824
		Robert Fowler (32 shares)	
Unity	John Carstairs	John Carstairs (32 shares)	30th Oct. 1824
		David Morris (32 shares)	
Molly	James Smith	James Smith	4th Nov. 1824
Victory	David Taylor	Andrew Heugh (32 shares)	8th Feb. 1824
		David Taylor (32 shares)	
Fox	Wm. Moncrieff jun.	Wm. Moncrieff sen. (16 shares)	10th Feb. 1825
		Wm. Moncrieff jun. (16 shares)	
		David Moncrieff (16 shares)	
		John Moncrieff (16 shares)	
Laurel	Andrew Watson	Alexr. Watson	14th July 1825
Brothers	James Murray	Thomas Murray (32 shares)	15th July 1825
		James Murray (32 shares)	
Agnes Lindsay	Thomas Anderson	James Anderson (32 shares)	16th July 1825
		Thomas Anderson (32 shares)	
Alexander Leckie	Alexr. Wood	Alexr. Wood	18th July 1825
George	John Parker	John Parker (32 shares)	9th Nov. 1825
		Alexr. Parker (32 shares)	
James & Alexr.	David Morris	John Carstairs (32 shares)	24th Dec. 1825
Henderson		David Morris (32 shares)	
Vine	John Pratt	Alexr. Pratt	25th March 1826
Olive	John Davidson jun.	John Davidson (32 shares)	29th March 1826
		William Davidson (32 shares)	
Pomona	Robert Watson	Robert Watson (32 shares)	1st April 1826
		David Watson (32 shares)	
James Leckie	Alexr. Pratt	Alexr. Pratt	15th July 1826

Some boat-names were carried on from generation to generation in the same family, a notable example being the *Morning Star* – a name given to a succession of boats owned by descendants of James Watson and Margaret Reid. The following anecdote illustrates how attached a family might become to a particular name. During the First World War the drifter *Craignoon* was sunk by the Austrian navy in the Adriatic, and as a replacement her skipper Alex. Rodger purchased the *Morning Star* from James Watson (Smith) ('Star Jeems'). After the war James Watson and his son David acquired a new steel drifter, and naturally wished to call her *Morning Star*. Skipper Rodger, however, refused to change the name of his boat, and two drifters with the same name would have been a source of confusion, so another solution had to be found. Rather than adopt an entirely new name, the Watsons hit on the idea of using Latin instead of English to convey the same idea, and called their new drifter the *Stella Aurora* (K.Y. 45).

Those interested in the later types of fishing-boat, such as the Fifie, steam-liner, steam-drifter, motor-boat, trawler, bauldie, etc., can consult a number of useful reference books, such as Peter Anson's *Fishing Boats & Fisher Folk on the East Coast of Scotland* (London, 1930), or Peter Smith's *The Lammas Drave and the Winter Herrin'* (Edinburgh, 1985).

Appendix 4 Fishing Grounds and 'Meids' in the Firth of Forth

Certain areas of the Forth have been renowned as fishing-grounds from time immemorial: none more so than the 'Traith' or 'Treath', the 'Hirst' and the 'Auld Haikes'.

The Traith is an area about one mile off Pittenweem harbour. To Pittenweemers it has always been known as the 'Fluke Hole', but in the mid-nineteenth century it acquired yet another name, as the *Pittenweem Register* reported on March 30th, 1850: 'Pittenweemers are now calling the Fluke Hole or Treath, California, because of the large amount of herring taken there in recent years'.

The Hirst is further east, between Crail and the May Island, and was a popular spawning ground for the herring before they left the Forth. In his poem *The Herrin'*, written in 1937 at the height of the winter herring fishing, Peter Smith portrayed this exchange between a retired fisherman at Anstruther harbour and a skipper about to put out to sea:

> 'Try not the Hirst', the veteran cried.
> The skipper smiled – then lood replied.
> 'Your guid advice I hear, auld man,
> Yet, there they congregate tae spawn,
> The herrin'.
>
> And tho' baith time and tide are late
> Doon there this nicht my nets I'll shate.
> My wife and bairnies, big and wee,
> And a' my crew depend on me,
> For herrin'.'

The Auld Haikes is still further east, between Fife Ness and Kingsbarns. So prolific in herring was this area that even in the eighteenth century it was jocularly known as 'the best farm in Fife'. A couple of letters in the *Caledonian Mercury* of September 10th, 1774, describe a herring bonanza in the Haikes of such magnitude that the writer was offered 30,000 fish for a bottle of gin! A rare example of co-operation between the fishing-villages of the East Neuk is afforded by the story, oft-repeated, of the horseman from Crail who, in the appropriate season, would gallop along the one long main street of Cellardyke with the ever-welcome news that there was 'herrin' in the Haikes!'

Of course, to ensure a good catch it was not enough simply to make for one vaguely-defined area of the firth well-known to every other boat's crew. Each skipper had his own favourite spots where he always fished well, and he made his way to them with the help of bearings taken from prominent landmarks, both natural and manmade. These were his 'meids', an old Scots word meaning 'mark' or 'measurement'. At the inshore fishing, chimneys, houses and monuments might serve; further out at sea church steeples and background hills were useful too. Most meids consisted of two objects in a line, but better still was a 'sharp meid' consisting of two sets of objects in transit.

On December 12th, 1929, the *East Fife Observer* published a list of old meids of the Firth of Forth, many of which even at that date were known only to the oldest fishermen, as they might refer to people or places no longer in existence. A selection of these is reproduced below, with explanatory comments. They commence at Crail and work westwards, taking the hill known as Kellie Law – some four miles NW of Cellardyke – as the most prominent feature in the landscape:

Crail Lichts in ane – The line of the leading lights to Crail Harbour.
Kellie ower the Thorn – Kellie Law over a clump of trees appearing over the village of Kilrenny.
Kellie ower the sledgates – Kellie Law over the Sea Ware path (locally, the 'Waur Peth') at the east end of Cellardyke, opposite the Cardinal's Steps at the Town's Green.
Kellie ower St. Irnie's – Kellie Law over Kilrenny kirk.
Kellie ower the Toor – Kellie Law over the tower which formerly stood at the Braehead, Cellardyke, at the foot of the Windmill Road.
Kellie ower Geordie Fooler's hoose – Kellie Law over George Fowler's house (Bayview House) at the Braehead.
Kellie ower the Auld Infant School – Kellie Law over the site to the east of the former Martin's factory in East Forth Street, where the early nineteenth century infant school was demolished to make way for houses.
Kellie ower Cellardyke Kirk – Kellie Law over Cellardyke Kirk.
Edge o' the Grund – An area offshore where a depth of 12 or 14 fathoms was reached.
Enster Lichts in ane – The Chalmers or 'Hannah Harvie' Lighthouse at the west pier, Anstruther, and the east pier light, in line.

Kellie ower Waid Academy – Kellie Law over the secondary school which stands to the north of Anstruther harbour on the back road to St. Andrews.

Kellie ower Enster kirk – Kellie Law over Anstruther Easter kirk (St. Adrian's).

Kellie ower the Burn Kirk – Kellie Law over Anstruther Wester kirk (formerly St. Nicholas's), which stands near the mouth of the Dreel Burn, and now functions merely as a church hall.

Kellie ower Hughie's – Kellie Law over the former manse of Anstruther Wester kirk (now the Craw's Nest Hotel), where from 1838 to 1872 the parish minister was the Rev. Hew Scott D.D., author of *Fasti Ecclesiae Scoticanae*, a history of the clergy of the Church of Scotland.

Kellie ower Black Rock – Kellie Law over Johnny Doo's rock at the Billowness, Anstruther Wester.

Kellie ower Cook's hoose – Kellie Law over 'High Cross', home of Mr. David Cook.

Kellie ower Kirklatch – Kellie Law over the farm at the east end of Pittenweem.

Kellie ower Miss Annie's – Kellie Law over Milton, Pittenweem, home of Miss Annie Martin from 1834 to 1864.

Kellie ower Catch-a-vote – Kellie Law over a cottage at the west end of Pittenweem.

Kellie ower Wullie Sim's – Kellie Law over a small farm called Pathhead to the west of Pittenweem.

Kellie ower Pan Brae – Kellie Law over a cliff to the west of Pittenweem where at one time there had been salt-pans.

Largo Law to the Heugh – Largo Law (behind the village of Upper Largo) showing over Kincraig Cliffs (near Elie).

The May Island, not unnaturally, also figured in many of the meids:

Neipy Fit – North Ness over the North Brow of the island.

Auld Licht tae the Little Ane – The lower light to the old tower once used for the Beacon Light. The lower light was discontinued after the Carr Lightship came into service.

Lum i' the Loan – One of the big chimneys of the electric power station on the south side of the firth, seen in the gap or valley of the island.

Mill Door Open – An opening or cave-like door seen on the west side of the island adjoining the pond.

White Saund Open – A small opening which discloses remarkably white shingle between the North Ness and that part of the island called the 'Stand': a landing-place at the west side.

Lichts in ane – The great upper light and the lower light (long since discontinued) in line.

Bass tae the Nor' Ness – The Bass rock over the North Ness of the island.

Bass tae the Sood Ness – The Bass Rock over the South Ness.

Other meids on the south side made use of North Berwick Law, the Craig islet near Fidra, and Pelder (Traprain Law).

The best meids of all, of course, were never revealed to outsiders, although they might be confided to a jealously-guarded notebook; and anyone foolish enough to enquire of a skipper returning to harbour where he had caught such an impressive 'shot' would, at best, be fobbed off with an evasive answer. With the demise of the anchored net and handlines, however, and the increasing sophistication of electronic aids, the 'Meids' of the old fishermen of the Forth have passed into the folklore of the fishing industry.

Notes

Chapter 1

1. George Gourlay, *Fisher Life, or The Memorials of Cellardyke and the Fife Coast* (1879), 62 (hereafter referred to as *Fisher Life*).

2. W. J. Eggeling, *The Isle of May* (1960), 28–9.

3. *Ibid.*

4. *Historical Monuments (Scotland) Commission. Inventory of Monuments in Fife*, No. 337, 169.

5. W. F. Skene, *Celtic Scotland* (1886–90), Vol. 1, 321; Vol. 2, 314–5.

6. *Historical Monuments Commission*, No. 331, 168 (I am grateful to Mr. Ian Fisher of the Commission for his illuminating comments on the Skeith Stone).

7. *Registrum Episcopatus Glasguensis* (ed. 1843), Vol. 1, App. 2 (*Vita Kentegerni*), lxxxiv.

8. *Liber Sanctae Mariae de Dryburgh*(Bannatyne Club, 1847).

9. Walter Wood, *The East Neuk of Fife* (1887), 19.

10. W. F. H. Nicolaisen, *Scottish Place-Names* (1976), 128.

11. W. J. Watson, *The History of the Celtic Place-Names of Scotland* (1926), 520.

12. *The First Statistical Account of Scotland* (1791), Number XLI, *Parish of Kilrenney* (sic), 409.

13. *Ane Addicioun of Scottis Corniklis and Deidis* (ed. 1819), 7.

14. *Register of the Great Seal*, Vol. 2, No. 1444.

15. *Fisher Life*, 1.

16. Personal communication from Peter Smith, Anstruther.

17. 'Auld Wull' (William Smith) in a series of articles entitled 'Cellardyke 70 Years Ago', published in 1927 in the *East Fife Observer*. I am indebted to Peter Smith for bringing these articles to my attention.

18. George Gourlay, *Anstruther, or Illustrations of Scottish Burgh Life* (1888), 50 (hereafter referred to as *Anstruther*).

19. *Historic Crail* (Crail Preservation Society, 1976), 4.

20. *Register of the Great Seal*, Vol. 2, No. 2292.

Chapter 2

1. Professor Gordon Donaldson, in *St. Andrews Formulare 1514–46* (Stair Society, 1942), Vol. 1, xii.

2. *The Works of John Knox* (Wodrow Society, 1846), Vol. 1, 151–2.

3. Robert Lindesay of Pitscottie, *The Historie and Cronicles of Scotland* (Scottish Text Society, 1899), Vol. 2, 83–4.

4. *St. Andrews Formulare*, 269–73. See also *Fisher Life*, 127–9.

5. *Acts of the Parliaments of Scotland*, Vol. 3, 167–9 (hereafter referred to as *Acts*).

6. J. H. Stevenson & M. Wood, *Scottish Heraldic Seals*, Vol. 1, Public Seals, 68.

7. *Reg. Great Seal*, Vol. 2, No. 2292; and *The Autobiography and Diary of Mr. James Melvill* (Wodrow Society, 1842), 259.

8. *Reg. Privy Seal*, Vol. 7, 5–6.

9. Angus Graham, 'Archaeological Notes on some Harbours in Eastern Scotland', in *Proceedings of the Society of Antiquaries of Scotland*, Vol. 101 (1968–9), 200–85.

10. Pitscottie, 108–9.

11. *Reg. Privy Council*, Vol. 1, 381.

12. *Ibid.*

13. Pitscottie, 281.

14. *Reg. Privy Council*, Vol. 1, 381.

15. Pitscottie, 317.

16. Walter Wood, *op. cit., passim.*

17. D. Hay Fleming (ed.), *Register of the Ministers, Elders and Deacons of the Christian Congregation of St. Andrews* (Scottish History Society, 1889), Vol. 1, 247.

18. *The Commissariot Records of St. Andrews. Register of Testaments 1549–1800* (Scottish Record Society, 1902), Vol. 8.

19. See Gourlay, *Anstruther*; Wood, *op. cit*; Aeneas Mackay, *A History of Fife and Kinross* (1896); D. Hay Fleming, *Guide to the East Neuk of Fife* (1886); Theo Lang, *The Kingdom of Fife* (1951), and Alison Thirkell, *Auld Anster* (no date).

(During Anstruther's Civic Week in July, 1984, members of the Spanish 'Orden Del Mar Oceano' – the oldest marine corps in the world – paraded through the streets of the town in sixteenth-century costume, hauling a huge cannon and helping the townspeople relive that dreich November day in 1588.)

20. Melvill, *op. cit.*, 330–1.

21. *Id.*, 11.

22. *Id.*, 6.

Chapter 3

1. Ranald Nicholson, *Scotland: The Later Middle Ages* (*The Edinburgh History of Scotland*, Vol. 2, 1978), 15.

2. *Id.*, 14.

3. *Acts*, Vol. 2, 235.

4. John R. Elder, *The Royal Fishery Companies of the Seventeenth Century*(1912), 14–15; and C. A. Goodlad, *Shetland Fishing Saga* (1971), 83.

5. George Gourlay, *Fisher Life*, 5. The 'Auld Haikes' and 'Traith' or 'Treath' are fishing-grounds near Fife Ness and Pittenweem respectively.

6. *Reg. Privy Council*, Vol. 7, 89.

7. J. D. Marwick (ed.), *Extracts from the Records of the Convention of the Royal Burghs of Scotland (1870–90)* (*Conv. Burghs*), Vol. 2, 203–4.

8. *Fisher Life*, 5.

9. *Acts*, Vol. 6, Part 1, 413.

10. *The History and Chronicles of Scotland written in Latin by Hector Boece, translated by John Bellenden* (1821), Vol. 2, 179.

11. Christina Larner, *Enemies of God: The Witch-hunt in Scotland* (1981), 82. See also David Cook, *Annals of Pittenweem* (1867), 53–5.

12. *Acts*, Vol. 6, Part 2, 712–3.

13. Rev. John Brand, *A Brief Description of Orkney, Zetland, Pightland-Firth and Caithness* (1701, reprinted 1883), 31.

14. *The Diary of Mr. John Lamont of Newton 1649–1671* (Maitland Club, 1830), 95.

15. D. Hay Fleming (ed.), *Register of the Ministers, Elders and Deacons of the Christian*

Congregation of St. Andrews, Vol. 2, 800 note.

16. *Selections from the Minutes of the Presbyteries of St. Andrews and Cupar 1641–98* (Abbotsford Club, 1837).

17. *Selections from the Minutes of the Synod of Fife 1611–87* (Abbotsford Club, 1837), 139.

18. *Conv. Burghs*, Vol. 3, 536.

19. Louise Taylor (*ed.*), *Aberdeen Shore Work Accounts 1596–1670* (Aberdeen, 1972), 484.

20. *Reg. Privy Council*, 3rd series, Vol. 2, 494.

21. Scottish Record Office, E69/10/2.

22. T. C. Smout, *Scottish Trade on the Eve of Union* (1963), 57.

23. *Id.*, 139.

Chapter 4

1. 338–9.

2. 343–4.

3. 119, note 7.

4. *Fisher Life*, 11.

5. Quoted in *Fisher Life*, 10.

6. *Miscellany of the Scottish Burgh Record Society* (Edinburgh, 1881), 227–8.

7. George Gourlay, *Our Old Neighbours, or Folk Lore of the East of Fife* (1887) (hereafter referred to as *Our Old Neighbours*), 125.

8. *Memoirs of the Insurrection in Scotland in 1715, by John, Master of Sinclair* (Abbotsford Club, 1858), 15.

9. *First Statistical Account, Kilrenny*, 410–11.

10. *Fisher Life*, 150.

11. Duncan Fraser, *The Smugglers* (Montrose, 1971), 26–7.

12. Customs & Excise Records (CE1), Friday, July 14th, 1738.

13. Id., Wednesday, February 10th, 1742.

14. Sir Bruce Gordon Seton & Jean G. Armit (eds.), *The Prisoners of the '45* (Scottish History Society, 3rd series, 1928), 133.

15. *A List of Persons Concerned in the Rebellion Transmitted to the Commissioners of Excise by the Several Supervisors in Scotland in Obedience to a General Letter of the 7th May 1746, and a Supplementary List with Evidences to Prove the Same* (Scottish Record Society, 1890).

16. *Anstruther*, 20.

17. See Gourlay's works, *passim*.

18. *Morison's Dictionary*, quoted in D. Hay Fleming, *Guide to the East Neuk of Fife* (1886), 39.

19. *Fisher Life*, 15–19.

20. William was probably the son of that name born in 1730 to Thomas Watson and Ann Craigie.

21. David Loch, *Essays on the trade, commerce, manufactures and fisheries of Scotland* (Edinburgh, 1778–9), Chapter 3, Section 1, 247.

22. *Fisher Life*, 55.

23. Catherine Tarvit and her future husband David Gellatly were the present writer's great-great-great-grandparents.

24. The 'fiery presbyter', as George Gourlay calls him, was no stranger to controversy during his thirty-seven year reign as minister of Kilrenny. Many a young fisher couple preferred a clandestine marriage in Edinburgh to Mr. Beat's ministrations, and in 1783

not even a petition signed by seventy heads of households in the parish could make him desist from grazing his horses and cows on the churchyard grass. The threat of legal action against him was met by a cool counter-threat that, in that event, he would cease to administer the poors' money. His relationship with the kirk-session was not always cordial, and he fought some bruising battles with the heritors of the parish (not least over the grazing of his 'Bestial'!). The death of his first wife was followed barely five months later by his second marriage, and a third wife followed hard on the heels of the second. It was this last spouse, Euphemia Scott, who had Mr. Beat's sermons posthumously published in Edinburgh in 1799. Our picture of him is based on a self-portrait executed for his friend Mr. Douglas in Cellardyke, who passed it on to John Kay for inclusion in his *Series of Original Portraits and Caricature Etchings* (Edinburgh, 1837).

Chapter 5
    1. *Fisher Life*, 34–5.
    2. *Our Old Neighbours*, 108–9; the *Weekly Scotsman*, Saturday, November 7th, 1936; Christopher Rush, *Peace Comes Dropping Slow* (Edinburgh, 1983). Details of casualties, and of Captain Bligh and the *Glatton*, are taken from *Logs of the Great Sea Fights 1794–1805*, Vol. 2, ed. by Rear-Admiral T. Sturges Jackson (Navy Records Society, 1900).
    3. *Fisher Life*, 46.
    4. *Id.*, 115.
    5. David Watson and Elspeth Salter were the author's great-great-great-grandparents. David and Euphame were the brother and sister born in 1782 and 1784 respectively to David Watson and Grizel Tarvit.
    6. *Fisher Life*, 58.
    7. *Id.*, 59.
    8. *Id.*, 82–5. For details of John Sutherland's trial see the *Edinburgh Evening Courant* of Saturday, March 17th, 1838.
    9. Personal communication from his great-granddaughter Mary Murray, 2 Murray Square, Cellardyke.
    10. *Fisher Life*, 62.
    11. *Id.*, 78–9.
    12. Details from Old Parish Registers of Kilrenny.
    13. West Register House, AF/38/88/1.
    14. *Ibid.*
    15. *Ibid.*
    16. *Ibid.*
    17. West Register House, AF/38/88/2.
    18. *Ibid.*
    19. Quoted by the Rev. George Dickson in his article on Kilrenny for the *New Statistical Account* of 1845.
    20. David Low was born at Brechin in 1768 to a family with Episcopalian and Jacobite leanings. At the age of 19 he was ordained deacon and placed in charge of the remnant of the old non-juring congregation of Perth. Two years later, by now an ordained priest, he obtained the vacant living of Pittenweem, where he was to spend the remaining 66 years of his life. In 1819 he was appointed bishop of the united dioceses of Ross, Moray and Argyll, but continued to minister to his faithful congregation at Pittenweem. His unassuming manner and seemingly inexhaustible fund of anecdotes about the Jacobite families of his native county won him a wide circle of friends and admirers, including even the Church of Scotland clergy of the East Neuk towns. For an affectionate portrait

of this remarkable prelate by a friend and parishioner of some forty years' standing, see Matthew F. Conolly, *A Biographical Sketch of the Right Reverend David Low, D.D., LL.D.* (Edinburgh and Cupar, 1859).

21. *New Statistical Account* Vol. 15 (Wick), 144–5.

22. James Bertram, *The Harvest of the Sea* (London, 1869), 269.

23. *Our Old Neighbours*, 24.

24. *Fife Herald*, Cupar, Thursday April 10th, 1834. (The 500 may be a misprint for 50, but the main point remains the same.)

25. Lumsden, *op. cit.*, 15.

26. *Id.*, 32.

27. *Id.*, 17.

28. *Id.*, 21.

29. *Id.*, 24–5.

30. *Id.*, 29.

31. *Id.*, 30–2.

Chapter 6

1. *Our Old Neighbours*, 105.

2. *Fisher Life*, 47–51.

3. The *Register of Sasines, Fife, 1831–40*, in the Scottish Record Office, gives us a potted history of Robert Fowler's house at the top of the Urquhart Wynd (west side). Robert was the son of Thomas Fowler and Janet Anderson, who acquired the house on April 13th, 1787, from Janet and Barbara Watson, daughters of the late Oliver Watson, Mariner. Janet was married to William Dick, tailor in Pittenweem, and Barbara's husband was Andrew Crawford, mariner in Cellardyke. Robert Fowler's son David would later become owner and skipper of Walter Hughes's old brig the *Hero*, while a younger brother, Alexander, would die at the age of only 26 aboard the *Northern Bride* on the River Hooghly in India.

4. *Fisher Life*, 80.

5. R. L. Stevenson, 'College Memories', in *New Amphion* (Edinburgh University Union, 1886), 227–9.

6. J. M. Barrie, *An Edinburgh Eleven* (London, 1929), 52–5.

7. 'Auld Wull', in the *East Fife Observer*.

8. *Id.*

9. Frank T. Bullen, *The Log of a Sea-Waif* (London, 1899), 166.

10. See Matthew F. Conolly's *Biographical Dictionary of the Eminent Men of Fife*. In 1849 Thomas Brown was appointed inspector of the poor in the parish of Kilrenny, and in 1862 he became deputy postmaster of the burgh.

11. The 'braboners' or weavers of Kilrenny first banded together to form a craft association on February 7th, 1643, and the association was to last until only five years before this census, being disbanded on June 9th, 1836. See William Harvey, 'Sources of Local History: Two Fife Minute Books', in the *Scots Magazine*, August 1932, 365–374.

12. Wood, *East Neuk of Fife*, 399.

13. 'Auld Wull', *op. cit.*

14. Scottish Record Office, Dept. of Agriculture & Fisheries Records, AF/38/89/1.

15. *Fisher Life*, 98ff.

16. Hugh Miller, *My Schools and Schoolmasters* (Edinburgh, no date), 42–3.

Chapter 7

1. Rev. Alexander Gregory, *A Brief Account of the Religious Awakening in Cellardyke* (Edinburgh, 1860), 4. I am grateful to the librarian of New College, University of Edinburgh, for tracing this rare pamphlet for me and providing me with a photocopy.

2. *Id.*, 6.

3. *Id.*, 7.

4. Quoted in *The East Fife Observer: A Review of Twenty-five years* (1914–39), 43.

5. Gregory, *op. cit.*, 30.

6. *Id.*, 31.

7. *Ibid.*

8. *Kilrenny Kirk-Session Records* (Scottish Record Office, CH2/215/4), August 7th, 1862.

9. *Kilrenny Burgh Records* (St. Andrews University Library), December 22nd, 1865.

10. Quoted in the *Scotsman* of Saturday, April 17th, 1819.

11. West Register House, CS 236/G/22/11.

12. *Our Old Neighbours*, 4.

13. See page 84–5.

14. *Kilrenny Burgh Records*, January 16th, 1871.

15. West Register House (AF19/2/6).

16. West Register House (AF19/38/1).

17. *Fisher Life*, 105.

18. *Id.*, 119.

19. Personal communication from Peter Smith, Anstruther.

20. Rev. Hew Scott D.D. (minister of Anstruther Wester church), *Fasti Ecclesiae Scoticanae: the Succession of Ministers in the Church of Scotland since the Reformation* (new ed., Edinburgh, 1925), Vol. 5.

21. Published in 1885. William Smith, the son of James Smith and Margaret Corstorphine, was known as 'Wullie Teenie' after his wife Christina Melville, to distinguish him from the numerous other William Smiths in Cellardyke.

22. *Lights and Shadows*, 190.

23. Quoted from an advertisement for the Waid Academy in George Gourlay's *Anstruther*.

24. Malcolm Gray, *The Fishing Industries of Scotland, 1790–1914* (1978), 156.

25. W. S. Miln, 'The Scotch East Coast Herring Fishing', *Fisheries Exhibition Literature* (London, 1884), Vol. XI (quoted in Gray, *op. cit.*, 100).

26. *Tocher* (School of Scottish Studies, Univ. of Edinburgh), 20:1975, 151 (reminiscences of Thomas Carstairs, born in Cellardyke in 1877, and interviewed in 1957 by A. J. Aitken).

27. *Lights and Shadows*, 190.

28. Charles Marr's parents were George Marr and Janet Fowler. His wife Isabella Watson was the daughter of William Watson and Margaret Reid.

29. Peter F. Anson, *Fisher Folk-Lore* (London, 1965), 100.

30. Matthew Conolly, 'Supplement to the Biographical Dictionary of Eminent Men of Fife', in *Fifiana* (Glasgow, 1869). Conolly mistakenly calls Alexander Rodger 'David', confusing him either with his father or his brother.

31. Basil Lubbock, *The China Clippers* (London, new ed., 1984), 92.

32. *Id.*, 142.

33. *Our Old Neighbours*, 85.

34. Robert Cunningham (Fowler) (1786–1874) was the author's great-great-great-grandfather.

35. *Our Old Neighbours*, 87.

36. G. Blainey, *The Rush That Never Ended* (2nd ed., Melbourne, 1969), 118.

37. *Dictionary of Australian Biography Vol. 6: 1851–1890* (Melbourne, 1976), 350–1.

38. *Ibid.*

39. John F. Mitchell and Sheila Mitchell, *Monumental Inscriptions (pre–1855) in East Fife* (Scottish Genealogy Society, 1971), s.v. Kilrenny churchyard, No. 139.

40. *Kilrenny Kirk-Session Records* (CH2/215/5), September 10th, 1894.

41. *Kilrenny Burgh Records*, November 30th, 1897.

42. Gourlay, *Anstruther*, 2.

43. *Ibid.*

44. *Our Old Neighbours*, 104.

45. See Mary Murray *In My Ain Words: An East Neuk Vocabulary* (Anstruther, 1982) for a native speaker's comments on the Cellardyke dialect. In 1978 a Dutch linguist, J. Hettinga, carried out fieldwork in Anstruther and Cellardyke, and his research findings are summarised in J. Hettinga, 'Standard and Dialect in Anstruther and Cellardyke', in *Scottish Literary Journal* Supplement No. 14 (Summer, 1981), 37–48.

46. The 'Golden Strand' was a tiny stream of clear water which trickled into the sea to the west of Kilrenny Mill farm, near the old bleaching green, and well to the east of the last house in Cellardyke. It was filled in as a result of land reclamation measures (personal communication from Peter Smith). One of the Cunningham family later owned a steam drifter called the *Golden Strand*.

Chapter 8

1. *East of Fife Record*, January 5th, 1900.

2. *East of Fife Record*, January 10th, 1902.

3. West Register House, AF19/111.

4. *East of Fife Record*, September 12th, 1902.

5. *Kilrenny Burgh Records*, September 10th, 1907.

6. Quoted in the *East of Fife Record* in October 1914.

7. *East of Fife Record*, May 20th, 1915.

8. *East of Fife Record*, December 23rd, 1915.

9. *East of Fife Record*, April 22nd, 1915.

10. *East of Fife Record*, June 24th, 1915.

11. *East of Fife Record*, September 30th, 1915.

12. *Kilrenny Burgh Records*, September 14th, 1914; June 29th, 1915; June 25th, 1918; July 30th, 1918.

13. Roy Jenkins, *Asquith* (London, 1964), 480n.

14. Malcolm Gray, *The Fishing Industries of Scotland, 1790–1914* (1978), 155.

15. Personal communication from Alex. Gardner, East Forth Street, Cellardyke.

16. Frank Prothero, *The Good Years, a History of the Commercial Fishing Industry on Lake Erie* (1973), 20.

17. Personal communication from the author's mother.

18. Quoted in the *East Fife Observer* of June 24th, 1943.

Index